Responsible Government
in a
Revolutionary Age

# Responsible Government
# in a
# Revolutionary Age

*Edited by* Z. K. MATTHEWS

ASSOCIATION PRESS · NEW YORK

SCM PRESS · BLOOMSBURY STREET · LONDON

Responsible Government in a Revolutionary Age

*Copyright © 1966 by*
*World Council of Churches*

Published by Association Press, 291 Broadway, New York, N. Y. 10007

*Library of Congress catalog card number: 65–10116*

*Publisher's title stock number: 1585*

 72

PRINTED IN THE UNITED STATES OF AMERICA

# PREFACE

In 1962, the Central Committee of the World Council of Churches authorized the Department on Church and Society to begin preparations for a world conference to be held in 1966. The theme that was finally selected was "Christians in the Technical and Social Revolutions of Our Time." The department was also requested to undertake such preparatory studies as would help the conference in considering the central issues for Christian social ethics in contemporary society. In 1963, the Working Committee of the department recommended the preparation of four books of essays on the following subjects:

    I. *Christian Social Ethics in a Changing World*
    II. *Responsible Government in a Revolutionary Age*
    III. *Economic Growth in World Perspective*
    IV. *Man in Community*

We are pleased to commend these books to Christians around the world, and we invite them to share with us their reactions and opinions on the issues raised therein. Although the books are primarily intended as preparatory reading for the 1966 conference, it is hoped that they will also be used for discussion in local and regional groups around the world, after the conference as well as before.

Not since the Oxford World Conference on Church, Community and State, in 1937, has there been a similar world-wide effort to rethink Christian social responsibility. The study volumes for that conference dealt largely with the theological issues of social ethics within the context of the churches' encounter with the challenges of that time. Since then, new technical and social revolutions have overtaken societies all over the world, and new issues of social ethics have arisen as the churches have responded to them. The first of the present volumes deals with the theological problems of social ethics as such, while the others concentrate on relating theological insights to the actual problems of Christian responsibility in the contemporary situation of world political, economic and social change.

These symposia do not pretend to represent the full range of viewpoints held within the ecumenical fellowship on these questions. This is impossible in the space of four volumes on such large themes. The aim is rather to reveal the wide range of attitudes and opinions held, giving special attention to new and challenging points of view.

The responsibility for the structure and contents of these volumes is shared by the international editorial committees, which met in 1963 and 1964 to prepare the outline of each book and to review the first drafts of the contributions; by the chairman or editorial conveners of these committees, who have since become the editors of the books; and by the staff of the Department on Church and Society, who necessarily had to undertake the large part of the detailed editorial work and correspondence. Each writer remains responsible for the content of his contribution.

We are grateful to all those who have contributed to the volumes and to those who have commented on the essays in draft form. We acknowledge with appreciation the contribution of the Church and Society staff—Professor Mauricio Lopez, the Reverend Thomas Okuma and, in particular, Miss Margaret Sinclair, one of the early workers in the Universal Christian Council for Life and Work, who forsook her retirement for three months to assist us in preparing the manuscripts for publication. We depended throughout on our secretarial staff, Miss Audrey Smith, Miss Christa Stalschus and Miss Judith Brown, who typed the many drafts of these manuscripts.

M. M. THOMAS, *Chairman,*
Working Committee
Department on Church and Society

PAUL ABRECHT, *Executive Secretary*
Department on Church and Society

World Council of Churches
Division of Studies

# CONTRIBUTORS TO
# THIS VOLUME

PROF. Z. K. MATTHEWS (Editor). Secretary for Africa, Division of Inter-Church Aid, Refugee and World Service of the World Council of Churches; formerly principal of the University College of Fort Hare, professor of law and administration, head of the Department of African Studies; formerly leader of the African National Congress of South Africa; member of many governmental commissions on higher education in Africa; author of, among others, "An African Policy for South Africa" (*Race Relations*, Vol. XVI, No. 3); "The African Response to Racial Laws" (*Foreign Affairs*, Vol. XXX, No. 1); "Christian Education in a Changing Africa" (*International Review of Missions*, Jan. 1963). (Church of England)

MR. M. M. THOMAS Director of the Christian Institute for the Study of Religion and Society, Bangalore, India; chairman of the Working Committee for the Department on Church and Society of the World Council of Churches; secretary of East Asia Christian Conference; author of many books on the church and problems of nation-building: *Mud Huts and Steel Mills* (with R. Taylor); *Christian Participation in Nation Building* (with C. Devanandan); *Political Outlook in India Today* (with R. Chandran); *Problems of Indian Democracy* (with C. Devanandan); *Christian in the World Struggle* (with D. McCaughney). (Mar Thoma Church)

PROF. HELMUT GOLLWITZER Professor of systematic theology in the Faculty of Philosophy of the Free University of Berlin and the School of Theology, Berlin; author of *Coena Domini; Und führen, wohin du nicht willst Forderungen der Freiheit; Marxistische Religionskritik und der christliche Glaube; Die Existenz Gottes im Bekenntnis des Glaubens*. (Evangelical Church of Germany)

DR. MAX KOHNSTAMM Vice President, Action Committee for the United States of Europe; Personal Secretary to Queen Wilhelmina of Holland, 1945–48; Secretary, High Authority of European Coal and Steel Community under Jean Monnet; closely involved in the post-war organization of European communities; author of *The European Community and Its Role in the World* (The John Findley Green Foundation Lecture, 1963).

Dr. Kenneth W. Thompson Formerly of the political science faculties of Northwestern University and the University of Chicago; author of *Christian Ethics and Dilemmas of Foreign Policy; Political Realism and the Crisis of World Politics; American Diplomacy and Emergent Patterns; Man and Modern Society* (with Karl de Schweinitz); *Principles and Problems of International Politics* (with Hans J. Morgenthau). (United Church of Christ)

Dr. J. B. Soucek Professor of New Testament theology at Comenius Faculty of Protestant Theology, Prague; formerly president of the Student Christian Movement of Czechoslovakia; author of theological works in Czech. (Evangelical Church of the Czech Brethren)

Prof. André Philip Professor in the Faculty of Law and Political Economy at the Sorbonne; formerly Minister of Justice in the first free French government; one of the leaders in the movement for European cooperation; leading French Socialist and author of many studies on contemporary political and social issues; his books include: *La démocratie industrielle* (1955); *Pour un socialisme humaniste* (1960); *L'histoire des faits économiques et sociaux de 1800 à nos jours* (1963); *La gauche—mythes et réalités* (1964). (Reformed Church of France)

Rev. Richard Andriamanjato Pastor, and mayor of Tananarive, Madagascar; Member of Parliament of Malagasy Republic; graduate in theology and philosophy at the University of Strasbourg; member of executive committee of the All-Africa Conference of Churches and speaker at the First Assembly in Kampala (1962); member of the Working Committee of the Christian Peace Conference and speaker at the second conference in Prague (1964); author of "Le 'tsiny' et le 'tody' dans la pensée malagache" (*Présence Africaine*, 1957). (Reformed Church of Madagascar)

Prof. Mauricio Lopez Secretary of the Department on Church and Society of the World Council of Churches; formerly the Latin American secretary of the World Student Christian Federation; leader in many Latin American student conferences and consultations; articles and lectures on the church and the Latin American social revolution: coauthor of *Race, a Signal* (1961) and *Witness in Six Continents* (1964). (Evangelical Church of Argentina)

Mr. T. B. Simatupang One of the four presidents of the Indonesian Council of Churches, with special responsibility for Church and Society; deputy chief of staff of the Indonesian Army during the struggle for independence; author of *Report from Banaran* (on Indonesia's armed struggle for independence); and other books on the military-political problems of newly independent countries after armed struggle: *Pioneer in War, Pioneer in Peace*, also articles and lectures on the problems of the churches in a revolutionary, modernizing, nonwestern society. (Indonesian Christian Church)

PROF. JOHN H. HALLOWELL Professor and chairman of the Department of Political Science, Duke University, Durham, North Carolina; author of *Main Currents in Modern Political Thought* and other books on Christianity and political theory. (Protestant Episcopal Church, United States)

PRINCIPAL CHANDRAN DEVANESEN Principal of Madras Christian College, Tambaram, India; leading layman of the United Church of South India; M.A. (Cambridge) and Ph.D. (Harvard); author of *The Cross Is Lifted*. (United Church of South India)

DR. M. ABEL Professor of politics and public administration at Madras Christian College, Tambaram, India. (United Church of South India)

DR. PETER D. LATUIHAMALLO Professor of Christian ethics at Sekolah Tinggi Theologia, Djakarta; chairman of the Indonesian Council of Churches and chairman of the Department on Studies and Research; Member of the Indonesian Parliament and of the People's Consultative Congress; member of East Asia Christian Conference Commission on International Affairs and Religious Liberty; contributor to "Christianity and the Asian Revolution" and to "Weltkirchen Lexikon." (Protestant Church in Indonesia)

DR. A. F. CARRILLO DE ALBORNOZ Director of the World Council of Churches Secretariat on Religious Liberty; doctorates in civil law and philology (Madrid), philosophy (Louvain) and divinity (Innsbruck); author of *Roman Catholicism and Religious Liberty* and *The Basis of Religious Liberty*. (Protestant Episcopal Church, United States)

MR. SEAN MACBRIDE Secretary-general of the International Commission of Jurists; long and distinguished career as a senior counsel of the Irish and Ghana bars; took an active part in the movement for Irish national emancipation; as founder and leader of the Republican Party, he was a member of the Irish Parliament from 1947–58; Minister for External Affairs from 1948–51; held various offices at the Council of Europe and other international organizations. (Roman Catholic Church)

PROF. HENRI BURGELIN Professor Agrégé of history, assistant to the Faculty of Letters and Human Sciences at the Sorbonne. (Reformed Church of France)

DR. JOHN KAREFA-SMART Professor at the School of Public Health and Administration, Columbia University; formerly Minister of External Affairs of Sierra Leone; coauthor of *The Halting Kingdom—Christianity and the African Revolution* (with Mrs. Rena

Karefa-Smart); consultant to World Council of Churches Assembly, Amsterdam, 1948, and Africa consultant to World Council of Churches Rapid Social Change Study 1956–57. (Evangelical United Brethren)

REV. ALAN BOOTH London secretary of the Commission of the Churches on International Affairs; formerly general secretary of the Student Christian Movement of Great Britain and Ireland; author of *Christians and Power Politics* (1961). (Methodist Church in Ireland)

MR. THOMAS SIEGER DERR Chaplain and member of the Department of Religion at Smith College, Northampton, Mass.; graduate in political science, Harvard, and in theology and Christian ethics, Union Theological Seminary. (United Church of Christ)

PROF. YOSHIAKI IISAKA Professor of political science at Gakushuin University, Tokyo; leading young layman of the Kyodon (United Church of Japan); secretary for East Asia Christian Conference; secretary for International Affairs and Religious Liberty; author of *Christianity in the Contemporary World; Political Ethics of Karl Barth; Political Ethics of Emil Brunner; Against Power and Authorities; The Problem of Shintoism Today* (editor). (United Church of Japan)

PROF. MICHAEL P. FOGARTY Montague Burton professor of industrial relations, University College of South Wales and Monmouthshire; has been member of British Institute of Management, assistant editor of *The Economist,* chairman of Catholic Social Guild, author of many books including: *The Just Wage* (1961); *Internal Wage Structure* (1963); *Personality and Group Relations in Industry* (1956); *Christian Democracy in Western Europe, 1820–1953* (1957); *Under-Governed and Over-Governed* (1962). (Roman Catholic Church)

REV. EDWARD ROGERS General secretary of the Christian Citizenship Department of the Methodist Church, Great Britain; chairman of the Department of ICA, British Council of Churches (1960–64); chairman of Commission of Migration, British Council of Churches; author of *A Commentary on Communism; That They Might Have Life; God's Business; Poverty on a Small Planet* (published in the United Kingdom as *Living Standards*). (Methodist Church)

REV. GERHARD BASSARAK Director of the Evangelical Academy, Berlin-Brandenburg; formerly traveling secretary of the Student Christian Movement in the German Democratic Republic; international secretary of the Prague Peace Conference. (Evangelical Church of Berlin-Brandenburg)

# CONTENTS

## PART II

### The Revolutionary Character of Present-Day Society and the Problem of Political Order

## PART III

### Growth of Government Responsibility and Political Power and the Claims of Human Freedom

## PART IV

### The Nation-State: Its Values and Limits in the Contemporary World

# FOREWORD

by Z. K. MATTHEWS

EVEN the most casual observer of the world scene, whatever his vantage point, is struck by the remarkable differences between the world of the first half of the twentieth century and that of the second. Modes of travel have evolved from the oxcart to the supersonic airplane; means of communication from the post card to Telstar; the organization of industry from the machine age to the age of cybernation; the conduct of government from the maintenance of law and order to the assumption of responsibility for the welfare of individuals and groups within a nation.

While some changes are normal in every society, those that have taken place in the modern world in recent years can only be described as revolutionary. They have been rapid, widespread and thoroughgoing. More changes have been packed into the last fifty years than have occurred in centuries in the past. They have affected the so-called western world of Europe and North America but, perhaps even more drastically, Asia, Africa, Latin America and the Middle East. They go to the root of every aspect of life; they call not for a minor tinkering with the social structure, the economic order or the political system, but for a radical transformation of individual and group attitudes, ideas and values; not for a mere pouring of new wine into old bottles, but for a thorough rethinking and re-evaluation of the traditional, in order to bring about the realignment of social, cultural, economic and political life to achieve a new world order.

The present volume is concerned with the problems of government in such a revolutionary age. Although this is not always recognized in schools of law or of political science, probably nothing has changed more radically in the last fifty years than the nature or the business of government. The claims of governments upon the lives of their subjects are much more comprehensive and arbitrary than in the days when Dicey expounded the doctrine of the Separation of Powers and the principle of the Rule of Law. In the interest of the security of the state, modern executives infringe with impunity upon the powers of the judiciary and of the legislature. Preventive detention acts, arbitrary arrests, imprisonment without charge or trial, the use of questionable methods to obtain evidence —all these are becoming more and more common and are justified on the grounds of public or national interest. Such actions raise the question of the nature of responsible government in a revolutionary age, and it is to this question that contributors to this volume have been asked to address themselves.

In order to ensure a realistic and comprehensive discussion of the issues involved, the contributors have been drawn from as wide an area as possible. They have brought to bear on the issues varying types of experience and differing perspectives. The reader will be struck by the spirit of ferment and urgency that emerges concerning the countries of Asia and Africa, which have only recently achieved their independence. Through the eyes of these contributors, we see how new societies are compelled to grapple with such basic issues as the powers of government, the fundamental principles for drawing up a constitution, the problem of passive resistance and violence, the promotion of social justice and the relation between political independence and economic development. On the other hand, in older countries, which have enjoyed the advantages of a relatively stable society and orderly government, the social change resulting from technological and scientific developments is fundamentally altering the nature and the scope of government.

There is no fundamental conflict between these two approaches; they merely reflect differences in how the world looks to those who view it from different angles. Obviously, it must not be assumed that, because a problem has been solved in one way in one part of the world, it will be solved in the same way everywhere. While the principle of the Rule of Law may be regarded as fundamental to good government in one area, in another it may be execrated as the basis of a formal legal tyranny. While the party system may appear to belong to the natural order of things in one society, it may be looked upon in another as an obstacle to peace, order and good government. While the separation of church and state may be an article of faith in one society, it may appear strange in another, in which belief in God is regarded as one of the basic principles of the Constitution. The transplanting of social, economic and political systems from one country to another, without careful scrutiny of the assumptions on which they are based or the conditions under which they were developed, may do more harm than good. This must not be interpreted to mean that countries with different historical and cultural antecedents cannot learn from one another. That would be to succumb to the *apartheid* heresy.

The contributors to this volume were provided with a broad outline of the pertinent questions to be dealt with, but no attempt was made to prescribe the manner in which their assignments were to be treated. Each wrote as the spirit moved him. There is a striking variety of approach, even among authors writing on the same subject. Practically every paper leaves many questions unanswered; none gives an exhaustive treatment of the topic. The result is a document that raises many issues calling for further elaboration and discussion. It is commended not only to our fellow-Christians but to all who take part today in the debate concerning world peace and responsible government in a revolutionary age.

## The Structure of the Volume

The volume is divided into five sections. The first is concerned with the problem of world peace, since this is the substratum on which the superstructure of all human progress must be founded. Hanging like a sword of Damocles over the whole world today is the radical change that has taken place in the nature of war. As Dr. Kohnstamm of Holland and Prof. Gollwitzer of Germany point out, in the past, and in appropriate cases, war could be regarded as an instrument of desirable change; but this is no longer true, because atomic war between the great powers—but involving both great and small nations—can lead only to total destruction. While there may be skirmishes or localized conflicts between small nations in Asia or Africa, in which only conventional weapons are used, there is the ever-present danger that escalation may lead to the total destruction from which the world has been saved only by the balance of terror between opposing nuclear powers. But is this balance of terror a sufficient basis for lasting peace? Is this the atmosphere in which the jungle of opposing forces can be converted, however gradually, into a political community that transcends national borders, in which countries are bound together by ties of interdependence and the pursuit of common objectives in social and economic development? Judging from the varied answers of our contributors, there is a considerable division of opinion among Christians on these and related questions.

The contributors to this section also raise certain unresolved questions regarding international relations that create tensions and hinder the search for peace. The problem of German unification, the possible increase in the number of nuclear powers, the gulf between the rich and the poor countries, the possibility of violence in the struggle against racial discrimination and *apartheid*—all these emphasize the need for a new political morality in keeping with the conditions of the modern world. In the search for this, church members can "become pioneers in building political community across borders that now restrict the active exercise of responsibility of man for man." [1]

The second section of the volume is concerned with the revolutionary character of present-day society and the problem of political order. The struggles of nation-building in the newly independent states reveal that independence is not the panacea many had imagined and has not brought in the millennium promised by some in the struggle for national liberation. The search for national unity, the struggle for economic development in order to raise the standard of living, the attempt to develop new relations with former metropolitan powers, with no traces of neocolonialism—all these have led to an emphasis upon national security that can easily develop into a new form of political tyranny.

Europe, also, is in a full-scale political and social revolution, and, in western Europe, this has produced the movement for politi-

---

[1] See MAX KOHNSTAMM: "The West and the Search for Peace in the Nuclear Age," p. 83.

cal and economic integration in the Common Market. Professor André Philip suggests that this means in the first place the end of the traditional revolutionary spirit of Europe and the acceptance of a new technical revolution. "We no longer dream about a future revolution, because we are already living in one, in a continual process of destroying the existing structures and rebuilding them; and man's role is to influence events in such a way as to turn them in the direction he considers favorable." [2] He contrasts the European situation with that in the developing countries, where he sees in these changes a great challenge to liberal parliamentary democracy. However, it might be countered that relations between the executive and the legislature in the developing countries are not so different from those in Europe, because the leaders of these countries are trying to apply European political ideas in their own areas and to their own problems.

In the third section of the book, the subject under discussion is the growth of government responsibility and political power and the claims of human freedom. It is interesting to contrast Professor Hallowell's chapter on the Rule of Law with the essays dealing with the situation in India and Indonesia. The Indian contributors note that, as a consequence of technological developments and the progressive integration of social and economic life, power is becoming concentrated in fewer and smaller centers. "Consequently, the obstacles to individual freedom have become all-pervasive and more formidable than in the nineteenth century." [3] The Indonesian writer places great emphasis upon the influence and prestige of President Sukarno in his implementation of guided democracy on the basis of the Pantjasila. Both writers believe in the necessity for a strong government in the circumstances prevailing in a developing country. Hence the assertion, "A powerful and positive government is neither incompatible with nor malignant to the self-consciousness and freedom of the individual as long as it respects the claims of the individual personal significance and endeavors to create a congenial atmosphere in which the individual can realize social and economic progress, higher standards of living, a

---

[2] See ANDRÉ PHILIP: "The Revolutionary Change in the Structure of European Political Life," p. 120.

[3] See CHANDRAN D. S. DEVANESEN, and M. ABEL: "The Powers of Government and the Claims of Human Freedom," p. 200.

more effective political order and greater social justice." [4] Everything, of course, depends upon the "as long as" and who is to
decide whether the government is faithfully discharging its obligations to the individual. Not everyone would hold to the belief that
the necessary restraint upon governmental authority and its possible abuse can be adequately secured by inclusion of fundamental
rights in the Constitution. Eternal vigilance may be the price of
freedom, but citizens must be permitted to exercise that vigilance
in the protection of their liberties. The increasing tendency of some
governments, in both developed and developing countries, to abro-
gate this right of vigilance, on the pretext of national security or
integration, is causing concern in many parts of the world. This
section ends with an illuminating discussion of religious liberty
and its relation to other freedoms and of the part the church can
play in fearlessly proclaiming "fundamental principles for the human community, regardless of whether these principles are agreeable to the people in power or not." [5]

In the fourth section, the writers grapple with the problem of
the nation-state. Many new nation-states are being formed—in
Africa alone, some thirty-five nation-states have emerged within
the last ten years. What are the values and the limitations of this
form of political organization? In Europe, the nation-state does
not provide answers to all the problems of economic and social
life: modern technological developments demand the formation
of much larger political and social units. The futility of war as an
instrument of policy also compels an abandonment of old political
frameworks and a realignment on a new basis. In the developing
countries, the nation-state has a particular fascination, and nation-
building proceeds with great determination and enthusiasm. Are
these developments contradictory to one another? In Africa, President Nkrumah has already raised the idea of a United States of
Africa under one government, instead of the present multiplicity
of scarcely viable states.

Professor Burgelin, in his essay, deals with the positive and negative aspects of nationalism. He believes that nationalism is limited

---

[4] *Ibid.*, p. 202.
[5] See A. F. CARRILLO DE ALBORNOZ: "Religious Liberty, Human Freedom
and Responsible Government," p. 243.

by new factors such as the growing concern for world solidarity, the progress of science and technology, with its increase in personal production and consumption, the increasing number of international groups nourishing this sense of solidarity, and the entrusting of certain responsibilities to supranational political organisms. Admittedly, national consciousness can be "a strength, an essential factor in the smooth running of political and economic institutions," [6] but even this can be too heavy a price to pay if it interferes with the development of a wider outlook. Within some countries, it may be desirable both for international order and for internal order that more and more powers should be taken away from national political systems. We must be on our guard against the consequence of nationalism in a new form through the formation of larger and powerful national states that compete with one another—the United States and her satellites, Russia and her satellites and the nations of the "third world." "If international cooperation is to lead to peace, progress and economic development, it is essential that nationalism shall not spring up again on a larger scale, where it is now tending to decline, and that it shall not triumph in those regions that do not yet know all its evils." [7] This is a problem that must engage the attention of statesmen in the developing and the developed countries. Obviously, churchmen must be deeply involved in the effort to define the limits and the obligations of the nation-state for our time. The role of supranational political institutions and regional organizations in fostering a wider outlook is an important dimension of this concern.

The final section of the volume considers the church and the Christian citizen in the world. It opens with a review of positions held within the ecumenical movement on political questions in the twentieth century. Professor Iisaka of Japan deals with the necessity for Christians to take an active part in political life, even in areas like Asia, where Christians constitute a tiny minority. Reverend Edward Rogers, with his wide experience of directing the Christian Citizenship Department of an influential church in the United Kingdom, shows how Christians can bring their influence to bear on public questions, and how pooling resources and infor-

[6] See HENRI BURGELIN: "Nationalism and the National State," p. 270.
[7] *Ibid.*, p. 275.

mation adds to "the value of . . . judgments . . . for the guidance of our people and strengthens the impact of any comment presented to government or to official social authority." [8] Reverend Bassarak of East Berlin, in the final contribution, makes it clear that the Christian, because of his faith, cannot stand outside the tensions and ambiguities of our world. The implication is that the Christian must take a stand when great public issues are under discussion. But the question remains: What criteria will he use in determining his obedience in action?

Quite clearly, the new and many-faceted debate about the Christian responsibility in political life raises questions that cannot yet be answered about the Christian understanding of man as a political being. Our hope is that the present volume will be a stimulus to much further reflection and analysis, which might clarify the spiritual and moral basis of responsible political life for mankind in a complex world.

---

[8] See EDWARD ROGERS: "Christians and Political Responsibility," p. 369.

# PART I

## THE WORLD POLITICAL SITUATION
## AND THE SEARCH FOR PEACE

# I

# AWAKENED PEOPLES, DEVELOPING NATIONS AND THE DYNAMICS OF WORLD POLITICS

by M. M. THOMAS (India)

THE Papal Encyclical *Pacem in Terris* describes three revolutions of our age that have made a tremendous impact on world politics: the awakening of the working class to a new sense of dignity, the emancipation of women and their increasing role in public life and the awakening of subject nations and races to their rights to independence and equality of status. When we set these revolts of suppressed groups within the framework of a world that technology is transforming into a neighborhood, we are confronted with the new dimensions of the problem of building a world community. This essay will concentrate on the third revolution—the emergence of nonwhite peoples into world politics.

### The Struggle of Awakened Peoples and Races for Their Human Rights

The struggle of the peoples of Africa and Asia against colonialism and foreign political domination and of nonwhite races everywhere against racial paternalism, discrimination and segregation, are two aspects of the same revolution. Pope John XXIII saw them together as the expressions of the same aspiration of men for freedom from the subjection of "political powers located outside . . . [their] own country or ethnic group," and for "the rank of citizens in independent nations." [1]

Daisuke Kitagawa, in *Race Relations and the Christian Mission,*[2] also sees this relationship, pointing out that behind Afro-Asian solidarity lies the dynamics of racism:

Today in Africa and throughout the world, members of coloured races are being united. It is wishful to think that they are not necessarily united against the white race, for quite frankly they are. The element of counter-racism is very strong. . . . To be sure . . . [the] conferences of Afro-Asian nations have not openly declared "racial war" against the West. However, racial feeling is one of the strongest factors that keeps the otherwise precarious solidarity among Afro-Asian nations from breaking down completely.

The struggle against racial segregation in the United States has been inspired by the political emancipation of African people, and its leaders have acknowledged their debt to Mahatma Gandhi, who used the techniques of nonviolent resistance on a large scale in India's struggle for national freedom. James Baldwin says, in *The Fire Next Time,*[3] that the decision of the American Supreme Court ten years ago against segregation in schools cannot be understood apart from "the fact that Africa was clearly liberating herself, and therefore had, for political reasons, to be wooed by the descendants of her former masters." [4] This view is generally

---

[1] "Men all over the world have today—or will soon have—the rank of citizens in independent nations; no-one wants to feel subject to political powers located outside his own country or ethnic group. Thus in many human beings the inferiority complex which endured for hundreds and thousands of years is disappearing, while in others there is an attenuation and gradual fading of the corresponding superiority complex which had its roots in social-economic privileges, sex or political standing.

"On the contrary, the conviction that all men are equal by reason of their natural dignity has been generally accepted. Hence racial discrimination can no longer be justified, at least doctrinally or in theory. And this is of fundamental importance and significance for the formation of human society according to these principles which we have outlined above. For, if a man becomes conscious of his rights, he must become equally aware of his duties. Thus he who possesses certain rights has likewise the duty to claim those rights as marks of his dignity, while all others have the obligation to acknowledge those rights and respect them." (*Pacem in Terris,* Part I).

[2] New York: Friendship Press, 1964, pp. 26-27.

[3] London: Michael Joseph, 1963.

[4] Dr. Paul Sigmund, of the Department of Politics of Princeton University, makes the following comment: "I personally would doubt that the

accepted by American Negroes, and it is a fact, as Kitagawa charges, that the sense of common struggle has brought "the people of Negro racial background in Africa and the United States closer together" in a new way, which it has not been possible for "the missionary movement of the last century and the first part of this century" to do.

The movement in the world toward full political rights for all citizens within independent nations is the direction in which world politics is moving and makes men conscious of the remaining vestiges of old western colonialism, which keeps one people subject to another, and of neocolonialism, which keeps peoples from the right to determine their own political and economic life.

No doubt, the peoples who still remain under an old type of colonialism are few. But the fear of neocolonialism will continue among the new nations; it will be enhanced by the frustrations of nation-building and reduced by its achievements.

The practice of some nations of giving only second-class citizenship to certain racial or ethnic groups because of their color is becoming therefore more and more intolerable and something that the people, thus deprived of their human dignity, are prepared to fight. There are indications that the struggle for racial equality will be a prolonged one and that it is likely to become a dominant factor in world politics in the years to come.[5]

---

decision of the Supreme Court in 1954 was much influenced by the emergence of Africa; at that point, the African independence movement was not sufficiently important to act as a major influence on the thinking of the Justices. Much more important was a long train of judicial decisions widening the implications of the constitutional guarantee of equality embodied in the Fourteenth Amendment to the American Constitution."

And Dr. Leroy S. Ronner, professor at the United Theological College (Bangalore, India), writes: "I think your assertion that American Negroes have felt a closer affinity with Africans as a result of the Civil Rights movement is generally wrong. It is certainly true for the Negro extremists of the Black Muslim variety, who regard the NAACP, CORE, SNICK and all other organizations which have a large white constituency as traitors to the Negro cause. But there is evidence that the majority of the Negroes—James Baldwin is chief among them—are protesting, not on the basis of the rights of the black race, but on the basis of their citizenship as Americans."

[5] Dr. Rupert Emerson, of the Department of Government, Harvard University, comments: "It is perhaps no more than wishful thinking, but I hope that the statement that race conflict is likely to become a more dominant factor in world politics in the years to come will prove to be wrong. If the

In the United States, the rights of the Negro "to go to school, to get a job, to vote and to pursue his life unhampered by the barriers of racial segregation" have the protection of the federal law. Yet, those rights may have to be secured by bitter struggles against state laws, organized white racists like the John Birch Society and the Ku Klux Klan, vested social interests and the legitimate fears of demoralization that inevitably follow in the wake of the disintegration of a traditionally segregated society. The combination of conservative extremism with religious pietism and individualist morality that found expression in the campaign of Goldwater, although he was massively defeated in the Presidential election, remains a potent force in American politics and may keep alive white racist groups in other parts of the world.

The growth of extremism on both sides of the race conflict is evidence of the failure of liberalism to achieve its ideals of equality and fraternity through moral persuasion, education and agitation, within the framework of the Constitution. The use of extraconstitutional means of exercising power is more or less taken for granted by most, if not all, of the groups fighting for racial equality. The only question is whether these means should be nonviolent (the "extremism of love," as Martin Luther King, Jr., calls it) or should involve the use of arms.

In general, Negro leadership has advocated a combination of constitutional process and the Gandhian technique of nonviolent group resistance as reinterpreted in the light of the Christian faith. In his book *Stride Toward Freedom,* Martin Luther King warns the American Negro against following the path of violence and says that, where violence is used, "future generations will be the recipients of a desolate night of bitterness, and our chief legacy to them will be an endless reign of meaningless chaos." He offers nonviolence as the path whereby the Negro can bring justice "for both himself and the white man." In his speech accepting the

United States can manage really to get over the hump of dealing with its own racial problem, I should think that a tremendous advance would have been made, since the great bulk of the colonial problem is already disposed of. South Africa certainly remains a danger spot of very real consequence, but I hope that it will become possible to deal with it not in terms of racial division in the rest of the world but on some more general ground."

Nobel Prize, he reiterates his faith in nonviolent means not only for the situation in the United States but for that in Southern Africa as well.

In certain parts of Africa, the situation is in fact more fraught with violence than in the United States. South Africa, with *apartheid* and its militant defiance of international opinion; Rhodesia, where the whites are determined to continue minority rule and recently declared their independence as a white nation-state; and Angola and other Portuguese territories are dangerous spots, where the struggle for racial equality and human rights may take a violent turn, especially as the newly independent African nations find the situation increasingly intolerable. (The United Nations seems helpless in the face of the needs of subjected African peoples. The big western powers do not take seriously the economic boycott of South Africa.) It is in this context that the words of the Kenya Home Minister must be read: "The remaining colonial territories in Africa will not be liberated until the independent African states jointly are prepared to wage war against South Africa." Sixteen independent African states are committed to liberate black Africa, and have already met twice, in Addis Ababa and Cairo, to organize their forces. The African members of the Commonwealth have been successful in pressing on Britain its responsibility for establishing in Southern Rhodesia an independent nation with majority rule. The policy of some African states, of withdrawing from international conferences because of the participation of South Africa or Portugal, is self-defeating. But at least it shows the frustration caused by the racial situation in Africa.

Many erstwhile followers of the nonviolent Chief Luthuli and his African National Congress, like Nelson Mandela (tried, convicted and sentenced to life imprisonment), have been converted through long years of frustration to the inevitability of armed uprising inside and armed intervention from without. They have organized the Spear of the Nation movement, whose aim is sabotage and armed overthrow of the South African government. This kind of conversion from nonviolence to violence is taking place every day. The consultation on Race Relations in Southern Africa, held under the auspices of the World Council of Churches and the South

African Institute of Race Relations, in Mindolo (Zambia) in 1964, declared:

The urgency of the situation in South Africa is further increased by the conviction of leading Africans that, as all peaceful measures tried by African political organizations over a period of many years to bring about an ordered change have proved abortive, only one avenue remains open—that of violence. On the other hand, it is precisely this conviction and possible resultant action which consolidates the white electorate, hardens its general attitude and leads to ever-increasing measures which eventually precipitate the danger they wish to avoid. For many Christians involved in the struggle for a just solution, the question of possible violence as the only remaining alternative has become an urgent and ever-pressing one. Reports indicate that many are convinced that war has already begun.

This picture may be too pessimistic, and I have not, perhaps, given due recognition to the achievements of liberal humanism. But, unfortunately, liberalism is breaking down through fear of the dynamism in the revolutionary upsurge of suppressed groups; it cannot face the fact that such hate and violence can exist in decent men! Liberal Christians are so conscious of their own guilt that they feel unable openly to condemn the extreme fascism expressed in *apartheid*. Those theologians who say, "Let the sinless among us condemn South African whites," tend to paralyze even those Christian groups that want to act. They are profoundly wrong in thinking that, because all men are equally sinful before God, they should not distinguish between the greater and the lesser evil in any situation, and then take the necessary action justified not by their own works, but by faith. There still seem to be some theologians who have not learned the necessity of dealing with the relativities of politics and society. There is no evidence that the forces of liberal humanism, Christian humanism, or even nonviolent militancy have fully understood the working of the political, economic and social powers that are seeking to consolidate white extremist elements, especially in Africa. Men are thus left struggling for their rights, with the path of violence their only choice.

*The Relationship Between Developed and Developing Nations*

In an article entitled "Brazil: An Underdeveloped Giant Wakes Up," [6] Caio de Taledo gives a few lines of a revolutionary song of Brazil, "Song of the Underdeveloped."

> But one day the giant awoke,
> He ceased being a sleeping giant,
> And lo! a dwarf arose;
> He was an underdeveloped country!

The description fits all the peoples of Africa, Asia and Latin America. They have all become conscious in a new way of their rich spiritual and cultural heritage, and feel themselves to be giants; but they know also that, given the modern criteria of economic and technological power, they remain dwarfs. And it hurts. The struggle of the poor nations today to develop themselves and to raise their people's standard of living not only determines in large measure the direction of politics within them but also shapes the character of international relations, especially those between the developed and developing countries of the world.

There has always been poverty and famine in the countries of Africa and Asia, accompanied by a spirit of resignation, often reinforced by religion. Today, this spiritual situation has changed. The struggle for national independence, the emergence of independent nation-states and the process of nation-building have disturbed "the pathetic contentment of the masses," who now realize that poverty is not their inevitable fate, but can be overcome through organized effort. Therefore, "the revolution of rising expectations" is part of the self-awakening of Africa and Asia and of the search of Afro-Asian peoples for their self-identity.

When hungry men begin to discern that a higher living standard is a fundamental human right, any obstacle to its realization, either within the nation or in other nations, seems like injustice. While this sense of injustice feeds on memories of colonial exploitation, by which the nations of the West developed their own economies,

---

[6] *motive,* Nov., 1963; *Student World,* No. 1, 1964.

it is not primarily a product of the past but a new awakening of men to their own human selfhood. Therefore, any slackening in the world's effort to promote the economic welfare of all peoples becomes intolerable. The new sense of economic injustice will have no less revolutionary results than did the old feeling of direct exploitation.

The nations of Africa, Asia and Latin America realize that their economic development is primarily their own responsibility. They seek to remove the causes of economic stagnation in their culture and society and to mobilize the financial and technical resources by increased agricultural and industrial productivity and social welfare. But they know only too well that they cannot succeed without international economic cooperation.

A large volume of opinion in the developed nations today is urging increased aid to the developing nations in their economic struggle. Such opinion has found expression not only in such voluntary movements as the Freedom from Hunger campaign but also in putting pressure on governments and business to evolve systems of financial aid and technical assistance to underdeveloped countries that show a sensitive awareness of their political and social goals. The United Nations is committed by its Charter "to promote social progress and better standards of life and larger freedom" and "to employ international machinery for the promotion of the economic and social advancement of all peoples" (Preamble). Bilateral and multilateral international machinery has been developed to support national development plans. However, they all remain inadequate, and then are sometimes subordinate to political and ideological interests, unrelated to the problem of economic development. Further, public opinion in this field is so closely circumscribed that the richer nations have not yet taken the more costly step of making the interests of developing nations a criterion, if not *the* criterion, of policy in international trade, common markets and world economic development. Even in international economic relations, charity and justice must be closely related. International charity must express itself in impersonal institutional structures and the obligations of international justice if it is to have the character of true charity. It is in this connection that the recent Geneva Conference on World Trade and Development and the

Final Act of the Conference deserve attention.[7] But the general reaction to it in the developed nations confirms that they have not adequately recognized the deeper implications of the ever-widening gap between the rich nations and the poor on world politics and on the issues of war and peace.

The gulf between the rich and the poor countries can be gauged by the fact that "the joint income of the developing countries, with two-thirds of the world's population, is not much more than one-tenth of that of the industrialized countries." As world economy swiftly expands, the result of vast scientific and technical progress widens the gulf still further. The value of world exports has been more than doubled since 1950. But the developing countries' share in them has been declining steadily "from nearly one-third in 1950 to only slightly more than one fifth in 1962" and at a time, we should note, when development in the poorer countries requires imports of capital goods and technical skills from developed nations. The growing gap between their import and export earnings has put the severest strain on development plans.

Many factors in underdeveloped economies no doubt contribute to this situation. But even when "their plans, policies and institutions are designed to achieve the transformation of their economic and social structures and to provide for maximum saving, investment and output to a pre-determined order of priorities for a targeted rate of growth," their realization has been hindered "by the instability of international markets for primary products and by conditions restricting the access of primary commodities and semi-manufactures and manufactures to the markets of the developed countries."

The Geneva Conference spelled out some of the "specific policies" of wealthy nations that hinder the plans of developing nations and affirmed that, "In order to facilitate the industrial exports of developing countries, their products should have freer access, particularly to the markets of the developed countries"; and it is recognized that "substantial imports of manufactures and semi-manufactures may involve some readjustment in the industrial structures of the developed countries."

[7] *United Nations Conference on Trade and Development: Final Act.* Duplicated report.

It is not yet clear, however, that the richer societies are prepared for this necessary "readjustment." The main resolutions at the conference were, in fact, generally carried by the votes of the majority of the economically underdeveloped nations, and it is therefore too early to assess their value. The hostile reaction in developed nations of the West, moreover, seems indicative of their irritation at the sight of the poorer nations forming themselves into a bloc and demanding sacrifices from the richer—almost as a matter of fundamental right. *The Economist* [8] commented on the conference that "the underprivileged nations at Geneva have been winning votes by losing heads." But, whether by exercising heads or votes, or by losing them through more explosive measures, the poor nations are determined to battle with the rich to realize the economic means of the fuller life. *The Economist* rightly said, "There are limits to the extent to which you can bully someone into giving you money for nothing, when you leave no bargaining power but a hubbub of voices." But this bullying spirit on the part of the powerless is an important factor in determining new trends in world politics. There is little doubt that the poor nations are determined to use their numerical majority in the continuing international machinery that has been set up. As they state in a joint declaration, "the developing countries attach cardinal importance to democratic procedures which afford no position of privilege in the economic and financial, no less than in the political sphere." And they do envisage that "the progressive strengthening of the machinery that is now contemplated" will lead to an international cooperation that will "serve as a decisive instrument for ending the division of the world into areas of affluence and intolerable poverty. This task is the outstanding challenge of our time."

By common consent, the forging at Geneva of the United Front of the Developing Nations was "the outstanding feature of the entire conference and an event of historic significance." The "seventy-five developing countries" have pledged themselves to strengthen it as "an indispensable instrument for securing the adoption of new attitudes and new approaches in the international economic field." And many rightly believe that this new bloc is the most dominant emerging force in world politics.

---

[8] London: June 6, 1964.

Ideological and political blocs along other lines continue to have validity. But it is also clear that, with the unity of the poor and the division between rich and poor becoming more dominant, they will cut across other divisions and make them less important. We find, for instance, that Japan, though a nation of nonwhite people, voted against, or abstained from voting on, many of the crucial resolutions at Geneva, because it is a developed nation. Free World alliances simply broke down in the conference, dividing themselves into rich and poor. Russia had its embarrassing silences, as it could not identify itself fully with the poor nations. Here the ideological rift between the Chinese and the Russian Communists has a certain relevance. As Edward Rogers writes in *Living Standards:* [9]

If the gap between rich and poor continues to widen, and if the world does polarize into opposing camps, the almost certain outcome will be war. From that point the estimation of probabilities moves into the realm of science fiction—where it had better stay. The advanced nations could win a nuclear war, ending, if they were lucky, with a world crippled, decimated in population and pock-marked with lethal radio-activity. The poorer nations could by force of numbers win a conventional war, dragging down the West to the level of their own poverty, and in the terrible enterprise destroying for generations their own prospect of escape from its thrall. Either prospect is grim. A serious, urgent campaign against poverty is the alternative to war.

### Search for a New Political Morality

In the industrialized West, the debate in the field of political and economic morality has for long been primarily between individualism and collectivism—in politics between a multiparty system of democracy, with its emphasis on individual freedom safeguarded by the Rule of Law, and a one-party structure of communist government, with its emphasis on the state and law as the instruments of the party that represents the people's collective interest and purpose; and in economics between *laissez-faire* capitalism and socialist planning. In the world today, capitalism and socialism have ceased in practice to be watertight systems, with capitalism accepting a good deal of state initiative and socialism accepting the stimulation of private enterprise and the price mechanism; and the

---

[9] London: SCM Press, 1964, p. 82.

ideological issues, though very much alive in some quarters on both sides, have not much moral significance. It is a different matter with the debate on political morality and the discussion of the nature and function of the state as conceived and practiced by the democratic and communist regimes. The ideological power blocs led by America and Russia continue to determine the character of the world political discussion.

Three new facts, however, are beginning to influence the debate on political morality. First, the awareness that nuclear technology, by increasing the utter destructiveness of a nuclear war, has eliminated it as a political weapon. Second, the logic of technological development and the move toward affluence, which, coupled with natural human urges, have led Russia to liberate itself from Stalinism and to ease its internal controls and tensions. This has altered its position in relation to other countries of the Russian bloc and has caused the breach with China; it has diminished the communist threat and made America readier to look toward peaceful coexistence with communist societies. Third, the struggle of Africa, Asia and Latin America to build up viable and dynamic political structures that are effective in consolidating self-conscious religious, linguistic and ethnic communities as national communities, in order to satisfy their expectation of higher standards of living and to meet the demands of the masses for fuller freedom and opportunities to participate in state and society at the level where power is exercised, has challenged static definitions of constitutionalism and the Rule of Law and has brought about a new consciousness of the dialectical relation between freedom and justice in a dynamic political situation. As a result, new forces and new perspectives have been introduced into the debate on political ethics.

When nuclear war can only annihilate both the victor and the vanquished, it certainly cannot be a continuation of politics through other means; and the idea of a "just war" loses its meaning. Can any political decision be more immoral than the decision to unleash a nuclear war, which would exterminate the major part of mankind and leave the rest hopelessly diseased?

The elimination of nuclear war from among the political weapons does not mean eliminating possession of nuclear bombs. Such possession does impress as a symbol of a nation's economic and military strength, and its prestige effect has tremendous political power. That is why nations are eager to enter the nuclear bomb club. But, at the same time, the peoples of the world strongly resist the entry of more nations into the nuclear arms race.

As a result of the nuclear impasse, several things have happened. First, world peace has acquired a new priority in world politics, which has led to the breakdown of the rigid ideological military blocs led by America and Russia and to a general acceptance of coexistence and cooperation between different social and political systems and ideologies. Second, it has deepened the awareness of all people of the interdependence of nations, the interconnection between the struggles for world peace and social justice everywhere, and the virtual elimination of the distinction between foreign and domestic affairs within the nations. The bargaining power of the non-nuclear nations has strengthened and increased their freedom to be rid of traditional structures of international law and to look for more dynamic relations in national and international life. Non-alignment in international affairs has a new respectability, and the new nations have scope to experiment with new political structures and ideologies and to build up their own political ethics.

The new nations need to develop new political ethics applicable to their own particular situations. They cannot, it is true, throw away the insights of political morality that have emerged in the debate between the advocates of liberal democracy, socialist democracy and communism. But the dynamics of their situations are in many ways very different from those of the West.

These differences arise in several ways. First, the revolutionary changes that came to the West one after another over a long period are coming to the new nations simultaneously and within a much shorter time. Demands for increasing agricultural and industrial productivity, for the participation of all the people in government, for more equal distribution of the wealth of the country and for public responsibility for health, education, social welfare and security, all pressing together, make strong state initiative and state-imposed discipline in large areas of public life essential, not primarily on ideological, but on sheer pragmatic grounds. It is significant that the United Nations Conference on World Development and Trade in Geneva assumed that state sectors would be required along with private sectors in the economic life of the developing nations. Second, industrialism, socialism and community development in relation to the traditional religious and cultural background pose many problems. If they are to attain stability, these new techniques and ideas must have indigenous cultural roots and a certain continuity with indigenous humanism through reform of traditional religions and cultures. In this process, it is necessary and legitimate to reinterpret as far as possible the techniques and ideas themselves in indigenous forms. But, inevitably, the spirit of traditional collectivism and authoritarianism will also seek to absorb the imported techniques and institutions, yet leaving aside the spirit of western humanism that lies behind them.

We face new situations where the relation between order, freedom and justice has to be worked out in new dynamic patterns without being too meticulous about using only well-tried political molds imported from the West. There has been a series of experiments in building political structures that represent attempts to adopt the insights of the West to new situations. Nehru's democratic socialism, Nasser's Arab socialism, Nkrumah's African socialism, Sukarno's guided democracy, Castro's communism and Mao's communism cannot be classified in the traditional categories of the West. Even India's parliamentary democracy has had to be adapted to the needs of a developing situation, by recognizing techniques of the states' planning of economic life; and Chinese communism has developed its own distinct patterns in seeking to revolutionize the agrarian pattern of a traditional Confucian society.

I do not claim that all these patterns should be accepted indiscriminately as equally legitimate and moral; or that morality should be dispensed with; and that stability and/or an alliance with either the communist or the anticommunist power bloc alone should become the criterion. But the moral evaluation of the emerging systems must be based on a new set of criteria that are creatively relevant to the context, and not merely on formal western categories. The new criteria will include the essence of democracy, but without identifying it with its traditional western forms. They will include, that is to say, the demand that the structure of any political order should, at some point, express concern for persons and their destiny beyond the state; that people should have the opportunity to participate in political power and to oppose power; and that power should be made responsible by minimizing the arbitrary exercise of it. But such criteria must also recognize that freedom and responsibility cannot be worked out except in the specific context of the search for the dignity and identity of new groups that lies behind the dynamic of awakened peoples, developing nations and reviving cultures. It is therefore a complete mistake to impose an ideal on the situation, pitting the individual against the awakening class, nation or race, or debating the moral priority between freedom and justice; the main concern should be to relate the forces and ideals that are already in operation in the actual complex situation.

No doubt, the idea of a responsible society that emerged from the discussions at the Amsterdam Assembly of the World Council of Churches can be developed into a criterion of the kind we seek. But, at Amsterdam, the main debate was between democracy and communism and therefore, as it emerged, the idea of responsible society did not reckon with the situations of the new nations. As a result, it is too comprehensive and balanced and too much lacking in the sense of the tragic tension existing between the urgently necessary and the ultimately significant to be relevant to the moral complexities of our situations. It is perhaps not impossible to work toward a new criterion of political ethics, expressed in a new understanding of responsible society, and relevant to the moral dynamics of the new situations.

What I have in mind is best expressed in a statement of the East Asia Christian Conference on "Responsibilities of the World Community for Asia's Political and Economic Development":

Abstract judgments of these different systems serve no useful purpose. Each has grown out of political forces and social needs of a particular situation. Moreover, they all have one common aim: to create an independent nation-state serving the urgent social and economic needs of their peoples. While each nation should be free to develop the patterns of political life which suit its genius best and correspond to its stage of political maturity, this freedom cannot be absolute. It should be exercised with understanding of certain basic political and moral requirements of community, both national and international. Christians concerned with the spiritual and ethical foundations of society have a duty to work within the limitations of the different situations for the basic principles of a responsible state even though they may be expressed in different forms of state and can be realized only partially in any.[10]

The statement goes on to speak of three values of responsible political life that should be the concern of the newly independent nations: 1. "The State must be based in some measure on the consent of the people." 2. "The State must express in its own structure its recognition that man has ends and loyalties beyond the State." 3. "The power of the State should never be absolute and must be limited by political means, legal processes or custom." But the statement recognizes that no political order can realize these values in its structure unless, in the first place, it is able to convince the people of its effectiveness in promoting national solidarity, economic development and social justice.

In fact, the real debate among people and parties accepting the responsible state as the goal of politics is not about moral priorities but about the chronological ordering of things. The question is whether radical structural changes and rapid development in society can and ought to be achieved with the minimum possible curtailment of individual freedom, with built-in safeguards for their restoration; or whether there are many situations that make it legitimate for responsible people to conclude that a government has to be at least pragmatically authoritarian to effect the necessary social transformation and that the urges of human freedom have a better chance of asserting themselves when the forces of development have achieved strength and when the larger inequalities between classes, castes, races and other groups in a society have been overcome. It is important that this debate continue within the framework of a responsible search of the nations for a new political morality. This is not said to minimize the threat of totalitarian ideology and politics, either of the left or of the right, but to distinguish a type of authoritarianism of the left that may be a necessary means toward an eventual strengthening of responsible state and society in some of the developing countries.

---

[10] *Christian Community Within the Human Community,* Minutes of the EACC Assembly, 1964. Part II.

## Chinese Communism Today and the New Polarization of World Politics

The struggle against colonialism and racial discrimination, the united front of the poor nations to secure a fair deal from the rich in matters of aid and trade and the efforts to build state structures that can effect modernization of traditional societies—all these have their distinctive characteristics, cutting across one another. Nevertheless, they are closely related and, broadly speaking, strengthen one another and work together to form some sort of new international proletariat, fighting for their liberation against the West. In this context, Chinese communism, with its concept of world polarization and its program of pushing this division of the world between the rich and the proletariat to extreme limits, poses a serious threat. It does so precisely because it speaks relevantly to the militant mood of the nonwhite peoples and the poor nations in their search for effective fighting power, and because it appeals to the human urges behind that mood. In the present situation, China seems to have great power to convince the leaders of the several liberation movements in Africa, Asia and Latin America that totalitarian communism and war are the only effective means of successful liberation. China's testing of the nuclear bomb has enhanced its prestige and its image as a rapidly growing military and industrial power and impressed the Afro-Asian nations with its capacity for militant leadership. In contrast, India and some other countries have represented a more liberal view of state structure and a more nonviolent form of political struggle; and they are committed to using nuclear science only for peaceful purposes. Will such nations retain an influential role, and will their ideas have some chance of success among the awakened peoples and developing nations of the world? Will Chinese communism move in the direction of the liberalization these countries represent, or will the extremist spirit overcome them, too? It is anybody's guess. The answer depends on many factors and forces within these nations. But much also depends on whether the white races and the developed nations, be they capitalist or socialist, will recognize the human urges behind the revolutionary awakening of peoples throughout the world and make the readjustments and sacrifices necessary in their own lives, enabling their countries to participate, in an imaginative and costly way, in the struggle of all peoples for a new society.

Perhaps, in the new decade that we enter, the churches' main task will be to prove that Christian and human solidarity can render unnecessary (or at least less destructive) wars and violences that seem inevitable today.

*Postcript:* Comment by Professor S. Rouner of the United Theological College, Bangalore, on the middle section of the preceding paper. He writes to Mr. Thomas as follows:

"There is an interesting shift in your argument from the concept of *rights* to the concept of *responsibility*. My feeling is that the basic issue is also one of responsibility rather than rights. You raise —by implication—the complicated philosophical question as to whether an individual or a nation has a 'right' to wealth. Your argument is that the affluent societies have it, and the poorer nations have a right to demand sacrifice by the rich. You go so far as to argue that the economic policy of the affluent cannot be regarded as moral in the fullest sense until they accept the national goals of the poor as their sole consideration in economic policy, rather than the present mixture of self-interest and interest in the future of the other fellow.

"Basic to the argument about rights is the democratic credo that 'All men are created equal.' This is not an empirical statement, but a legal principle essentially, which has now been applied to some social areas, and tentatively to economics in the principle that all men have a *right* to equal opportunity, or a 'fighting chance.' If they lack the ability or the situation which gives them a genuine 'fighting chance,' the welfare state declares, rightly, that society has a responsibility to see that none of its members suffers great hardship economically. This is not far from the communist goal of 'to each according to his need.' And I take it that what you mean to say here is that the rich ought to recognize the needs of the poor, and are responsible for meeting them—and I couldn't agree more.

"I am uneasy about the use of *rights,* however, because—while it highlights the sins of the rich, it tends to cast a cloak of piety over the sins of the poor. It has the revolutionary advantage of pitting rich against poor and clarifying the problem, but it tends to authorize any demand made by the poor on the rich. Psychologically speaking, it is an expression of the resentment of former colonies against the colonialists who often bled them. Because the colonialists feel guilty for their sins, the charge of 'economic colonialism' becomes an effective weapon of the poor in urging their demands. It also tends to further the false economic assumption that the major problems of the poor can be met by large increases in aid of one sort or another from the rich.

"Economic rights are tied almost solely to nationalism. The poor are concerned only with their rights as a poor nation. They are not concerned, for example, with the internal problem of poverty in the 'rich' nations, or with the complex difficulties which the 'rich' have in maintaining economic stability. Their demand is based entirely on self-interest, but they do not recognize self-interest as valid for the rich. The rich, because they are 'rich,' have no right to self-interest.

"From the perspective of the poor, the ethics of the situation is clear to the point of being maddening, further adding to their resentment. But economically there is a certain lack of realism involved, because the poor know that their economic problems are so much greater than those of the rich that they find it hard to understand that a rich nation has many genuine economic problems. Price supports for grains in America is probably a good example. Unless the poor are prepared to admit the right of the Americans to deal with this as a real economic problem, the real difficulty of sharing America's incredible agricultural overproduction isn't going to make much headway.

"I would say, rather, that the question of rights is rooted in the deeper question of responsibility. The real problem of relationship between rich and poor is a problem of mutual responsibilities, both to one's own people and to each other. Each nation's primary responsibility is to its own people, economically, politically, culturally, etc. This is what makes it a nation. This much 'self-interest' is valid for everyone. What we are all gradually learning is that our national identity takes place under a more inclusive and increasingly felt identity of mankind. We are our brother's keeper. We must reach out politically and economically, and we must do it responsibly. America must solve the surplus agricultural problem not only for its own sake, but for India's (etc.) sake as well. India must be prepared to recognize that this is an American problem and not impose an Indian solution on it, in the same way that America must recognize that India's planned economy affairs are appropriate for her and not insist that India's internal affairs be ordered along an American pattern. India has a right to urge on America a solution of the problem, because it is a mutual problem; in the same way, American AID [Agency for International Development] people urge particular solutions on the Indian economy because they are involved in it.

"I agree entirely that the whole question of mutual economic responsibility takes place within the context of the moral requirement of the rich to aid the poor. Let there be no question about that. But any economy, rich or poor, is a dynamic thing, subject to its own particular operations, and liable to collapse if dealt with insensitively. The poor always envy and resent the rich for being rich when they are poor, and this resentment is a crucially necessary ingredient in any movement for economic justice, for the rich seldom share unless they have to. In this context, perhaps the emphasis on rights is both inevitable and necessary. But there is at least some evidence in the modern world that the rich are also 'awakening' to their responsibilities. And as this awakening increases, the poor will begin to realize that their own needs are part of the larger problem of a new economic pattern based not on the divisive cry of *meum* and *tuum* but the problems of the entire international community."

# 2

# THE CHRISTIAN IN THE SEARCH FOR WORLD ORDER AND PEACE

by HELMUT GOLLWITZER (Germany)

## The Problem of World Peace

THE most profound change in world politics today, in comparison with earlier periods in the history of mankind, would seem to consist in the fact that the traditional function of war, as a political method, has changed. Because of the development of armaments, war is no longer a calculable means to an end; it is no longer a means the precise object of which is discernible. This is an extraordinary innovation. We are living in a time of transition, during which humanity must get used to this situation and work out the consequences of it. To live in a time of transition means, in the first place, that, while modern war can no longer be relied upon as a political method and constitutes a risk we can no longer take, there still remains the possibility of traditional warfare, whether between countries that so far have no modern weapons, or as civil war, or between countries or groups of countries which are equipped with modern weapons, but which deliberately fight a limited war. Countries that are equipped with modern weapons cling to the hope that it may still be possible to adopt this third course so that they may not be forced to choose between capitulation and suicide (uncalculable atomic war) whenever armed conflict occurs. They retain conventional weapons and armies in order that they may have a choice of some other weapon before the last step is taken and in order to be able to meet on a conventional plane those countries that have no atomic weapons. There is little likelihood of a conventional war between the great atomic powers; and there is even less likelihood that, if such a war did break out, anyone would succeed in keeping it under control and in preventing it from developing into a nuclear war; that is, from changing from a war to achieve an object into a war of annihilation as an end in itself.

Second, a time of transition means that military armaments still serve their traditional purpose of deterrence. But they can no longer serve as a means of waging war to a particular end, because the end is no longer calculable. A deterrent is a threat to use force. Between the atomic powers today, it threatens a use of force that is no longer calculable, but suicidal. Whereas previously the warning conveyed by the threat was "Do not drive me to the use of force!" today it is "Do not drive me to madness!" The deterrent works because the seriousness of the threat is uncertain and because there is a possibility, not clearly defined, that if too great a demand is made upon him and appears to affect his existence, the enemy may prefer madness and the risk of suicide to capitulation. Only if the atomic equilibrium were upset and one of the two great powers should feel secure from retaliation because of the superiority of the weapons it had developed could nuclear armaments again serve the second purpose, and the power that started the war would not need to fear an incalculably deadly reaction.

A time of transition is characterized, in the third place, by the existence of a large number of sovereign states, with all their complexities of foreign policies and conflicts. In fact, however, the sovereignty of many small states is limited first and foremost by their continued inability to compete in armaments and by the treaties that some of them have made for their protection with one or the other of the atomic powers. Despite the dictates of common sense, and despite the fact that the future of all mankind is endangered, the egoism inherent in the sovereign state drives governments to overcome these limitations of sovereignty and to engage in conflicts with other states by the traditional methods of war and of the threat of war. As a result, because of their military superiority, and because of their interest in avoiding an atomic war, the two great atomic powers are forced to assume the role of world police and to seek to prevent the outbreak of armed conflict between smaller states. They fulfill this role only imperfectly; first, because their mutual competition causes them to take sides in conflicts of foreign policy between smaller states with which they are closely connected and to supply them with arms, thus keeping the conflicts virulent instead of ending them (for instance, the conflict between Israel and the Arab states); and second, because in view of their disunity and the danger of a nuclear war, they cannot exert the pressure of an ultimatum, threatening to make war on the smaller states unless they stop using force to settle disputes with neighboring states.

Hitherto, war has been the *ultima ratio* of politics—a means of order. It could serve to defend as well as to change the existing order. In a time of transition, this way of keeping order has become too risky. Yet, as long as there are reasons to have recourse to war, the temptation to resort to it remains. The danger of atomic warfare, which everybody fears, has not so far proved a sufficient incentive for states to remove the causes of war with the energy that common sense demands.

It is true that the existence of atomic weapons today has a peace-preserving significance. The great powers have gone to war in the past for far more trifling reasons than exist in our day. The incalculability and the horror of an atomic war effectively strengthen the interest of the atomic powers in preserving peace and preventing war. But the peace maintained in this manner is extremely unstable. A one-sided lead in armaments, the unthinking and irresponsible action of any one government, outbreaks of extremism on the part of governments or nations, could lead any day to a sudden change from a supposed peace, guaranteed by atomic weapons, to the most terrible catastrophe, involving the whole of mankind, as a result of these same atomic weapons. If the atomic deterrent is reckoned to be needful today, it must, at the same time, be recognized that it is *even more* needful to find ways of replacing it as a guarantee of peace by a better one. The retention of atomic weapons cannot be justified, as was the case with armaments in the past, by the eventuality of an outbreak of war.

Atomic weapons can be justified morally and politically only as a passing phase until the atomic deterrent gives way to a better guarantee of peace.

It remains to be seen whether, after this time of transition, we shall attain a new and more stable order. On no account can we envisage the possibility of a return—perhaps by atomic disarmament—to a situation in which war is a means of keeping order. To do so, the clock would have to be put back to a time before the discovery of atomic weapons. For the same reason, the unilateral abolition of atomic weapons by one of the two great powers, even if conceivable, could no longer end the danger of atomic war. On the other hand, the renunciation of nuclear armaments by other states would have a very positive significance. In fact, however, willingness to make such a renunciation is diminishing among the smaller states, and the danger of anarchy in nuclear armaments is constantly increasing. Moreover, it must always be borne in mind that, with the advance of technical development, atomic bombs will not, in the long run, constitute our only threat. It is possible, as Bertrand Russell once said, that we shall live to see inventions that will make us look back with longing "to the days of the old, homely hydrogen bomb." Accordingly, the aim must be workable international regulations, from which no state can withdraw, and which will also bring further technical developments under international or supranational control. It is imperative that steps be taken toward achieving this aim before further developments overwhelm us. One of the greatest dangers for the future of mankind is the superiority of particular interests that is still prevalent today, together with the delusion that we can afford this superiority under the protection of the balance of atomic power.

### The Christian Attitude Toward War in a Nuclear Age

In a time of transition, the traditional Christian attitude toward war has to be re-examined. There are still situations in which it is possible to apply the war ethic of the major churches and to maintain that "conventional wars" can still take place and that the military deterrent can serve its purpose. Yet such situations continue to exist only provisionally. Just as, in the past, the Christian attitude toward war has been concerned not only with the *threat* of force but with the *use* of force, so today it cannot be confined to thinking about the problem of a balanced atomic deterrent, but it must also take a definite stand in the event of an atomic war.

Within the ecumenical movement, widespread agreement may gradually be reached that, in the event of atomic war, the distinction between a just and an unjust war is no longer tenable—even if it ever was justifiable or practicable (I myself feel that there are many impressive arguments for such a distinction). There is now no possibility of an atomic war being a just war. This assertion has far-reaching implications. It means that the peace-keeping influence of the atomic deterrent is exercised through mutual menace. God's law says No to atomic war. Thus, God's commandment places the church in the same dilemma as confronts the politicians through fear of atomic warfare.

The church must speak out clearly against atomic war. In doing so, it will only delude and deceive itself if it underestimates the difficulties in which it thus places statesmen. God's No means No. Atomic war can no longer be a means of enforcing justice, as a *bellum justum* was in the past. It can no longer be a means of defense or of restoring a legal position. The church must not cloud this clear issue but must be its servant; it must pierce the smoke screen that politicians and the armed forces are always inclined to set up in a time of transition. This No to atomic war has not been arbitrarily arrived at by the church but is a command given to it by God. Therefore, the church must first of all carry out its commission and tell the politicians what God's command says to all: that atomic warfare lies outside the limits of those forceful methods by which we may protect our goods and our rights. God's law is not against all use of force; but whoever has recourse to atomic warfare will have God against him. Only after such plain speaking can the church proceed to take part in deliberations about the way in which this is to be translated into political practice; that is, what policy is adopted when God's No is not ignored and when that policy takes its bearing from him in a world in which atomic weapons have become a decisive and irrevocable factor. If its No is not to look like arrogance or self-righteousness or fanaticism, and if its ethic is not to be one of abstract principles removed from reality and "governed by sentiment" instead of a concrete "responsibility ethic" (Max Weber), the church must take part with all seriousness in these deliberations.

The church must oppose all the sharpening of antitheses that is characteristic of the Cold War. It must steer clear of them and must not identify itself, because of its own interests, with one of the parties in the Cold War.

The major churches must take more seriously than they have in the past the ethos and the arguments of Christian pacifist groups and must make use of the experience of these groups and see that it bears fruit. Because atomic war can no longer be used as an *ultima ratio* for the preservation of justice through force, the major churches are coming closer to the position always held by the historic peace churches—that war cannot serve justice.

The major churches must firmly withstand the temptation to continue transmitting without reflection the traditional war ethic or even to reinstate it because it still appears to be suitable in some circumstances. Rather, they must recognize the theoretical and practical problems of this ethic and think out these questions anew. They must intercede in all countries for the legal protection of conscientious objectors, and they must recognize conscientious objection among their own members as a legitimate form of Christian obedience.

All churches must take a decisive stand for the maintenance of peace and the achievement of a stable, peaceful order. They must demand that even justifiable interests and aims be sacrificed for this purpose. They can do this not only in the statements of church leaders but by urging this attitude on their members and congregations as God's command and therefore the duty of the Christian in our time. Disarmament, peace settlements, the sacrifice of national interests to the cause of peace, the renunciation of war, the termination of the Cold War, the understanding of national as well as Cold War disputes—all these must deeply penetrate the consciousness of our congregations. Otherwise, it is no longer possible to be a true Christian in our time. The Christian Church must be the pioneer of efforts for peace in every place and in every country. It must impress this conviction especially upon those of its members who are active in politics and must ask them specifically how far their political words and deeds conform to it. If we apply this standard to our congregations today and to the actions of Christian politicians (or of those who call themselves Christians), it becomes clear how far removed we still are from it.

We do not know how much time we still have. We must not delude ourselves and others about security. We must not confine our interests to the functioning of the nuclear deterrent, refusing to let our imaginations visualize a real case of war. Rather, we must think and act on the same lines as the Fire Service. Its calculations are not based on the hope that a fire will never occur. It regards the occurrence of a fire as a distinct probability (even if it appears to be quite improbable) and its conduct is determined thereby. Since the irrationality of those who wield power has been proved in history, the outbreak of a catastrophic nuclear war in our generation is more probable than not. The timid efforts to relax tension during the last few years have not really altered this fact.

In view of the seriousness of the possible catastrophe that hangs over us, Christians must ask themselves, before it comes, what they have contributed to its prevention and must act in such a way that they do not need to confess (as the German churches did after the catastrophe of 1933-45): "We accuse ourselves of not having testified more courageously, prayed more faithfully, believed more joyfully or loved more ardently."

## The East-West Conflict

If atomic war is the worst enemy of mankind today, the maintenance of peace and the achievement of a stable and peaceful order become more important than the victory of one ideology or the other. This thesis has important implications.

For the church, it means first a completely different recognition of nonviolence as a means of achieving justice, on the lines followed by Gandhi and Martin Luther King. Since the time of Augustine and Constantine, the church has looked mainly to force as a means of maintaining justice in a world in which evil is a reality and has understood nonviolence only as an abdication of justice. At a time when war can no longer serve this purpose, the church has an urgent need to remember that justice can also be protected by nonviolence, in the form of passive resistance. It is not merely a question of refusing to use force; it is a question of active willingness to suffer in connection with nonviolent demonstrations that seek, by putting pressure on rulers responsible for injustice, to bring about a restoration of justice. In a sense then, nonviolence is also a weapon; but it is one that (in accordance with the Christian faith) is more appropriate to Christians than is the use of force. For the opponent is not treated as an enemy; the aim is rather to win him over by shaming him into right action. Those who adopt this course fear that the use of force will only increase evil and hatred, and so they put their faith in the power of love. The war ethic of the major churches has hitherto been far too subservient to the superstition about force and has accepted the view that justice without force is lost. Minority groups, on the other hand, such as the Jews and Negroes in the United States, and religious minorities, have had less temptation to resort to force and know more about the power of suffering and of love. Now the whole church must learn from them. It must embrace the cause of nonviolence; it must oppose the still-prevalent belief that justice cannot be achieved without force. It must oppose the view, in the struggle between the West and the communist powers, that armaments are the sole salvation and that the victory of the other side is the worst possible evil.

The antithesis between East and West becomes relative when one realizes that atomic war is the greatest external evil that threatens mankind today. But this realization must not, in any way, result in the surrender of one side to the other. It will still be possible to defend one side against the other by the military deterrent ( and, in any event, there is no hope of diverting the nations from this course). But the aim will no longer be victory—the elimination of the opposing power; it will be coexistence, and a coexistence that permits communication. Although we are still a long way from this position, it is still, with atomic war threatening us like the sword of Damocles, the only possible one to adopt.

In the conflict between East and West, Christians and Christian churches have widely supported the West and have furthered western concerns. This has been taken for granted with a certain naïveté based on the antagonism to religion that is inherent in Marxist communism. It is worthwhile to speculate whether the churches would have reacted so definitely against communism if communism had remained neutral toward religion or had even supported the churches. The opposition of certain systems of government to the demands of Christian ethics and to the Christian view of man has not hitherto prevented the churches from condoning such systems. As long as they themselves were not oppressed but privileged, the churches have, to a large extent, ignored slavery, the exploitation and pauperization of the masses, the suppression of free expression of opinion, the education of youth to hate, the arbitrariness of police methods (which include torture), prostitution and the degradation of man. All these things, if practiced by communism, are universally denounced in Christian sermons and in the Christian press of the West. A particularly striking example of this in our century is the different attitudes shown by the Roman Catholic Church (and reflected also in most other ecclesiastical publicity) toward the Batista regime and the Castro regime in Cuba. That communism, wherever it has been established, in spite of having done much harm, has also removed a great deal of evil that previously existed (the poverty of the masses, serfdom, the creating of enmity between the nations, the degrading position of women in the East, open prostitution) goes for nothing in the eyes of the average church member. The same could be said of the improvements that have resulted from the abandonment of Stalinism in communist countries—they have hardly been acknowledged by Christians in the West, let alone thought of as the answer to prayer for the people in the East. The sincerity of the Communists in their open rejection of religion is, from the political viewpoint, their folly. It prevents communism from winning the allegiance of the religiously tied masses and from making full use, for its own benefit, of the historic corruptibility of the churches.

The recognition of this corruptibility is both alarming and significant in respect to the Christian attitude toward communism. There are other reasons, besides its fixation on atheism, why we must, as Christians, object to communist doctrine. The communist superstition about force, about the end justifying any means; the communist ideal of the complete collectivization of man; the communist failure to recognize human dignity and the rights of the individual; the claims of the Communist party to a monopoly of knowledge of absolute truth and of uncontrolled authority not subject to any higher justice—all these are characteristics of communism that make it impossible for the Christian to be a Communist, as long as communism is as it is, and they also oblige a Christian to disagree with it. But our disagreement is untrustworthy as long as we tolerate feudalistic, fascist or similar regimes (which are characterized by the same terror, the same deprivation of human rights, the same hallowing of any means in order to retain power), and as long as we stand alongside them and even support them, for no other reason than that these regimes outwardly support the churches and have not developed an antireligious doctrine. The Christian Church's criticism of capitalism has never had the same force and sharpness as its criticism of communism. Thus, the church comes under heavy suspicion that its criticism is only an expression of egoistical ecclesiastical interests, and that it takes its principles of social ethics seriously only when the church itself is injured by a regime. Only when the church overcomes its moral corruption (which is the result of its alliance with the powers of state and of society) and opposes the misdeeds of its friends as sharply as those of its enemies can its criticism of communism carry weight with Communists. Only then can that criticism make a selfless contribution to the improvement of communism and to its liberation from erroneous ideas.

Is it, then, possible for communism to change? There was (and still is) a panicky view of communism, which the philosopher Karl Jaspers expressed in his book *The Atom Bomb and the Future of Mankind*.[1] Here Jaspers advocates the thesis that modern totalitarianism, unlike former despotisms, if not removed in time, produces an irreversible distortion of human nature. From the standpoint of the dignity of man, this would mean that life was no longer worth living. Yet, according to Jaspers, the point is not whether mankind should live at all, but that it should live lives worthy of human beings. Therefore, if a decision must be made, it is more fitting to sacrifice the whole of mankind (through an atomic war) than to let it fall under communist totalitarianism

[1] Munich: 1958.

without this final act of resistance. Such a viewpoint ascribes to communism monstrosities as great as the achievements on which communism prides itself. This view is just as godless, just as atheistic, as communism itself. Unfortunately, even Christians have adopted this apocalyptic vision,[2] without asking how it is related to the Christian belief in God's lordship over history and to God's gracious covenant with mankind in Jesus Christ.

One may ask in the abstract the question that is raised in novels such as George Orwell's *1984,* whether it is possible for human power to transform humanity into a race of termites and thus to dehumanize it. The experiences of our time, even under the regimes of Hitler and Stalin, give us no grounds to answer this question in the affirmative. However terribly human power can dehumanize the individual and groups of human beings, it has not succeeded so far in dehumanizing whole nations. Although the means of power in the future will be much greater than in the past, and therefore the danger to humanity (as well as the opportunities) will correspondingly increase, the developments of the last decade give us no right to see communism as the only source of these dangers. Rather, this decade has already shown that communism is a world historical phenomenon in a totally different sense from that of the organized criminality of national socialism. Communism is capable of change and looks to the future. It is in no greater measure than any other movement the subject of history; it is equally the object of historical development and of pressure from the traditions of the nations it rules, with their needs and their desire for liberty. For good or ill, these nations have invested their work and their lives in communism, and they work at it in order to make it more bearable or useful for themselves. It does not occur to them that the seizure of power by the Communists may be the twilight of history, as Jaspers implied. On the contrary, they hope—and we must hope with them—that their life will continue, and that even under communism they may achieve a decent way of life.

Christians who live in communist countries also take part in this effort to achieve a decent way of life. We would suggest that,

---

[2] See, for instance, EMIL BRUNNER: "If Communism Were Victorious," *Neue Zuricher Zeitung,* Zurich. May 28, 1961.

as they engage in this task, they—as well as Christians elsewhere in the world—should bear the following points in mind.

1. The right social contribution of Christians is always and everywhere directed toward the humanizing of society, toward the establishment of freedom and equality before the law for the members of society, toward the maintenance and the improvement of the law and toward the formation of areas of freedom in which the individual can act responsibly. In a society based on law and justice, Christians will realize that they are responsible for the maintenance of justice and freedom, of obligation and of the limitation of power. In a totalitarian society, they will realize that they are responsible for achieving these good things; that is, for gradually breaking down totalitarianism.

2. Communism could lose its totalitarian character. The possibilities for such a development are inherent in its doctrine, but, more particularly, the pressure of historical events could bring this about.

3. Whether communism will always retain its hostile attitude toward religion no one can say. It is conceivable that many factors, including the existence and collaboration of a live Christendom in its midst, could cause the withdrawal, or at least the total decay, of that attitude.

4. In terms of human dignity, the communist countries today are certainly not to be depicted black and the other countries white. Christians must not support such black and white distinctions, which could incite the nations to atomic war. They are as slanderous as the picture of conditions in the capitalist world adduced in communist propaganda.

5. The problems of the last third of the twentieth century will trouble the communist countries as much as the noncommunist countries. Presumably, they will bring about profound changes in everything that today comes under the heading "communism" or "capitalism." To overcome these problems, both communist and noncommunist countries have positive and negative presuppositions, though of a different kind. Khrushchev called upon his deputies to learn from the Capitalists. There is equal reason for the West to observe communist developments carefully and to ask, What can we learn from the Communists?

6. Today there is no longer a single, uniform type of communism, as Lenin and Stalin visualized it. It is likely that, in the future, there will be a series of very different types of communism, including some whose philosophy of life will be far less committed than that of the Soviet Communists. This is already so in Cuba and in Latin American communism generally. Thus, a crucial barrier, which has prevented Christians from participating in communist revolutionary movements, will fall. There is much to be said for the view that, unless there is a revolutionary upheaval, it will be impossible to bring about radical reforms in Latin America. The last and, presumably, final breakdown of Kennedy's Alliance for Progress will raise again and more urgently the question of Christian participation in communist revolutionary movements. There is need for a careful and profound theological examination of this whole question.

The political as well as the economic interests of the great powers (particularly those of the United States in Latin America) are affected by these revolutionary movements. The church must not be a party to "mythologizing" the discussion, but must help to "demythologize" it, by making it clear that this is not a question of choosing between communist tyranny and freedom consonant with human dignity, or between ungodliness and Christianity. Rather, it is a question of conflicting power interests and, at the same time, a battle to ensure the possibility of existence for the impoverished masses. If conservative forces do not achieve the necessary reforms, that is no doubt deplorable; but it is not a matter for condemnation if reforms are achieved in a revolutionary manner, as in Cuba and China. In such circumstances, the Christian task is to cooperate in order that the transitory despotic phase may be alleviated and shortened.

In any event, none of the objects of this controversy is worth an atomic war. The competition between communist and noncommunist efforts to solve the social problems of our time must take place in friendly coexistence. This peaceful coexistence is thus a nonwarlike state of combat; and the outcome will depend on which solutions prove best. Its motto must be: Whoever wins in peacetime, let him win! Christians will await the outcome with neither a panicky fear (in the event of a communist victory) nor a messianic hope (if victory should go to the West); for whoever wins, we shall not be out of the wood. Much will remain for Christians to do. And, presumably, there will be no victor, but new situations that cannot at present be foreseen.

In respect to the East-West conflict, the churches must help their members during this phase of world history to take an unbiased view of developments. Panicky fear of a victory for the opposite side leads to biased thinking, which sees only the crimes of the other side and is blind to those of its own, and which even declares everything to be good and just that furthers the interests of its own side. By such an attitude, Christians betray the freedom given to them in the gospel, and the commission that God has given to each in his political camp. Because of communist hostility to religion, Christians in the West identify themselves more easily with the measures of their governments than do those in the East. For instance, most Christians in the West violently condemned the Soviet oppression of the Hungarian people in October, 1956, and attributed its inhumanity solely to communist views. Yet they remain blind to—or justify with arguments that are equally applicable to the Soviet measures—the brutality with which Portuguese colonialism reacted to the insurrection in its African colonies, the aggressive behavior of the United States against little Cuba (behavior that was also contrary to international law), and the intervention of the United States, motivated solely by power politics, in the Vietnamese Civil War, against the will of the majority of the suffering people there. Only when we Christians seize the privilege, which the gospel has given us, of a frank and just viewpoint and a candid word of criticism of our own side, will we truly serve our own countries.

## The German Question

It is conceivable that the division of the German people into two states, which was the result of the defeat of Germany in the Second World War, could become permanent, and that out of this might develop two politically separate nations, just as, in the past, the Swiss, the Dutch and the Austrians broke away from the German body politic and became politically independent nations. The contrast between the social systems of the Federal Republic of Germany and the German Democratic Republic could further such a development. The division of Germany has already lasted so long, and the different conditions of life for East and West Germans during the last fifteen years have led to such estrangements between them, that many Germans fear (and many non-Germans hope) that, if the situation continues much longer, no reunion will be possible. The consequent formation of two independent nations will relieve Europe of the pressure of a nation of eighty million people in its midst.

I regard such a development as unlikely. Admittedly, at the moment, there is no militant nationalism and no inclination for a passionate policy of reunion, or for jeopardizing the present prosperity and the relationship with the western nations. Indeed, the signs of alienation between the two parts of the nation cannot be disputed. If the communist order in the German Democratic Republic had the sympathies of the people, this alienation would increase. But that is not so. Antipathy toward the communist system leads to opposition to the development of two separate nations. Besides, the peculiar situation of West Berlin—a part of the Federal Republic in the middle of the German Democratic Republic— acts as a rivet for the two parts of the nation. The consciousness of belonging to a nation and the consequent desire for political unity are constantly present beneath a covering of indifference (in West Germany), resignation and estrangement. Whether this is regretted or welcomed, it must be reckoned with as a political factor. To preach against nationalism and to challenge the Germans to accept the division as a penance for their responsibility for the Second World War will alter nothing; nothing can prevail against the potential dynamic of such national consciousness. Moreover, this potential dynamic, which no one can control, carries with it the danger that it may become virulent at a moment favorable to itself but unfavorable to world peace. Accordingly, the reunion of Germany in a form tolerable for Europe and making equal demands on the West and on the East must be seen as an urgent task in world politics—not in order to please the Germans but in order to prevent an outbreak of madness on their part at a moment when it would be disastrous for peace.

The West German Federal Republic strives for the union of the German Democratic Republic with the Federal Republic; that is, reunion in the form of *annexation*. The government of the German Democratic Republic, being that of the smaller, weaker state, is not interested in reunion but in self-assertion; that is, in the continuing existence of two German states. Because of this interest, and according to the stability of its own regime, only limited and strictly controlled alliances between the two parts of the nation are acceptable to it. The East German government conceals this fact behind proposals for the "confederation" of the two states—proposals that are not, presumably, meant to be taken seriously and can be made without risk, because it is assumed from the outset that the Federal Republic will decline them. Both governments, each in its own sphere, have as good as stifled consideration of any other solutions of the problem and have made it impossible to discuss them effectively. Moreover, because of the existence of two separate German armies, each pledged to the concept of Germany held by its own regime, the two governments live in continual fear of military aggression (a fear that dominates, no doubt for objective reasons, the government of the German Democratic Republic more than the Federal government). This fear contributes greatly to the hardening of the differences within Germany and to the aggravation of the cold civil war between the two German states.

For a long time, it was hoped in Germany that reunion would eventually be brought about by a decision of the forces of occupation. It can be said with certainty that this will not happen. Such a decision would lead to free election in both parts of Germany, when it may be expected that, because of their antagonism to the communist system and the attraction of the prosperity and civil liberties of the Federal Republic, the majority of the population in the German Democratic Republic would vote for the Federal Republic. In the same way that the governments of the United States and of South Vietnam broke the 1955 Geneva Agreement by not holding elections in Vietnam, because most of the South Vietnamese population would have decided for communist North Vietnam, so the Soviet government does not allow the question of pan-German elections even to be discussed, because they would mean the loss of the German Democratic Republic to the West. It is extremely improbable that a situation could ever arise in which the Soviet government would accede to this western demand. To do so would be equivalent to complete capitulation to the West, and only a condition of total weakness (which is improbable) could bring it about. A partial interest in such a proposal was conceivable during the first ten years after 1945, when the Soviet Union allowed the German Democratic Republic to leave the communist camp, perhaps in order to build up a neutral, united Germany as part of a neutral European buffer zone between the Eastern bloc and the North Atlantic Treaty Organization. This opportunity was not taken by the West and the Federal Republic at that time, and today its recurrence is highly unlikely. Moreover, only a Soviet leader who is in an outstandingly strong position could demand this sacrifice from his party. Stalin had the power and would probably have been ready to do so. Khrushchev and his followers did not have this power over the party and over the countries of the Eastern bloc and were no longer able to do what Stalin could do. Even to discuss it would probably have led to their being overthrown.

Thus, there exists a dilemma: on the one hand, the interests of European peace, and therefore of world peace, demand reunion as a solution to the German question; and on the other hand, there is at present no way of achieving it. In this situation, we can strive only gradually for the solution of the German question. This should not be a disaster—not even for the Germans, because their forced participation in both opposing social systems could bear positive fruit. The East Germans will not suddenly be reunited with West Germany, but must participate in the development of communism. As reconciliation is gradually achieved, and contacts are renewed between the two parts of the nation, that which has stood the test in the socialist order will be preserved for a future order in a united Germany. In this way, much could be gained for an agreement between eastern and western Europe, and the German people could be compelled to contribute to bridging the gulf between East and West. This is a task for which they are equipped by their position and their true interests; but it is one that they have not been able or willing to carry out, because their aversion to communism and their fear of it led them after 1945 to strive only for the fullest possible integration with the West.

It is impossible to foretell whether this process will eventually lead to the reunion of Germany. For the time being, the aim can only be to end the cold civil war in Germany; that is, to bring about internal understanding between the Germans. The offers made in this direction by the government of the German Democratic Republic serve only to support and strengthen it. For this reason, the Federal government answers them with blunt refusals; and, as a result, it is not itself in a position to institute this process. On the contrary, it opposes it and measures each step only by its aim—to destroy the government of the German Democratic Republic and to bring about its union with the Federal government. By confining itself to demands that the opposite side cannot fulfill, it hardens the dilemma described above instead of contributing to the search for a possible solution. Only if pressure is brought to bear on the two governments by non-German powers (particularly by the two atomic powers) can the necessary process be initiated. Critical situations must not be shirked. There is a possibility that such a desire on the part of the non-German powers may meet with opposition in West Germany. The ground for a popular revolutionary outbreak against it has already been prepared there, for the Federal government and, and on the whole, the press in West Germany have managed to secure the support of the mass of the population for their own policy and to prevent them from recognizing how complex and hopeless that policy is. They are thus unaware of the true attitude of other nations to the German question and of the requirements for a peaceful and peace-promoting solution of it. Pressure from non-German powers would therefore come as a surprise; and the first reactions of the West German population would be violently nationalist. This situation must not be shirked; and it will be far easier to control in the present circumstances than it would have been at the time of the Weimar Republic.

Unfortunately, it cannot be said that the Christian churches in Germany are in a position to further this necessary process of understanding among the Germans. Immediately after 1945, German Catholicism saw that the cleavage of Germany and the founding of the Federal Republic offered great advantages. It therefore opted for the extension and rearming of the Federal Republic and its integration with the West and identified its interests with those of the West German governing party (Christian Democratic Union/Christian Social Union). German Protestantism was unable to follow this course in the same carefree way, because the birthplace of the Reformation was in communist hands. The Evangelical Church in Germany was therefore forced to see itself as having, by virtue of its position, a special task—to act as a rivet between the two separate parts of the nation. But, from the beginning, its sympathies were understandably on the side of the Federal Republic. This prevented it from seeing that task in its full magnitude, its difficulty and its promise, and from tackling it with a balanced view of its own sympathies and antipathies. Thus, the church foundered on the task; and today it is as much divided as the rest of the German people. West German Protestantism (from church leaders and bishops to ordinary members of the congregations) lives under the influence of its government's political propaganda. Its horizon is as limited as that which the government and the press have successfully drawn for the West German citizen. Admittedly, there are exceptions: not only an insignificant number of ineffective outsiders, as in German Catholicism, but also the stronger, critical movement, which originated in those ecclesiastical groups within Protestantism, that dissents from the common view. But these groups have not yet accomplished very much. Unfortunately, there is therefore no ground for the hope that Protestant ecclesiastical circles will exert effective pressure to put an end to the cold civil war in Germany, or that they will prove an effective obstacle to nationalist reactions in the event of non-German pressure on West German policy. To put it bluntly: If it should prove possible to prevent the rise to power in West Germany of a man like Franz Joseph Strauss, this could not be attributed to the fact that evangelical Christians are educated in their churches to watch out for such a person and to resist him.

This does not mean that the experiences and insights gained in the German Church struggle of 1933-45 have been completely lost. They included, among other things, a recognition that the Christian congregation has political responsibility. In West Germany, the middle class is still the influential class, and within this class, Protestantism of the Lutheran stamp still has great influence. Consequently, Protestant Christianity shares responsibility for the development of the German question. The church struggle has had a positive effect in that there was *no* general relapse of German Protestantism, after 1945, to its pre-1933 conservative, antidemocratic attitude, which was sympathetic to the monarchy, the Army and national strength. The picture of German Protestantism today, as reflected in the clergy and synods, is wholly different from that before 1933 and is much more strongly composed of "right," "left," conservative, pacifist and socialistically inclined groups. As a result, since 1945, the discussion about the political tasks of the Christian congregation in this concrete situation has sometimes been very violent. At present, it has somewhat abated, but it has not died. Although the discussion could not prevent a great mass of church people and clergy from coming under the influence of the official government doctrine on the questions here discussed, one is nevertheless glad that such a discussion exists. It is to be hoped that, because of the struggles that have been fought out in their midst during these years, Protestants in Germany will be in a position to help, at critical moments in the future, in preventing fresh catastrophes in German history.[3]

---

[3] These pages have not been written with the idea that the three problems discussed are the *only* major questions in world politics today. Other questions (such as that of the rapid increase of population) are of equal importance. I selected these three because circumstances have made me more familiar with them. Others must contribute other things.

# 3

# THE WEST AND THE SEARCH FOR PEACE IN THE NUCLEAR AGE

by MAX KOHNSTAMM (Holland)

## Atomic War: Total Destruction

HUMAN history has been from the outset a history of war, of organized violence between human collectives. Modern technology has made war ever more destructive; atomic arms represent the last and decisive step along this road. War—Cain killing Abel—has always been tragic and terrible, but it has now become so different that it is confusing to use the same word for it. For atomic war means total destruction, in which conventional concepts such as "victors" and "vanquished" no longer have any meaning. The survivors of an atomic war will envy the dead. War has become "impossible" in the sense—but only in that sense—that there is nothing reasonable left in the concept of war as total destruction. Any future atomic war may mean the end of human history—at least in the sense of continuity of development. Mankind is therefore placed in a new revolutionary situation in which the prevention of war becomes the most important preoccupation of social and political thought and action.

This new situation raises the question of the cause and function of war in history. How we answer it is deeply influenced by our understanding of man. The Bible shows man as created after the image of God but, at the same time, involved in the ambiguities of life—a mixture of freedom and destiny. Therefore, Kant's assertion [1] is acceptable: for any human being, the mere existence of another human being constitutes a threat; only rules and laws, which both protect man and are binding upon him, make community possible. For human collectives and their relationship the situation is the same.

European history is the history of the emergence of communities, mostly national in character, making life without violence possible through law and its enforcement. But no parallel development took place in the relationship between these communities or nations. International law never obtained binding or protecting force. Therefore, to any nation, the existence of another nation remained a threat. In the absence of binding and protecting law, peace could never be more than an armistice.

Since life is always changing and dynamic, no order that excludes change can last. Therefore, provisions were found to be necessary inside a community, enabling the law to be adapted to changing circumstances. Arbitrary change destroys the security that law must provide, but the absence of provisions for change leads to a breakdown of law, to civil war and to revolution.

In the relations between nations, processes for the peaceful changing of the existing order have never been evolved. The use of force or the threat to use force have been the only ways in which to bring relations between human collectives into conformity with changed social forces or with political conceptions and insights. The absence of any process allowing peaceful change formed another cause of war between nations. And the function of these wars was to bring about changes in the relations between nations, necessitated by the dynamics inherent in life.

Atomic weapons have turned war into total destruction, without removing war's cause or replacing its function by some other process. The present armistice may last a while—others have—but someday war may well break out again, unless its cause is removed and processes instituted to replace its function.

---

[1] *Zum ewigen Frieden.*

## Nuclear Arms and Peace

It is sometimes said that the very horror of atomic arms has created the foundation of lasting peace. By turning war into total destruction, nuclear arms have certainly made war totally "unthinkable," but have they really made war impossible?

No doubt, nuclear arms have made war unprofitable and unthinkable, both for attacker and for attacked, by increasing, to a degree never before attained, the power of the means of destruction over the means of defense. The protection and movability of weapons have been developed to a point at which, even when an unexpected attack had almost totally destroyed the civilian life of the attacked, the attacked would still be capable of almost totally destroying the attacker; on this balance of terror rests the present armistice.

If the present superiority of offensive over defensive weapons were ever overcome, this balance would be undone (for example, by a perfect antimissile missile). In the hands of *one* nuclear power, these new defensive weapons would lead to the supremacy of that power, placing the decision over war and peace solely in its hands. If both Communists and the West were to have these weapons, war might return to more or less conventional forms. (More or less, because tactical nuclear arms would continue to exist, making war more murderous than the most recent conventional wars have been.)

Scientists think such developments in weaponry, overcoming the present advantage of offensive over defensive weapons, highly unlikely. If this is so, can we then not expect that this balance of terror itself will maintain the peace?

No doubt, we owe our present armistice to the existing balance of terror. But it seems irresponsible to conclude that the balance of terror can be a sufficient basis for lasting peace. Such a conclusion would have to rest on the assumption that human collectives will continue always to behave rationally, even in the absence of binding and protecting law and of any process for peaceful change; there is no support for such an assumption in history. Moreover, the world would remain at the mercy of an accident or an error of judgment. We should certainly be profoundly grateful for the present armistice and for the balance of terror on which it rests. But, in view of what would be at stake in a nuclear war, every Christian must seek a basis on which lasting peace can be established, replacing the present precarious armistice.

Can technical solutions such as nuclear disarmament liberate the world from the danger of total destruction and provide a basis for lasting peace? To answer in the affirmative is to mistake the symptoms for the cause of the illness. Once nuclear disarmament had abolished the balance of terror, war would be more likely to happen than at present. And, once war broke out again in conventional, non-nuclear form, nations capable of producing nuclear arms would produce and use them again. Neither the knowledge to make these arms nor the technical means to deliver them can be destroyed. Therefore, nuclear disarmament, preceding the removal of the cause and function of war, could mean only that the war of the future would begin as a conventional war, becoming total destruction as soon as one or more of the warring nations produced nuclear arms again.

There will always be a tendency to believe that wars result from weapons—a belief neither more true nor more respectable than the belief that illness is caused by fever, or fever by the thermometer. There is no simple way out of our predicament: Cain can no longer kill collective Abel without destroying his own world at the same time. Total destruction can be avoided only by removing the cause of war itself and by substituting for war's function peaceful processes of change. We must face up to this brutal reality and seize the opportunity that the present balance of terror provides.

Does this mean that there is nothing to be expected from disarmament or from armaments control? The life of a patient can be saved by reducing his temperature, on condition that the doctor, at the same time, deals with the causes of his patient's illness. Limitation of the armaments race can reduce the international temperature and contribute to the creation of a climate of *détente*. The recent reduction of the military budgets of the United States and the Soviet Union by tacit agreement is certainly helpful and can, like measures against the dissemination of nuclear weapons, lengthen the time at our disposal in which to work on the cause. But such measures are useful only as long as they are taken for what they are: action on the symptoms. Often the prudence of politicians in matters of disarmament is more responsible than the talk about it in the church.[2] The church should encourage those who work on the problems of armaments control and disarmament. But the church should also courageously point out that here, as in other matters, there is no *Weg zurueck, den weiten Weg ins Kinderland* (Bonhoeffer). God's history has put an end to that part of his history in which collective Cain, without destroying his own world, could make war on collective Abel, and is forcing us to deal now with war itself, not just with this or that weapon, however destructive that weapon may be.

## The United Nations and the Possibility of World Community

We cannot escape reality and return to *Kinderland*. We must accept the fact that we are confronted with the necessity of creating an international structure in which binding and protecting law removes the cause of war and in which the function of war is replaced by peaceful processes of change.

The road that leads to such an international structure may be long and difficult; but is it not a clear one? Is the United Nations not the beginning of it, forming the framework in which peace can and must be organized? Again, such a simple answer does not correspond with the complexities of the reality that confronts us. In history, binding and protecting law has nearly always originated in order imposed from above, by superior force, through domination. Slowly and gradually, interrupted and stimulated in turn by civil strife and revolution, small, powerful groups at first, and then, in modern history, all the members of the community, began to participate in the process of maintaining and adapting the law. This development, from order imposed by superior force to the

---

[2] A typical example of irresponsible talk is the demand often made by Christians that nuclear nations should declare never to be the first to use nuclear arms. We should be grateful that neither the Kremlin nor the White House has ever taken such talk seriously, because our present armistice (and therefore our chance to organize peace) rests on the fear that certain hostile acts (for example, the capture by conventional force of West Berlin by the Soviet Union or of East Berlin by the West) would be answered with nuclear attack. To eliminate this fear means to destroy the basis of the present armistice.

consent of the governed, has always been slow and difficult. At the heart of the problem lies a nearly insoluble riddle, something like a vicious circle that is extremely difficult to break.

No human community is possible without law, but law is nothing, or degenerates into sheer oppression, unless there is community. Domination—not consent—is natural to man. Only necessity will force him to seek consent; only necessity, facilitated by the bonds of a common history, by the growing consciousness of common interests and a common destiny, will slowly and gradually turn the seeking of consent into a habit. The existing nations of Europe have all been helped in breaking the circle by a common history, a common language, a common culture, often a common descent. What has been and still is true inside our nations is true in international relations. Peace and community between nations are not possible without binding and protecting law, but binding and protecting law cannot exist without community.

The organization of peace demands that, in the relations between nations, this vicious circle be broken. Only patiently and gradually can we build community and establish the beginnings of common rules and common institutions. These common institutions, making possible a process of consent, and the common rules resulting from such consent, will strengthen, in their turn, the consciousness of forming a community. It is a romantic fallacy to believe that the formation of community is a purely organic process, like the growth of a tree in a virginal forest, and that this process cannot be influenced by conscious political action. But it is a rationalistic fallacy to believe that there is nothing organic about this process, that community can be formed by an act of will, that it can be established simply by the promulgation of a Constitution, be it for Europe or for the world.

The United Nations has been formed in the expectation that the great powers together would impose law and order in the same way that law and order inside our nations were at first imposed from above. But the relations between the two biggest powers, the United States and the Soviet Union, and their allies proved to be the real problem. The United Nations Charter supposed that problem solved and therefore did nothing to solve it. The danger of war as total destruction springs from the conflict between the communist nations and the West. With the exception of the Korean War, where action was made possible by a tactical error on the part of the Soviet Union, the United Nations has never been able to intervene in a conflict in which the two blocs opposed each other.

It may seem noble to see the United Nations, not as it really is, but as one would like it to be: as a world government. But the United Nations, as long as there is no world community, cannot be a world government, capable of binding and protecting the nations of the world through the enforcement of law. And there will be no world community as long as the vicious circle of community, which is impossible without law, and law, which is impossible without community, is not broken through slow, patient and gradual action, undertaken wherever and whenever it is possible.

Is the United Nations, then, useless? Far from it. It forms a world forum. It can do something in lesser conflicts, especially if the two main world powers concur in, or at least accept, the action that is to be undertaken. But the United Nations cannot do away with the cause of law; law and order can only grow together with community; neither law nor community can be the result of the simple promulgation of a Constitution.

*It is the tension between the Soviet bloc and the West that threatens the world with total destruction.* There are now, and there will be in the future, wars that do not lead to total destruction, because the countries engaged in them do not possess or do not use nuclear weapons. Nuclear dissemination is on its way; some time in the future, other countries, especially China, will become nuclear nations, contributing to the threat of total destruction. But, as long as the present situation lasts, nuclear war can result only from conflict between the Soviet Union and the West.

In our day, only an international order based on equality before a common law and imposed with the consent of the governed can last. But a rudimentary order, under which the two nuclear powers would limit the use of violence by other nations, could provide a period of grace, during which a community composed of a larger group of nations could gradually be established.

The tension between the Soviet bloc and the West contains the threat of total destruction and, at the same time, prevents the establishment of such a rudimentary and provisional world order.

Undoubtedly, this tension has abated over the last decade. The leaders of the West are fully aware of the incredible horror of nuclear war. At the same time, the leaders of the Soviet Union, rejecting Lenin's thesis, no longer regard war between their country and the West as inevitable. Since the Cuba crisis, the Soviet Union seems to accept the present balance of military strength. Whatever the intentions of either camp, neither the Soviet Union nor the West seems to contemplate a crusade in order to impose by force of arms its domination over the other.

But, between the Soviet bloc and the West, one crucial problem remains unsolved: the division of Germany. Barbed wire that separates people of the same language and the same history cannot provide a solution. This division can never be accepted by those thus separated. In order to maintain this artificial division, the Soviet Union is forced to treat Germany as an object, as a nation whose fate must be settled by others, and to whom equality cannot be granted. Oppression is based on violence and breeds violence. The imposed division of Germany, as long as it lasts, will stimulate on both sides feelings of uncertainty, hatred and fear, providing all the elements for conflicts that could lead to war.

Clearly, the problem of the division of Germany cannot be solved by total destruction nor can it remain unsolved forever. Reunion of the Germans will become possible only if uncertainty and fear in the relations between East and West are gradually replaced by understanding and trust. Mutual anguish over total destruction is beginning to create an awareness that the Soviet bloc and the West have a common destiny. The great question, then, is: How can progress be made on the long and difficult road that leads from the present uncertain armistice, based on a balance of terror, to lasting peace, based on the Rule of Law?

## The Ideological Element in the Tension

Progress along this road depends, among other things, on our willingness to see things as they are, not as we in the West would like them to be, and upon our readiness to respect those with whom we must deal, in the same way as we wish them to respect us. This means that we must take their convictions seriously, even if we do not share them.

Undoubtedly, part of the tension between the Soviet Union and the West results from a real or supposed conflict of interests, comparable to conflicts of interests that existed or were supposed to exist between the European powers in the nineteenth century. But to underestimate the ideological element in the tension in no way suggests Christian charity. On the contrary, this attitude stands in the way of progress toward peace, as does the opposite attitude that treats as differences of principle matters that Christians should regard as matters of expediency (like the question of the ownership of the means of production). There is nothing in the biblical view of man that gives any grounds for looking upon ownership of production as a matter of principle. Production must serve man; man must serve production. How society is to be organized in order to achieve this end is a matter of expediency, not of principle. The biblical view of man puts us on our guard against all great concentration of power. But such concentration results inevitably from modern production methods, forcing us to deal with the problem of its control, whether power is concentrated in public or in private hands.

But where is the ideological element to be found? The basis of every political philosophy is a certain conception of man. The communist view of man differs fundamentally from the view of man on which western political thought is based. The ideological element of the tension between the Soviet bloc and the West is to be found in these differing views.

The political philosophy of the West urges that, for every power, there should be a counterbalancing power, and that there should be freedom to place every center of power and ideology under review (Reinhold Niebuhr). This political philosophy and the political institutions related to it are the results of a long and complex history. Whatever material and spiritual influences have shaped it, whatever part the Bible may have played among these influences, the important point is that the view of man on which the West's institutions and political philosophy is based allows both for the goodness of man's creation and for his involvement in the ambiguities of life. From this understanding of man spring the demand that man's freedom must have a good deal of room *and* a good deal of limitation, and the demand that man must be trusted and distrusted at the same time. The West thus maintains a consistent refusal to choose between two polar views: man as a child of light and man as a child of darkness (Reinhold Niebuhr).

The communist reading of man, on the contrary, does choose: man is good, man is a child of light. All the ambiguities of life can and will be overcome by putting ownership of the means of production into the hands of the state. Social revolution, leading through the dictatorship of the proletariat and communism to socialism, will overcome all the differences between essential and existential man, restoring him in this way to his full stature. He will then no longer need law or state. Communism must claim to be universal, because it posits a universally valid cure for universal ills. The West's understanding of man makes an identical claim; therefore, by its very existence, the political philosophy of the West constitutes a threat to communist philosophy and is inevitably regarded by communism as an attempt to prevent man from attaining his full splendor and goodness.

To stress this difference has nothing to do with the question whether the Soviet citizen is or is not a lovable, peace-loving person. But the difference has fundamental consequences for the conception of what a human community is, can and should be. As long as this view of man remains the basis of communist political philosophy, the Soviet Union must continue to want to weaken, divide and bury the West, using to this end all means, save those which are inefficient, such as nuclear war. The ideological element in the tension between communism and the West, involving the very basis of their different political philosophies, makes it impossible for them to form together a community based on common institutions and on binding and protecting laws, because their conceptions of community, law and democratic institutions differ as fundamentally as their views of man.

## Development Inside the Soviet Bloc and the Policy of the West

Communism must use oppressions to overcome the gulf that separates man as he really is from man as he is supposed to be. A refusal to account for man's goodness always leads to an attempt to destroy his freedom. But a refusal (like that of communist philosophy) to account for his sin, his involvement in the ambiguities of life, leads to exactly the same result. Thus, the communist view of man and a dictatorship of the Communist party are intimately related. Once a dictatorship is established, strong vested interests come into existence, aspiring to perpetuate the power of the apparatus and opposing a transition from dictatorial to democratic rule—a change that, even under the best conditions, is always full of risks and dangers.

Nevertheless, developments of the last decade clearly indicate that important changes are taking place. It does not matter much what is causing them. Is it education? Is it the transition from building up heavy industry to a consumer economy? Is it the result of conflicts of interests between the Soviet Union and China, which are conducive to heresy inside the Soviet Union and the Communist parties everywhere in the world?

The change from Khrushchev to Brezhnev and Kosygin, although certainly not the result of public debate, has nonetheless taken place in a more "democratic" fashion than any former change in the Soviet Union's leadership. Undoubtedly, the Soviet citizen enjoys more freedom as a consumer and more legal security than before. At least, inside the Communist party, a dialogue seems to have begun to replace the oppressive monologue of former days. There are many signs in literature and films that point to an inquisitiveness that does not accept official limitation of thought. A philosophical debate on alienation under communism is taking place inside some of the eastern European countries. Is man, after all, a more complicated phenomenon than orthodox communist philosophy allows for?

It is essential to estimate these changes correctly. If they are underestimated, opportunities for real contact and understanding will pass by unused. If they are overestimated, dangerous illusions about these opportunities will be created. In all probability, progress toward free inquiry and free discussion will not be rapid, and setbacks are to be expected.

Directly, the West can do little to influence developments inside the communist world. It can assist the process in certain ways: by facilitating contact, by helping to establish some freedom of action among the Soviet Union's eastern European allies. But it would be very unwise to try to separate these countries from the Soviet Union. Such an attempt could only increase, on the side of the Soviet Union, a distrust that would probably lead to increased repression of free discussion inside that country and in those of its allies. We should never forget that communist philosophy, of necessity, expects the West to be aggressive. The West cannot stimulate the process of change inside the communist countries by proving this conviction right, but only by proving it wrong.

Indirectly, the West can do a great deal. The weakest point, the real Achilles' heel of communist philosophy, might prove to be its claim to be able scientifically to predict developments. Communist philosophy predicts continuously increasing tension within the West, leading to economic catastrophe, to domination of one country over another and, finally, to wars between them. It predicts the West's incapacity to build an international community that establishes peace on the basis of law and justice.

Inside its own house, the West is totally free to act and to prove communist philosophy wrong. It can do so by remaining united and by establishing peace and community inside its own perimeter. It can do so by using its incredible power of production to increase social justice and by helping the less-developed areas of the world to overcome the problems of economic take-off.

In stimulating change inside the Soviet Union by indirect action, the West will need patience and tenacity. For a long time, it may have to live with the Soviet Union in the present precarious armistice, based on the balance of terror. The West will therefore be obliged to maintain its strength, while at the same time working patiently toward creating the conditions that will finally make it possible to solve with the Soviet Union and the countries of eastern Europe the outstanding problems—above all, the problem of the division of Germany.

The West needs strength and unity, because it is an illusion to believe that the Soviet Union has already given up or will easily give up the hope of burying the West—of overthrowing, that is, the most valuable element of the West's political thinking and political institutions: equilibrium between freedom and restraint, based on an acknowledgment both of man's created goodness and of man's fall.

The West needs unity and strength not only for this defensive purpose. It needs it positively in order to prove its view of man— to prove that, on this basis, a just internal and international order can be built. Thus it will stimulate the process of change in communist thinking by proving communist philosophy wrong, thereby making possible what is not possible today: the gradual development, between the Soviet bloc and the West, of a community based on common institutions and common laws.

## Uniting the West

Why unite the West? Would it not suffice as a first step to aim at creating a community of European peoples? It would not, because the economic, military and political tasks to be accomplished, in order to transform the present armistice into peace, cannot be accomplished by a European Community alone, even if the other nations of western Europe, and especially Britain, were to join it.

Together, the United States and Europe possess an overwhelming proportion of the productive capacity of the world and the greatest share of international trade. This certainly does not exclude other countries from responsibility; but Europe and the United States, acting together, are responsible for managing what has to be managed in our world economy. Acting together, they can maintain or create the conditions that are necessary for economic expansion, like, for example, a reasonable functioning of the world's monetary system, without which postwar expansion would soon be replaced by economic stagnation and chaos, as happened during the late Twenties and Thirties. Acting together, they can create the conditions that are necessary for economic development by providing aid and by organizing the world's raw material markets, which have a decisive influence on the economic possibilities of the developing countries. How this should be done and whether the West does it well or badly cannot be discussed here. But the United States and Europe, acting together, are undoubtedly capable of, and therefore have the responsibility for, doing these things. Militarily, the maintenance of the balance of terror, and therefore of the present armistice, is possible only through the closest military cooperation between the United States and Europe.

Such cooperation also forms a *conditio sine qua non* for all serious measures of armaments control and armaments reduction. No move toward the settlement of the main outstanding problem between the Soviet world and the West, the division of Germany, is possible without the cooperation of both the United States and Europe, because such a settlement would have to include guarantees for the Soviet Union and for Germany, which can be provided only by Europe and the United States together.

How should western unity be organized? As an alliance of the Atlantic nations or as a partnership between "two separate but equally powerful entities, each bearing its share of common responsibilities in the world," [3] as proposed by President Kennedy? The unity of the West is not a temporary but a lasting necessity; first, because it will take time before the process of change in the Soviet Union makes progress toward real peace possible; second, because this progress must finally lead to a community that encompasses both the West and the Soviet bloc.

Certainly, western unity cannot be the end of the road. Distances have disappeared. Between the Soviet Union and the West, war has already become "total destruction." In the future, nuclear dissemination will probably turn war, everywhere in the world, into "total destruction." The organization of peace will therefore finally have to be of global dimensions. The global organization of peace, even if at first imposed, cannot last without global participation. The vicious circle of community, impossible without law, and law, impossible without community, must be broken not only in the West or between the Soviet bloc and the West. It is a circle that spans the globe and threatens the earth and challenges mankind; and it must finally be broken everywhere around the globe. But, as in all matters regarding relations between men, general answers do not suffice and must be translated and broken down into specific actions in limited fields. The organization of the unity of the West on a lasting basis represents a specific and limited action of that kind; it is, at the same time, possible and necessary. The organization of western unity can constitute a break-through in the larger struggle for world community.

---

[3] Resolution of the Action Committee for the United States of Europe, 1962.

In the course of history, no alliance has ever provided lasting unity. Only a community can do that. In order to accomplish what must be accomplished, the present western alliance must develop beyond alliance into community.

Community exists only where there is delegation of authority, where certain important decisions are no longer taken separately by the participating nations, but by common institutions. Such delegation, difficult *per se,* is hardly conceivable unless a certain equilibrium of power exists between the participants. Power and justice are intertwined; so are power and responsibility. Therefore, the relation between a superpower such as the United States and a host of relatively small powers cannot lead to a real sharing of responsibility or to delegation of authority and to the establishment of binding and protecting law that is equally applicable to all. The present relation will remain a relation between protector and protected, providing a façade of consultation, but remaining essentially a colonial relationship that, even if in the interest of both, and containing an unusual amount of generosity on the part of the protector (as is actually the case), *will* not last, because, between, nations as between men, inequality creates tensions, which, if the inequality is not removed, finally disrupt the relationship.

Does the concept of partnership imply that the building of the Community of the West must wait until a perfect European Community exists? Certainly not. Interdependence between the European nations and the United States makes it impossible to form a European Community first and to settle only afterward its relationship with the United States. Moreover, developments in this world never happen in a neat, logical way. Even though some confusion will be created, the development of a European Community and the building of the Community of the West, based on an equal partnership between a European Community and the United States, must be pursued at the same time.

## The European Community: A Constructive Example

Today, the European Economic Community constitutes an economic reality and a political hope. This chapter cannot attempt to discuss its achievements and shortcomings, or its inherent potentialities and dangers. But it not only forms a necessary element in building the Community of the West, it also constitutes a major attempt to break the vicious circle in which community is impossible without law and institutions, and law and institutions are impossible without community.

The European Community, formed between nations bound together by common civilization, and separated by different languages and by a long history of war and domination, is reshaping the attitudes of its citizens. It is creating a material solidarity between them and establishes such a beginning of common law as is made possible by an elementary sense of community, born out of suffering and necessity. The constant dialogue between a European body that is responsible for suggesting solutions to common problems and the governments of member countries that express national points of view constitutes the Community's federating power. Gradually, the scope of common law is widened in conformity to a gradually developing sense of common interest and common destiny. In thousands of meetings between hundreds of national organizations (agricultural groups, trade unions, interest groups, political parties, etc.) during endless sessions of ministers and civil servants, through difficulties, conflicts and crises, the Community gradually fulfills the difficult task of changing man's mind. At first hundreds, then thousands, now hundreds of thousands of people regularly participate in the laborious process of widening our understanding of the European Community.

Only he who participates in what happens on both sides of a line of demarcation is capable of serving that which transcends it; and thus serves peace. . . . In personal life, as in political life, peace comes into being only where an old line of demarcation, even if it continues partially to exist, loses its importance and therewith its power to create strife and tension. (PAUL TILLICH: *Grenzen*)

The frontiers of Europe's nations, once lines of demarcation that were necessary to enable the responsibility of citizenship to become an organized reality, have grown into insurmountable barriers between men no longer able to solve their own problems within the national context.

As Pope Paul VI said in his Christmas message of December, 1964, the world has become too small for man to be a stranger to his fellow man. In the earthly city, only those bound and protected by the same law and sharing common institutions as members of the same organized community can fully exercise those responsibilities that turn a stranger into a fellow citizen. The European Community *is* breaking the vicious circle. It must, at the same time, contribute to the building of the Community of the West as a necessary step on a long and difficult road, but the only one that can lead beyond the present armistice toward peace.

## The Implication for Action by the Church

Only much further discussion and group study can determine the responsibility of Christians in supporting such movements for new and wider forms of community. But one thing seems certain: If the view expressed in this paper is correct, and if peace in the nuclear age depends less on the abolition of nuclear arms, or on armaments control, or on the United Nations charter, than on extending political community beyond existing national borders, then the church must take the processes of building political community more seriously than it has so far done. The church has, or should have, a much truer reading of men, and knows, or should know, much more about making man his brother's keeper than any political organization. Action by the church should not be confined to pronouncements and preaching, but should enter into the daily lives of its members. They must become pioneers in building political community across borders that now restrict the active exercise of responsibility of man for man. The whole life and organization of the church should—if the line of argument of this paper is valid—be reconsidered in the light of the services that the church could render to the world in moving toward community. Although steeped in the ambiguities of life, like all other human endeavors, such action could help to make possible the continuation, under God's patience, of life upon his earth.

# 4

# NATIONAL INTEREST AND INTERNATIONAL ORDER

by KENNETH W. THOMPSON (United States)

AMERICAN thinking on foreign policy has undergone at least four major and far-reaching changes since the First World War. For most Americans, that war was a struggle to safeguard western civilization and "to make the world safe for democracy." After the war, President Woodrow Wilson captured the imagination of a broad segment of mankind by his proclamation of a new international order. However, discovering the conditions of a lasting peace proved more difficult than defining the principles of a just war. In consequence, the Wilsonian "grand design" was rejected at home and abroad. This reaction stemmed in part from a rather general lethargy and yearning for normalcy and in part from the gap that separated Wilson's idealism from the facts of a stubbornly rationalistic world. A small but powerful body of American senators spearheaded the defeat of the League of Nations and the triumph of American isolationism.

But responsible Americans were unwilling to turn their backs on the rest of the world. Intellectuals and policy-makers launched a campaign to revive the spirit of American internationalism and to draw the blueprint for a more durable world order. The churches and universities constituted a rallying ground for discussions that were to lead to proposals for a new international organization. For such groups, the shadows of war that sounded the death knell of the League of Nations experiment were, at the same time, a clarion call to support a new enterprise in international cooperation. It is no exaggeration to say that the birth of the United Nations was made possible by the labor and love of these new champions of international responsibility.

Their efforts and the life of the United Nations itself evoked a third response: a realistic critique rooted in a reaction against the utopianism that surrounded the ideological justification of that organization. A worthy institution that provided the framework for international cooperation had come to be viewed as an end in itself. Those who announced that it spelled the elimination of rivalry among states soon discovered that it was actually a new arena in which great and small powers vied for influence and power, and that all the novel techniques of an international Parliament could not supplant peace-keeping through strength and the balancing of power. "Open diplomacy" had not removed the need for what Dag Hammarskjold described as "quiet diplomacy."

But, finally, the demands of a world in change called for a marriage of realism and idealism, for peace with justice. The newly emerging states were pressing their claims for a place in the sun. It was not sufficient for the United States to keep the peace with friends and allies. Because of the principles for which it stood— self-determination, individual rights, social advancement and economic progress—it had to be responsive to the winds of change. It took as its guide, therefore, both the restraints of national self-interest and the compulsions of being a friendly neighbor to those who were struggling for independence and self-government.

All those who have matured in the United States in the past twenty years have been influenced by the interplay of these several trends of thought. It would be folly to claim immunity from the tensions and conflicts between them. There are inevitably contradictions between putting national self-interest first and showing a decent, if not compassionate, regard for the interests of others. Moreover, thinking about the international realm is, of necessity, uncertain and ambiguous. Problems of judgment intrude, and the facts are never fully at hand. Citizens of a nation that enjoys, if but for one fleeting moment in history, a supremacy of world power, see the world differently than do those who speak for the smaller powers. They often overlook the legitimate claims of others and the changing needs of rising peoples and, as a result, must bear the burdens of dissatisfaction, resentment, suspicion and fear. The most they can hope for is respect, since appreciation and affection seem always to escape them. They must strive unceasingly to be just, in the consciousness that their justice is doomed to incompleteness. For, while helping others, they must satisfy their own people that they are being well served. While coming to the aid of friends in the new states, they cannot neglect ties with friends in ancient states. In explaining their purposes, they must speak to varied audiences at home and abroad. And, as they debate on the course to follow, in free and democratic elections, they must know that their words may seem harsh, selfish and vainglorious, and may offend those whom their chosen government would serve.

### Between War and Peace: An Interpretation of the Present Situation

Throughout history, nationalism, industrialism and, more recently, modernization have shaped international relations. The nation-state has remained the primary unit of political organization, even though some of its functions may be obsolete. In fact, in the newly emergent states of Latin America, Asia, Africa and the Middle East, new forms of nationalism, embodying rudiments of the old, comprise a dynamic new factor that will, for better or worse, affect every plan of international cooperation.

Industrialism is another force that helped to transform the face of western Europe in the eighteenth and nineteenth centuries. It has spread its influence irresistibly through Russia, Latin America and Asia. Its effects are evident today both in capitalist and communist nations: it has led to greater concentrations of population, to specialization and division of labor and to the need for community programs on behalf of less privileged groups. Marxism predicated that industrial and capitalist societies carry the seeds of their own destruction, that the rich would become richer and the poor poorer and that eventually the more numerous poor would arise and throw off their chains.

Marx's prediction has been largely refuted—at least within the more developed societies, which, despite abuses and social injustices, have found ways of regenerating themselves. They have succeeded in removing substantial areas of injustice through social legislation and reform. Now, Lenin's version of Marx—that rich nations would become richer and poor nations poorer, until the poor would be driven to revolt—is on trial on a world-wide scale. Can international society succeed in repudiating the Marxist prediction as national societies have done before them? In the absence of a world-wide sovereign legislature, the United Nations and multilateral agencies give the sanction of representative international bodies to this great task. The social costs of industrialization have been met on the national scene; men of good will are now striving to meet them at the international level.

Modernization is a world-wide social phenomenon that knows no national or ideological boundaries. In developed and developing countries alike, it sets the framework for change and influences the patterns of national life. It accounts for many of the circumstances that influence competition and cooperation, and, because it encompasses the most basic factors of change, it contributes to shaping the Cold War.

Competition and cooperation are present in every human situation. Man is a social animal and discovers his true nature in cooperation with others. The necessity of living together in a shrinking world prompts men and nations to link their aims and policies; it leads to the building of new institutions. Yet rivalries are inevitable in every social grouping. Preachments and injunctions, urging men to seek common purposes, are fragile and often futile, unless joined with firm programs and controlling incentives. Cooperation must pay—or seem to pay. The necessities of cooperation must be as visible as those of competition.

In the mid-twentieth century, change has added a new dimension to competition and a new urgency to cooperation. Communism and democracy are the political creeds not of the citizens of two countries but of men and women around the globe. In the past, rival nations fought for territory and prestige; today's struggle is for "the minds of men." Communism parades as a revolutionary faith whose loyal adherents are pledged to the overthrow of the *status quo*. Democracy holds to beliefs that are both old and new. It is the product of two thousand years of experience and reflection on the political consequences of the nature of man. Yet its belief in the inalienable right of men and nations to govern themselves is ever new and revolutionary. In this focus on the living as against the written creed, democracy comes into view as fundamentally a political philosophy of change. An open society in which channels of public opinion and contests for authority are untrammeled is attuned to the forces of change. Contending men and principles compete in the free market place of politics and ideas. Communism, which controls men and subordinates individual rights to the single goal of social and economic justice, devolves into structures of power organized and managed by the few in the name of the masses.

The contest between two ways of life and two contending political orders is not trivial and imaginary: it goes to the heart of man's striving to build a better life. The outcome will decide whether generations to come will live in freedom or under tyranny. Freedom and order are gained and preserved, not once and for all, but through eternal vigilance within each nation-state. When national determination flags, the cause of freedom is in jeopardy. On a world-wide front, the early resolution of the contest between democracy and communism is foreclosed by the concentration of power in two great world systems. Despite strident statements in our country about victory in the Cold War, successive Administrations have learned to live with the facts of power. Moreover, changes take place even within monolithic structures. The Russia of Stalin gave way to the greater liberalism of Khrushchev; Russia and China, despite their common aim of winning the world for communism, found themselves drifting apart. The lesson that this teaches is not that communism will "change its spots," but rather that no political system escapes the pressures for change and the demands of necessity. Particularly in revolutionary regimes, generation succeeds generation, and, with the passage of time, the ardor of buoyant and crusading political movements tends to be supplanted by the more pragmatic spirit of those who must cope with ongoing events. They find there is too much unfinished business in the daily lives of their people to warrant continuous crusades abroad. This has happened in present-day Russia, but evidences of such a change are not yet visible in China.

The most compelling incentive to international cooperation lies in the terrible predicament raised by a thermonuclear age. Modern instruments of warfare have turned the prospects of an enemy's destruction into the possibility of self-destruction. Limited engagements and local wars are not excluded where restraint is practiced, but over them all hangs the deadly peril of the thermonuclear holocaust. Communist and open societies share the same perils. The recent limited test ban is proof, if any is needed, that Communists are not immune to the demands of necessity. This revolution in modern weaponry may be the most far-reaching change of all, with untold consequences for the pursuit of international cooperation. It may drive men to policies and behavior that they have not been virtuous enough to achieve over the centuries.

The present conflict between the Soviet Union and the United States can be seen most meaningfully in terms of the factors that lie at the roots of foreign policy. The Cold War, now nearly two decades old, is clearly a conflict with at least two dimensions. At one level, it is a struggle for men's minds; at the other, it engages two great configurations of power that, by necessity or design, reach out to influence others. Soviet-American rivalry is primarily a problem in foreign relations.

Both the United States and the Soviet Union have been blessed with most favorable geographic situations. The United States is bordered on the north and south by friendly and weaker states and safeguarded on the east and west by two great ocean moats. The geographic area of the Soviet Union, about one seventh of the earth's surface, has historically swallowed up any would-be invader, although its western boundaries are exposed to the European plains. The natural resources of both powers are immense, and their technology is far advanced. In conventional military weapons, Russian strength probably exceeds American, but in the production of new weapons—first of an offensive type but, more recently, of a defensive kind—the Russians, despite their progress with satellites, have lagged behind. Russia's population is greater than America's, although its per capita technical skill is probably less. American political institutions should, in the long run, prove superior, but the Russians may temporarily enjoy the advantages that flow from a system in which instantaneous decision-making and kaleidoscopic initiative are possible. National morale, particularly in the hydrogen age, is difficult to measure before a crisis. The quality of diplomacy on both sides is subject to the broader tendencies and problems that have been described.

Americans live by the faith that other peoples will come to embrace a political creed that involves a decent respect for the dignity of man, and that an international order may be founded on respect for the rights and interests of other sovereign states. However, there are three difficulties that confound American policy-makers and often confuse our friends abroad.

The first is the difficulty of marshaling domestic support for American policies while at the same time putting America's best foot forward in the eyes of the rest of the world. To mobilize public opinion, Americans say things to themselves that, from the standpoint of other people, might better be left unsaid. (In this, the United States is, of course, not unique.) America is a vast, sprawling continent whose people display great diversity in political and religious beliefs; in its constitutional system, power and responsibility are broadly diffused, although less so in the conduct of foreign than of domestic affairs. As Americans seek to persuade one another of the right course to follow, they speak with many voices, some of them raucous and strident. The language of domestic politics is not that of political theory. It aims to unite people behind certain policies. It looks for a common denominator that can more often be found in broad principles and moral generalities than in directives for strategy that, like military policies, must be cast in practical alternatives to meet varying circumstances. It prefers militant slogans to qualified truths and a crusade to public conversation on a problem.

Above all, it is a permanent feature of the landscape of international relations that American foreign policy must draw its support from a union of experts, the public and friends and allies abroad. History demonstrates that no American statesman can ignore any point of the triangle without courting disaster. Before the Second World War, public opinion lagged behind the thinking on foreign affairs of experts and allies. After the war, and up to 1950, American policy—especially for Europe—was acceptable alike to the experts, the public and members of the postwar grand alliance. This day has passed, and the three groups have tended to diverge more and more. America's allies have increasingly come to view their national interests as not necessarily identical with those of the United States, and, ironically, at a time when American policies are vulnerable to criticism by experts at home and abroad, they enjoy broad endorsement at all levels of American life.

Another difficulty stems from the colonial dilemma, which touches conflicting interests throughout the world. The colonial problem stands at the top of every agenda for discussion of American foreign policy. Nationalism is on the march in Asia, the Middle East and Africa; and Americans implore one another to identify their country with these movements. Responsible officials are encouraged to issue proclamations throwing America's weight behind popular revolutions. Unhappily, the colonial problem is less tractable than such exhortations would suggest. For, at the same time the fight is being waged to end the old imperialism, a new expansionism is threatening. Some feel that, in order both to contain it and to maintain a minimal system of order and a stable balance of power, America must cleave to its trusted allies with whom it has interests and military bases in common. Yet, in itself, this is unlikely to be enough. The present equilibrium of power and the sense of justice will be upset unless America supports the new nations in the so-called underdeveloped areas. The United States faces a triple challenge: to stem the tide of Russian imperialism and world communism; to unite the other western states; and to draw closer to nonwestern peoples only recently emerged as independent states. It is the unenviable task of American statesmen to keep all three of these balls in the air.

Can we offer any guidance to these jugglers? Are there any guidelines or principles that might throw a spotlight into a few of the darker corners of this colonial problem? There may be. First, we must start with the assumption that the colonial problem is fraught with dilemmas with which America must learn to live. No dogmatic statements for or against colonialism will waft them away. Solutions must be worked out case by case. Second, timing is of the essence. Third, any general solution will rest in the coordinating of mutual interests, not in the wholesale sacrifice of one set of interests to another. For example, in North Africa, French,

American and African interests appear to coincide and to be met by "liberal solutions." This harmonizing of interests requires a judicious balancing of claims. Fourth, it is one of the ironies of history that force may be necessary to preserve arrangements, not in order to perpetuate them, but to make their orderly liquidation possible. Fifth, it will not do to call every conflict of view between America and its European allies a colonial issue.

## The Morality of National Security

A final difficulty has its roots in the moral problem. The question of right and wrong is continuously raised in international and individual relations. Nations, like individuals, claim either that they seek to do, or have done, what is right. The values embodied in American culture ensure that, far from being an exception, America persistently aspires to bring about justice and international order. We are pained when we are told that some aspect of our national conduct cannot be justified in international terms, yet we can take comfort from the fact that, throughout history, one of the most baffling philosophical problems has been whether an action can be called good if it serves the group or primary loyalty or whether it must serve a more inclusive purpose. Political morality, as distinct from pure law or justice, looks for the point of concurrence between the particular and the general value, rather than calling for the sacrifice of the part to the whole. Politics can count on a residual egotism or self-interest that represents the creative potential of individuals and groups. The nascent international community must guard against extreme forms of parochial loyalty that reserve the right to suppress weaker neighbors. Moreover, it must be able to harness, beguile and deflect the more limited national purposes, even though it cannot easily transcend them. In Reinhold Niebuhr's words: "The individual or the group may feel called upon to sacrifice an immediate value for the sake of the more ultimate or general interest. But the community cannot demand this sacrifice as its right." Nor, one might add, can another sovereign state.

The American credo of political morality, especially in recent years, has been more pretentious than this. It has often called upon others to sacrifice a limited advantage to some higher cause. Justice and international order are properly considered the broad framework of political morality, but the weight and particular content in any decision to be given to them can never be determined in advance. The values of community and order are frequently in tension with the principles of justice, which are liberty and equality. If a national community cannot ensure a tolerable measure of justice, even though it maintains order, in the long run its authority will tend to erode. Similarly, if the international order lacks the power and prestige to safeguard all its members, they will be tempted to seek justice in other ways. There is an indefiniteness in political morality because

various and frequently contradictory values are involved in political decisions, and the preference which is given one value and end over another must be determined by historical contingencies rather than fixed principles. There are fixed principles and norms in the political realm, but there is no fixed principle for relating the norms to each other. It is possible to define as "bad" only those situations in which one or more norms are completely wanting. . . .[1]

Policy-makers sometimes look for short cuts to the moral problem. They spend a great deal more time talking about the need for greater morality in political life than in determining what this would actually imply. They seize on popular expressions congenial to their tastes and interests, like "majority rule." The workings of political machinery are invested with all the trappings of a religious exercise, and political pronouncements are equated with the glorification of God. The problem of public morality calls for Christian humility rather than for moralistic self-righteousness, which can win few friends abroad and serves only to lower the currency of moral principles.

For more than a century and a half, national security has been primarily the concern of soldiers and statesmen. Since the Second World War, however, public opinion in the United States has engaged in a succession of great debates on military strategy. Collective security, support of the North Atlantic Treaty Organization and nuclear weapons policy appear constantly on the agenda of

---

[1] REINHOLD NIEBUHR: "Theory of International Politics," p. 11. Unpublished manuscript.

public discussions. And, significantly, no discussion of defense policy has omitted reference to moral issues. It is as if people in the United States reformulated Clemenceau's classic dictum to read, "National security is too important to be left to generals," and added "and it must be approached in the context of morality."

If the present crisis between Soviet Russia and the West were clearly either a clash of military systems or a struggle between political ideologies, we would doubtless face the future with greater confidence and hope. However, most of us must admit that we vacillate between a military and an ideological view of the situation. Our difficulty in arriving at acceptable policies arises primarily from our uncertainty over the nature of the crisis. In the early days of the Cold War the majority of informed observers were convinced that the Russian threat to western civilization was identical with the Nazi menace, and that the recipe for dealing with it was the same. They said that over two centuries of national experience had proved that a foreign policy unsupported by military strength is likely to be impotent. Nevertheless, after the Second World War, as after the First, the United States dismantled its military establishment as an indication of its peaceful intentions. Both Germany and the Soviet Union seized the opportunity to impose their will upon helpless nations that fell within their zones of control. They succumbed not because they were lacking in morality but because they had no means of securing their national frontiers.

The West has applied this lesson to the atomic and thermonuclear age. There are evidences that the Soviet Union more than once marched up to the brink, threatening to engulf Greece and Turkey, Iran and Berlin, only to march back again when it met resistance. Conversely, where resistance proved ambiguous, uncertain or divided, as in Egypt, Syria and the Far East, the Soviet sphere of influence flowed across boundaries that had long marked the limits of Russian power.

Those who look at the international situation from this point of view see the immediate military threat as unquestionably the gravest danger, and call urgently for the multiplication of more powerful weapons of destruction, for new strategies and for missile bases and a nuclear weapons pool. They believe that the irreconcilable conflicts and tensions of the Cold War will end only when one side or the other forges decisively ahead.

A second group urges states to display equal vision and energy in seeking political and economic solutions and in launching expanded military programs. It points to technical assistance programs of the Soviet Union, which has pledged $1.5 billion to the underdeveloped areas, and to the evidence of successful Soviet penetration into the Middle East. The tactics of Russian imperialism have shifted to subversion, infiltration and indirect aggression.

The value of ultimate weapons in these areas, with their great numbers of agrarian peoples spread over vast regions, seems doubtful at best. Crises have passed in Indo-China, Korea and Egypt without their being used. Because they neither possess nor see the relevance of these terrible weapons, the newer nations have led the movement to outlaw them.

However, the contradictory reactions of these states to thermonuclear devices are revealed by the grievous blow to the United States' prestige in the same countries when the Soviet Union launched the first satellite. Despite criticism throughout Asia and Africa of the United States' materialism and preoccupation with technological and military advance, confidence in United States policy was gauged by the very standards that were deplored. When the United States, through the United Nations, held the line in Korea, those who had been its sharpest critics (including some Indians who had judged the United States to be rigidly anti-communist and obsessed with the military threat) applauded the successful deployment of American power, particularly until the fateful crossing of the 38th parallel.

The relative validity of a military and an ideological characterization of the crises cannot be measured by a barometer registering the rise and fall of Stalinism in the Soviet Union. If Stalinism is synonymous with the brutal and heedless sacrifice of every other goal to those of the communist society, then it is as alive today as ever. The Russian military threat undeniably survived the death of Stalin; we have only to look at the sputniks and the hundreds of divisions guarding Soviet frontiers; to recall the threats and displays of force when crises arose in the Suez, Hungary and Poland, and during the Turkish-Syrian disputes; to recognize that moves and countermoves on the political and economic fronts are equally real; and the contest shifts almost imperceptibly from one type of warfare to another, or sometimes is joined simultaneously on all sides.

Three errors are commonly made in appraising the military component of foreign policy. First, military power is often confused with national power, and a nation's capacity to impose its will is equated with its military establishment. But military power is like a fist, the force of which depends on the health and vitality of the body politic and the whole society. Second, the military element is often viewed in too static terms. In two world wars, the democracies were the last to arm, but they gained the final victory. Third, it is difficult to analyze the most effective distribution of the components of military force. For example, what comprises a strong military force today? Is it large ground forces, hydrogen bombs or intensive research? Is a small, highly specialized army more desirable than a large number of ground forces, or are both essential? We know that an effective foreign policy must be supported by a military program that can safeguard national security, but decisions must be made about distributing resources among alternative means of defense, without any certainty of the kind of war in which they may be used.

Beyond this, the weapons of today may not be used in future wars because technology will have rendered them obsolete. It is said that conventional weapons are fast being supplanted by new and more deadly ones, and that therefore traditional armaments fail to provide an adequate basis for foreign policy. On the other hand, some military experts question whether atomic and hydrogen weapons will ever be used, because of the prospect of mutual annihilation. Does the stockpiling of an unlimited supply of weapons that no one dares to use furnish a state with the requisite military support? These are the horns of the dilemma that threaten to impale the defense strategists. The recent agreement of East and West to reduce stockpiles was based on the application of the principle of mutual dislike to this situation.

## From Coexistence to Cooperation

Despite the fact that nations continue to live between peace and war, profound world forces are at work bringing about a relaxation of tension. These include the rising pressures in communist and democratic countries alike for a more abundant life, the nuclear stalemate and fear of mutual annihilation, the disappearance of first-generation bolshevik revolutionaries and the coincidence of the leadership in Moscow and Washington of moderates and pragmatists. The break-up of great-power authority symbolized by the Sino-Soviet split and by Gaullism has had the effect of contributing to the *détente*. Yet coexistence remains at best provisional and unstable. Competition continues, and the struggle for power goes on unabated. What has changed is not the substance but the forms and modalities of competition. Neither side can afford to contemplate the escalation of conflict except as a last resort.

One result is that the scene of great-power rivalry has shifted to competition for influence in the developing countries. It is in Africa, Asia and Latin America that the merits of the various political and economic systems are on trial. Neither system is likely to afford a completely satisfactory blueprint. Emerging societies will fashion their own forms of government. Yet, as they evolve, they will, like every nascent political order before them, draw on the legacy of the past. Having tapped the wellsprings of social and political experience, thereby learning from the past, Americans in turn must play the role of partner, not patron, in helping others freely to shape their future. The United States could not escape this challenge even if it wished to do so. In an era of peaceful competition with a rival political system, it must pursue its purpose with dignity, restraint and justice.

Indeed, the hope for greater cooperation and more lasting friendship relates to the great purposes that Americans and other free peoples espouse. There is a profound and lasting identity between the ends of the American people and mankind everywhere. If this were not so, the American Constitution and Bill of Rights would not be mirrored so faithfully in the Preamble and first two Articles of the Charter of the United Nations. Both documents affirm the rights of men to choose their own form of government and to rule by the consent of the governed, the protection of the individual against arbitrary rule, freedom of speech and conscience, freedom from arbitrary arrest and the goal of social and economic justice. No national or international leader can long deny or thwart the realization of these fundamental freedoms, for they lie at the roots of civilized life wherever it evolves, including relations between the nations.

The attainment of an international order made up of nations that respect justice and the Rule of Law is, of course, a long-run objective. Some states must, in any foreseeable future, place order ahead of justice; they are constrained to give internal security priority over the creation of a multiparty political system. If freedom for a people to select their own government is merely postponed, a society can be seen as moving toward membership in a true international order. Their respect for law will evolve internally and be reflected in international conduct. They may serve to remind us all of the long and painful progress toward representative government.

Even where this identity of ultimate purposes is lacking, the benefit of contacts across national borders remains. The peoples of communist and noncommunist states have much to gain from one another. Cultural exchanges provide fruitful channels for clarifying goals and intentions and ensure that the benefits of science and learning for a more peaceful world will be shared. Peoples who come to respect fellow professionals in other lands are likely to help turn the tide toward more favorable attitudes based on mutual respect. Where great powers confront each other, mutual respect, while falling short of affection and good will, represents an important advance.

A world order, when it comes about, will result from a recognition of the infinity of common interests and ties that bind men together. Today, the threads that bind us together are a blending of fear and respect. The threat of mutual annihilation hangs over us all. The spotlight is relentlessly focused on the risks of nuclear war. Beneath the surface, less visible and acclaimed common interests are being forged. Scientists around the world are dedicating themselves to the search for new and better solutions to the major problems of welfare that face all mankind. Nations are drawn together by an infinity of threads that unite them as members of a single international order: health; commerce; the war against hunger; population; communication; transportation; and science. The realization of this order will come when the forces that divide can be supplanted by those that unite.

# 5

# EASTERN EUROPE AND THE WEST IN THE SEARCH FOR PEACE

by J. B. SOUCEK (Czechoslovakia)

IT IS generally agreed that the characteristic of the present world political situation that distinguishes it from former periods consists in the fact that the traditional function of war as an instrument of policy has changed and will probably soon entirely disappear. This statement is certainly true, but it should be supplemented by a parallel thesis: that the traditional way of overcoming conflicts and allaying enmities is also rapidly losing its applicability and usefulness. In human history, we can repeatedly observe how inveterate conflicts and enmities were put aside and even forgotten, or at least pushed into the background, when the two enemies had to face a new danger—a new enemy that menaced them both. Examples are not difficult to find. The alliance of the West with the Soviet Union against Hitler is one; the subsequent rapid reconciliation and alliance of the western allies with western Germany in the face of the presumed communist danger is another. One may venture the suggestion that this way of easing tensions and ending enmities is no longer practical without the greatest dangers for all concerned.

This thesis can be practically illustrated. When the gradual easing of tension between what are known as East and West acquired definite forms, particularly in the Moscow agreement to end nuclear tests, this fact was sometimes overtly or covertly interpreted to mean that the two world powers or blocs were preparing to unite against the "third world," or at least against China—that giant that is slowly acquiring the strength commensurate with its size and population. On the other hand, when the tension between the Soviet Union and China seemed to be at its peak, voices could be heard, particularly in western Germany (isolated, but not quite insignificant voices), speculating whether China could not be approached by the West in order to weaken the Soviet position. Both kinds of speculation are equally wrong and dangerous. And, if the recent changes in the Soviet Union were to mean that that power, while disapproving and regretting the present intransigent mood of the Chinese, wanted to make clear its utter refusal of any speculation as to the ulterior meaning of its coexistence policy, it would be entirely to the good. If this were not to happen, if the former East-West conflict were to be supplanted by a North-South conflict—the haves against the have nots—then another disaster of unprecedented dimensions would be building up, perhaps at some time near the end of the century.

## *The Impact of the New Nations on Old World Tensions*

These considerations are linked with the great change in the world scene that we observe taking place at an increasingly accelerated pace. We did, of course, expect that former colonies, dependent territories and nations of old cultures, where economic and political development had been slowed down in the course of recent centuries, would eventually acquire a fully independent status. But not many of us were prepared for the breadth and speed with which this process has been taking place. A "third world" is emerging, asserting its independence on all sides and, in all its poverty, outward weakness and inexperience, is rapidly becoming a force with which even the most powerful have to reckon. We might do better, however, to speak not simply of the "third world," but rather of a rising multicentrism in the world political scene. All this certainly contributes to the easing of older tensions, but much will depend upon the wisdom with which the great powers or power blocs are willing and able to use this opportunity, not simply to strengthen their own position or to build a common front against the newly emerging or rising nations. The only sane way open to them is to unite their resources to help these new nations to master the tremendous difficulties affecting consolidation and growth.

The rise of so many new nations has, inevitably, its dangers. Many observers are dismayed at the spirit of intolerant nationalism that they display. This is a real danger. But experience shows that our best hope of curing nationalistic disease lies in the creation of a feeling of security, equality and "acceptance" in the new or hitherto subject nations. The experience of Czechoslovakia provides an illustration. Nationalistic feelings were strongest in the Czech nation after it had emerged from the period of its great national decline. As it acquired greater strength and self-confidence, a broader outlook became increasingly apparent; and, during the first fifteen years of the independent Czechoslovak Republic after 1918, nationalism of the more extreme type was clearly on the wane. With the coming of Hitler and during the occupation, nationalist feeling understandably ran high. But, after the new liberation, and after a comparatively short period of equally understandable, though deplorable, nationalist outbursts, this feeling began to disappear with striking rapidity. Now, a nationalistic spirit is hardly to be observed anywhere, least of all among the young. If it exists at all, it is dormant. This state of affairs, as we well know, is to be observed in nearly all European nations that experienced the Second World War at first hand. The minds of the peoples of the newly-emerging nations on other continents seem to work no differently than do European minds; and the best way to help them to avert the danger of destructive nationalism is to help them to acquire, with the least possible delay, security and a healthy self-respect. There is, admittedly, a great obstacle in the way: not only the fact that these nations, for the most part, differ from us in their historical and cultural heritage, as European nations differ from one another, but the racial factor, which easily creates irrational feelings of otherness and dislike that are difficult to overcome, must also be considered. In this respect, too, we Europeans have the first and greatest responsibility. It was our own racial pride and insufferable attitude of superiority that created the extreme sensitivity of our brethren of other colors in relation to us, not to mention nations or other communities of our own race that, in various ways and with varying intensity, still refuse even to consider the idea of racial equality.

The process of emancipation in the formerly subject nations has no doubt been accelerated by the division of the world into two antagonistic camps, the East and the West; more specifically, by the help that the Soviet Union offered these nations, not by directly using its power for this purpose but simply by existing as the second great world center of power and by upholding these nations with its sympathy and political support. It is, moreover, equally clear that this development did not result simply in strengthening the power sphere of the Soviet Union as such; but, by its drive toward selfhood and independence, it has, on the contrary, helped to speed up the process of easing the tension between the two world powers or blocs.

## Common Influences at Work on Eastern Europe and the West

This easing of tension has other more profound and substantial causes than the mere respect for the rising nations or the intention to win them for one side or the other. It is an outcome of gradual, at first hardly discernible, but deep-seated internal developments in many countries, particularly the leading powers of the world. One of the contributing factors is certainly the realization that the Cold War is futile and that its rigid patterns and images are unreal. Seen in another and perhaps deeper dimension, it is evident that the internal foundations or projections of the Cold War, the hysteria of the McCarthy period in the United States and the rigid authoritarianism in the Soviet Union known as "Stalinism" or "cult of personality" were out of touch with reality and caused distortion and deprivation of life in the nations thus afflicted. The revulsion arising from these aberrations has given rise to a new critical spirit, which results in a re-examination of the established patterns of political, economic and cultural life and in a new willingness to learn, in an objective spirit, about conditions and trends in other parts of the world. A new sobriety and self-criticism and— most hopeful of all—a new probing into the ultimate problems of individual and social human existence are emerging. And, with it, there is a new willingness to take other men and their ideas seriously, even while holding fast to the essentials of one's own. This is fundamentally true of all countries, though the movement toward a new openmindedness sometimes seems more vigorous in our area of the world than elsewhere. In any event, what is gradually opening before us is the opportunity to gain a better and more objective knowledge of those who, until recently, were largely veiled from us by the notorious curtain; and to understand each other and to learn from each other. This mutual exchange, which is just beginning, will certainly confirm what many of us have sensed for some time now, over and above all differences of political and social systems—that the modern scientific and industrial civilization creates everywhere similar conditions, attitudes of mind and social and moral problems. The exchange of experience that is already taking place and the expansion of which is to be encouraged can contribute to the gradual creation of a new world unity. One word of caution must, however, be added. The trend toward variety, multicentrism and assertion of particular national traditions, which is so clearly apparent in eastern Europe, is sometimes considered in the West mainly or solely in relation to the question whether and how it could contribute to the disintegration of the cohesion of these countries and thus to the isolation and weakening of the Soviet Union. This is particularly apparent in the way these developments are often discussed even in the most serious West German political periodicals.[1] This amounts to seeing the new, promising developments in East European countries simply as opportunities to achieve, at long last, the western victory in the Cold War. That, however, is a forlorn hope. Even those of us who are by no means one-sidedly antiwestern or enthusiastic about communism resent such speculations and can see in them nothing but a retarding factor in the hopeful developments of our times. Undoubtedly, analogous speculations about a possible use of differences and dissensions in the western world can be heard in the East. Both, in the long run, are equally useless and harmful. What we need is true openmindedness and a readiness to understand and to welcome and encourage, without ulterior motives, all evidences of reasonableness and true humanity, wherever they may appear.

---

[1] The most recent example in my hands: K. BIRRENBACK: "Lockt der rote Handel?" *Die Zeit, Nr 48,* Nov. 27, 1964.

### The Decline of Nationalism in Europe

We have so far considered the problem of relations between old and new, rich and poor nations and the cognate problems of the relations between East and West and its recent modifications. The specific problems of the area that is nearest to the author, Europe, and, in particular, central Europe, have so far scarcely been mentioned, a fact that corresponds to the real shift of the world center of political gravity. Some thirty or even twenty-five years ago it was different. In the pre-Munich and Munich days, for example, we in Czechoslovakia felt that we were taking a stand that was of decisive importance, not merely for the whole of Europe, but even for the world. Decisions were being taken in central Europe that could lead either to world peace or to war. The disastrous agreement of Munich was made by the western and central European powers, while the two nations that were already the most powerful, the United States and the Soviet Union, were left outside. This was probably the last opportunity for western and central Europe to play a supremely decisive role in the world. The end, as we know so well, was disaster. After 1945, Washington and Moscow remained for a time the only decisive centers of power. It is only in recent years that new centers have emerged, to ease—but also to complicate—the situation. Europe is certainly one of these new centers that has acquired a new importance. Both the western and the eastern European countries cease to look politically like mere replicas of their respective protecting powers. But this is far from reinstating Europe in the status of being *the* center of world affairs. Its problems can rightly be seen and settled only within the framework of a superior world order. The times when large areas of the world could be regarded as an insignificant annex to European interests and European politics are irrevocably past.

Europe, however, remains, and will long remain, an important part of the world. Its ills and problems can still affect the rest of the world in a dangerous way. Europe is beset with problems and is, in many respects, sick. It is true that some of the problems or types of problems that plagued Europe thirty years ago or more seem to have been overcome. This is particularly true of the old-fashioned nationalism and of primitive nationalistic prejudice. In our part of Europe, we are experiencing in this respect a *détente* that we hardly dared to expect as little as twenty years ago—even if some of us did at that time cherish the hope that the terrible war might have one good effect—namely, to end nationalism. These hopes have not been altogether disappointed. In our country, we are experiencing an easing of relations with our Hungarian and Polish neighbors that seemed to be out of the question before the Second World War. It is not that the differences of temperament and national traditions have simply disappeared. Residues or echoes of old prejudice can still occasionally be observed. But the whole atmosphere, the overruling attitude toward neighbors who used to be regarded as national adversaries, or even enemies, has fundamentally changed. This is also true in respect to our German neighbors. It is a phenomenon that has probably not yet been thoroughly explained and understood that, soon after the end of the war, the wave of violent anti-German feeling rapidly disappeared. What remains is probably an uneasy feeling of uncertainty as to what this great and powerful nation, with its particular traditions, might not one day do again, to the surprise and detriment of others. But this uneasiness is far from hardened prejudice and still farther from hatred. As we know, the same development has been taking place between the Germans and their neighbors in the West.

### The Possibility of New Relations with Germany

The question remains whether this welcome development has also taken place or gone far enough in the relations between western Germany and her eastern European neighbors. There are signs that a good deal of prejudice remains or is being born anew. It is no longer merely national but is connected with a general aversion to the other side of the curtain. An essential part of this prejudice rests, without question, on sheer ignorance. This was always largely characteristic of the German attitude toward their smaller neighbors in the East. Language difficulties may to some extent explain it, but it is regrettable and dangerous; and, during the postwar era, there was the further difficulty of acquiring information about conditions on the other side of the dividing line.

Much of this kind of prejudice remains, together with precon- ceived, fixed notions, both old and new, even though the possi- bilities of becoming better informed have greatly increased. It is true that serious elements in the press and among the leading representatives of intellectual circles in western Germany are try- ing to acquire more objective knowledge and to appreciate with real understanding the position of their eastern neighbors. It seems, however, that, among the general public in Germany, prejudice and distorted images of our past and present prevail, and that they are being perpetuated by the less responsible manipulators of the media of mass communication. Certainly, much remains to be done and improved—on both sides. But, again, one gains the im- pression that the average Czechoslovak citizen has a more ade- quate image of German life and a more sober appreciation of the German situation than vice versa.

We are, of course, aware that the German attitude toward us in the East is largely conditioned by the difficult political situation of the German nation. Many of us have learned to know and under- stand Germany better than ever before and have acquired a new respect and sympathy for the great German traditions. This en- ables us to understand their sorrow at the division of their coun- try, which is not only a national disaster but involves grievous separation of friends and families. We know, too, that those who, after the Second World War, had to leave their homes in Czecho- slovakia and Poland have many bitter memories, not only of the expulsion itself but of the harsh manner in which it was often car- ried out. It was a measure that was never contemplated and was, in fact, unthinkable before the war. We must, however, remember that the nations east of Germany emerged from the occupation con- vinced that Germany, as represented by its leaders, had premedi- tated their annihilation, not only in the sense of forced assimilation but by literal extermination. Documentary evidence found after the war shows that this was no mere suspicion or figment of the imag- ination, but a plan actually prepared and thought out in amazing detail. The harsh measures against the Germans in 1945 would certainly not have been adopted except in an utterly abnormal situation, after a period of the extreme and unprecedented acts of extermination that the German government planned and organized without any effective resistance or protest on the part of the German people. To try now to undo what was done then is unthinkable, except in a situation of similar extremity and one, in all probability, even more terrible than that of 1939–45.

In some sense, this applies even to the other aspect of the German predicament—the division of the country. Nobody is prepared to regard this state of affairs as final and unchangeable. And those of us who have now learned to know and understand the German people better sympathize with the great and unceasing sorrow of the best and most responsible Germans on account of the division. This is certainly an anomalous and potentially dangerous situation—a sore that is poisoning not only the German but the whole European atmosphere. The question remains, How can this danger spot be removed? It is evident that it cannot be done by liquidating the German Democratic Republic; that is, by its capitulation, which would also involve a virtual capitulation of the Soviet Union and its allies and friends. This is unimaginable without the reversal of the results of the Second World War, i.e., without another war. The union of Germany can be achieved only within the framework of a gradual process in which the two great European camps continue to move nearer together and to diminish their antagonisms and differences. But it is difficult to imagine how this process, which has made important progress in the last few years, can bear fruit for Germany unless the Germans themselves—and that means the two German governments—take appropriate steps in that direction. This would mean abandoning many inveterate taboos. German rearmament, again, has played a fatal role in this respect. It was irresponsible to dismiss the warnings of the Soviet government to this effect as mere propaganda or as a tactical maneuver. These warnings were made in all seriousness; they correspond with the facts of the situation and have been fully vindicated by actual developments. Germany is much further away from its reunification than when it was disarmed, a fact that ought to be remembered also in the light of recent discussions about the creation of the MLF. In this connection, a question addressed to the contributors of this section is relevant: "What is the Christian understanding of 'peace'—whether as that which supervenes as the just and equitable resolution of conflict or the precondition of other favourable developments?" It seems hardly possible to answer in the abstract by a simple "this" or "that." Certainly, peace cannot be solidly established if manifest injustice or great hardship is lamely tolerated and allowed to continue indefinitely with no prospect of redress. This is why we agree that the present division of Germany is potentially very dangerous. On the other hand, the removal of this injustice or hardship depends upon a peaceful atmosphere or outlook (if one is not prepared to resort to force, which today would be madness). The division of Germany was an outcome, in the first place, of a war in which the rulers of Germany chose a path that inevitably ended in the position *Germania contra mundum*. And, in the second place, it was the fruit of the fatal estrangement between the victorious allies soon after the war. It is untrue to say that this division is the chief cause of the Cold War. It is, on the contrary, its most important and bitter result; before reunification can be achieved, the Cold War must be fully overcome. There cannot be any really fruitful preliminary steps toward it without a substantial modification in the Cold War atmosphere.

The predominant need of our era is to establish and secure peace in our time—and to leave doors open for those who will come after us to consolidate and perpetuate that peace. It is an absurd and sinister phenomenon of our time that things have been allowed to go on in Germany in a direction that has resulted in the peace and the union of Germany being regarded as virtually contradictory. This may sound like exaggeration. But those who have constantly observed the manifest dislike of many of the ruling circles in western Germany for any measure that might ease the tension—not to mention the stubborn veto of such concrete proposals for disarmament as the creation of atom-free zones—or the obvious nervousness with which these circles note signs of any *rapprochement* between Washington or London and Moscow, will appreciate the point.

### The Prophetic Mission of the Church

Peace, disarmament and the means and conditions for realizing these aims would be apt subjects with which to conclude this essay.

They have, however, been discussed in other contributions to this volume, and they have been the subject of many pronouncements of the World Council of Churches and its various bodies and commissions, of many individual churches or church federations and, last but not least, of the Christian Peace Conference. But I want to draw attention to an aspect of these problems that has for long troubled many of us.

There are many truths with which everybody seems familiar and which everybody repeats with the greatest conviction. We all know that war is a terrible thing; that under modern conditions it has become an absurdity; that the great need of our time is to recognize the emergence of the new nations and the increasingly conspicuous role they play and to understand the dangerous eventuality that the gap separating them from the leading industrial nations is likely to increase. Everybody agrees that there is much to be done about the two urgently serious questions—disarmament and aid to underdeveloped countries. But, in fact, little that is effective is being done, certainly not enough to avert the dangers that are involved. Those who draw our attention to the immense complexity of the tasks and problems that confront us in both realms are certainly right. It is easy to demand disarmament or efficient aid to underdeveloped countries or effective steps toward the overcoming of race discrimination and conflict, but it is difficult to discover what can be done concretely and then to do it. And those who point out that in all these difficulties the perennial reality of the sinfulness of man finds a new manifestation are also right. But is it enough to say this? Is it not the churches' role to breed the spirit of revolt against complacent acceptance of the inevitability of the sinful corruption of all human effort? Are we not aware, not only of the reality of sin but of the overruling reality of Christ's victory? In other words, have not the churches in these matters a prophetic mission as well—to encourage those who work for peace and for effective aid to needy nations to hope against hope and to attempt the seemingly impossible?

Alas, the churches have their own sad record of noble and great and even prophetic words that were not followed by action. And sometimes when the churches encountered the emphatic disapproval of the powerful, their actions belied their words. There are certainly encouraging instances of determined and effective action on the part of the churches. A conspicuous example is the firm stand taken by the leaders of the major American churches in the civil rights struggle. But how far and how quickly does such action penetrate the rank and file of the congregations? This is no complacent question addressed only to brethren in other countries. It is humiliating for us to discover that there are, within congregations of our own churches in Czechoslovakia, some otherwise loyal brethren who have evidently found it impossible—in spite of our bitter experience—to overcome their unworthy prejudice against the Jews. What is needed everywhere is the renewal of the churches, which means the genuine Christianization of us all.

But this cannot be achieved by simply taking note of this truth and waiting for the renewal. Renewal can come only within the framework of a determined, devoted effort to work for the aims that we have recognized as imperative for our Christian conscience. In this respect, the Christian Peace Conference, with its aim of reconciliation, may be an instrument of the coming renewal of the church—provided that it firmly resists the temptations of institutionalism and continues to refuse to retract its own pronouncements if they later seem inopportune.

The church so renewed will ponder a remarkable fact, which, from the point of view of our faith, may be the most significant sign of our times: The appeals and commands of the gospel as contained, above all, in the Sermon on the Mount, so long regarded as totally foreign to the problems of man in history, are now seen to illuminate the basic political issues of our day. These are not, perhaps, precepts to be followed verbatim, but in their ultimate meaning and in the direction to which they point. We can affirm without hesitation that human life cannot continue much longer unless, at critical moments, leading statesmen receive insights that in the last analysis are derived from the Sermon on the Mount. This should both humble the church and encourage it to be more bold and steadfast in its message to the world.

There is no question of the church's imposing its will on the world or of its playing a decisive role in world affairs. This possibility, always most ambiguous from the point of view of the gospel, has gone forever with the disappearance of the medieval *corpus Chris-*

*tianum.* But a renewed church can discern, encourage and sustain those forces in human society that work for understanding, peace and solidarity with the needy or oppressed of all nations and races and so try to enlarge the area of human dignity and freedom. It can encourage those statesmen who show by their acts that they have received some insight congruent with the true needs of mankind, and it can discourage those who persist in blindly seeking their own interest or glory. It can sometimes raise its voice in protest or in demands for definite action at a crucial moment. And it can always be a fellowship in which brethren from various countries and walks of life can meet and learn to understand one another. To foster in this way better mutual knowledge and understanding may be the most important service that the church can render, for it helps to create the only climate in which our stubborn world problems can be tackled with some prospect of success.

# PART II

THE REVOLUTIONARY CHARACTER
OF PRESENT-DAY SOCIETY
AND THE PROBLEM
OF POLITICAL ORDER

# 6

# THE REVOLUTIONARY
# CHANGE IN THE STRUCTURE
# OF EUROPEAN POLITICAL LIFE

by ANDRÉ PHILIP (France)

EUROPE today is undergoing a new technical revolution, the effects of which far transcend the changes that occurred at the end of the eighteenth century when the modern industrial age was born. What is happening today is no longer simply an advance in existing techniques (continuing the era of mass production) but a series of innovations that involve a general increase in production in Europe, a gradual raising of the standard of living and great transformation of social structures.

## New Developments in Population, Agriculture and Industry

We can examine this transformation from three essential aspects: population, agriculture and industry. First, population. The growth in the population of Europe slowed down during the nineteenth century; in France, there was even a marked fall in the birth rate. After the end of the Second World War, however, the birth rate rose in all countries, especially in France, with the introduction of the system of family allowances. This growth in population does not yet present problems like those that confront the developing countries. For the moment, it simply establishes a better balance between the generations; the proportion of old people is not falling, because the expectancy of life is longer; but the number of young people is increasing, a situation that, during the transition period, imposes a heavy burden on the adult productive population, which has to support both the old and the young. To-day, however, these young people (born during the last twenty years) form part of the producing section of the population; they do not form a separate independent group; they want to be in-tegrated into the community as a whole, to have a voice in its decisions and to share in its responsibilities. The first characteristic of Europe is therefore the growing tendency to appoint younger men to the responsible positions in our economic, social and politi-cal life. This trend has already begun and is likely to continue.

Simultaneous with the growth in population is the profound change that is taking place in our agriculture. Agricultural methods remained somewhat old-fashioned in most European countries, with the exception of the Netherlands and Denmark, which had already introduced far-reaching technical changes at the end of the nineteenth century. Today, agriculture is not only becoming mechanized; its methods and character are being completely trans-formed by the biochemical sciences. During the last few years, in certain countries, the increase in agricultural productivity has been greater than that in industry, with a series of consequences. Agriculture that produces more requires broader markets; it can no longer function within the framework of small national economies; that is why agriculturalists support the principle of European unifi-cation and are increasingly becoming export-minded. At the same time, the progress in technique means that fewer hands are needed on the land. The real agricultural population is falling rapidly all the time, as the younger generation leaves, in large numbers, for the towns. Those who remain must have technical training, and an increasing number of them are becoming specialists, technically trained and experienced in the work of agricultural production.

At the same time, these changes require the formation of in-creasingly large units; even in the countries that have very small farm holdings, the exodus from the country is leading to a redis-tribution of the land and a regrouping of the farms. This is accom-panied by a complete change in the attitude of the farmers, espe-cially the younger ones. Formerly, they were essentially peasants; as soon as they had saved a little capital, their aim was to buy more land. Having invested their savings in land, they had not much left with which to ensure the scientific exploitation of the soil, especially as the older generation hesitated to apply to the banks and to take out loans. The younger generation has no hesitation about borrowing from the banks or from the credit cooperatives; and they prefer to use their financial resources to purchase stock, equipment and agricultural machinery. Rather than purchase land, they are content to rent it as tenant farmers, provided that the rent is reasonable. In France, the young farmers have obtained governmental permission to set up local bodies called *les formats,* which have a right to pre-emption on all land put up for sale. This land can then be resold by the *format* to young farmers, or rented to them at a price fixed by a board of arbitration. Unlike the earlier farmers, these young men do not press very much for a rise in agricultural prices; they are more interested in increasing the quantities produced, in reducing the cost prices and in improving the conditions of production. They therefore form cooperative groups for purchasing or selling, and these groups are steadily gaining in influence in their networks of distribution, both of raw agricultural products and of foodstuffs. Sometimes, several families join to form a farm cooperative, working together on a larger farm.

With the development of the towns, too, many people are buying a second house in the country; this increases the demand for land for nonagricultural purposes and creates the danger of land speculation. The increase in the value of land results in higher rents, and this means unfavorable conditions for the farmers. It is therefore not surprising that the farmer movements are against all forms of speculation; some of them would even support nationalization of the land, to be rented out either to farmers for agricultural purposes or to building societies for the laying out of building sites.

Tremendous changes, again, are taking place in the techniques of industry and in the social structure of the people engaged in it. Europe is not as far advanced as the United States in the field of automation. The smallness of the markets prevented this, until there was progress toward European unity. Its effects are already apparent, however, in certain basic industries. At the same time, new industries (especially in the fields of chemicals and electronics) involve large investments, which require greater resources in capital and which completely change the techniques of production. These changes, in turn, have helped to stimulate European unity, because a large market with 200 million inhabitants is required for the great new industries. This large market is already bringing about some concentration and fusion between enterprises, and as soon as a company law, applicable to the whole of Europe, has been drawn up, large European companies will be formed. This will certainly present problems; a monopoly power may fix prices to the detriment of the consumer; and there must therefore be a European political power strong enough to control the great economic units and to subject them to a common legislation.

At the same time, a transformation is taking place in the social structures of European countries. It is true that the old working class, consisting of unskilled or semiskilled workers, still exists and will long continue to do so. But the number of people in this social group is tending gradually to fall, while the number of technicians, designers, supervisors, engineers and other executives in industry is increasing all the time, especially in the most modern enterprises. The former working class is therefore going through a difficult period. It is almost impossible for an older worker to rise from the status even of a skilled worker to that of an assistant technician, unless he undertakes three or four years of additional studies, and he feels that all opportunity of advancement in the factory is closed to him. Moreover, he is increasingly subjected (owing to the progress of scientific organization and rationalization) to monotonous work, every detail of which is fixed in advance by the central office. In many countries, especially in France and Italy, the working class is permeated with a feeling of melancholy. There is nothing revolutionary, however, about this melancholy. There was a time when the workers dreamed of replacing government management with administration through local worker councils, thus ensuring the direct management of industry by the trade unions. That was the age of revolutionary trade-unionism in France. Today, this has almost disappeared. Then came the dream of liberating the worker by nationalizing industries and introducing state appropriation of the means of production. There is now an important public sector in most of our countries. State investments cover nearly one third of the total national investments. But, although nationalization has usually proved technically successful and has resulted in progress and in a reduction in cost prices, it has failed socially. The worker now has to obey the state's engineers instead of those appointed by the shareholders. His own low status remains as it was before.

Information from Russia suggests that the problem of hierarchy in factories is equally acute there. Consequently, we must not hope too much for changes in political conditions or in the system of ownership. The old working class is marked by an attitude of resignation, or else it dreams of returning to preindustrial conditions. A recent inquiry into French industry showed that 80 per cent of the workers were dreaming of becoming artisans or small shopkeepers, in order to be free from the modern industrial machine and taking orders from a foreman, and thus to be their own masters again. This is symptomatic of a serious problem; but it also shows that the old working class is no longer a progressive, revolutionary class that wants technical development and innovations; it is, in fact, becoming conservative, trying to maintain the *status quo* and to defend the marginal enterprises.

An entirely different situation prevails in the new wage-earning class, which is growing annually in numbers and in influence. It consists of trained workers ranging from the assistant technician, the adjuster and certain office employees, in jobs where mechanization has not yet been introduced, right up to the technical director of the whole concern. There is a chance of advancement within the enterprise, or at least within the industry itself, and there is hope for everyone. The skilled worker's special knowledge and technical value entitle him to a higher rate of remuneration than the ordinary worker, and especially to security and an independent status, for there is a shortage everywhere of highly qualified workers, technicians, engineers and executives. It is an interesting fact, moreover, that the mentality of these qualified people is not capitalistic. The highest grades are recruited by promotion from the bottom. They want their company to earn enough to reinvest, while paying the shareholders a guaranteed dividend of 6 or 7 per cent per annum to keep them quiet, while they themselves concentrate on the technical development and extension of the enterprise, within the framework of the Plan for the country as a whole. It is note-worthy that, especially in France, these higher grades are well organized. A higher percentage of them belong to trade unions than among the working class. They sometimes take the initiative in struggles, or even lead strikes in support of their own technical concern for increased production against the purely financial inter-ests of certain bankers or financiers, who are concerned primarily with profits or with speculation.

## The Challenge to Political Institutions

The technical and economic changes that we have analyzed have certain political consequences. In the first place, they mean the end of the revolutionary spirit. It used to be comparatively easy to dream of a utopia that would be just the opposite in leadership and structure from the society in which one lived, thinking that a time would come when—through a revolution—one would pass from the old society to the new, defined in this way. Some people, who accepted the Marxist approach, believed that the contradic-tions within capitalist society would become increasingly acute, un-til one day a complete and radical transformation in the structures took place. No one believes in this historical determinism today nor in the possibilities of sudden change in a society that had hitherto been regarded as stable. We no longer dream about a fu-ture revolution, because we are already living in one, in a con-tinual process of destroying the existing structures and rebuilding them; and man's role is to influence events in such a way as to turn them in the direction he considers favorable.

There is therefore need for a continuous action and influence on events, supported by technical analysis of the problems we are trying to solve. Such action must be technical in character and in no way revolutionary or violent. Violence seems to be impossible, even apart from any ethical considerations. In the industrialized countries, the technical structure is too elaborate and the different elements overlap too much for any sudden break to be made with-out upsetting the whole system of production and consequently impoverishing the masses. It is through limited action, which does not jeopardize the structure as a whole, that improvements can be introduced, by methods that are bound to be democratic, attempting creatively to mobilize public opinion as a whole. We see very clearly the contrast between the old and the new revolutionary pattern if we compare social change in Europe with that in the new nations.

The old revolutionary utopianism and the use of violence that is closely linked with it are still found today in the underdeveloped countries; but that is because they are still at the stage at which Europe was living in the fifteenth and sixteenth centuries—the stage during which the national state was being created. These underdeveloped countries must get beyond the tribal stage and create a state that is powerful from the outset; for its intervention in economic life is indispensable in establishing the basis for any progress. This corresponds to the different forms of "benevolent despotism" that existed in Europe before the age of democracy. In fact, what is happening in the developing countries is the creation of the national state, the coming-to-power of a *bourgeoisie* that is usually not liberal, because it consists not of "managers" (entrepreneurs) but of state officials; and the terms "socialism" and "communism" that it uses in no way correspond to reality.

As in Europe in the fourteenth, fifteenth and sixteenth centuries, when a state was created, there are conflicts and struggles in these countries—often violent ones—and revolutionary ideas are inevitable while they get rid of a past that bars the way to progress. On the other hand, in the industrialized countries, no revolution is possible but only a continuous encounter with events in such a way as to influence the course of a technical revolution that is automatically taking place.

All over Europe, this technical transformation seems to be creating a crisis in parliamentary institutions, which are proving unsuitable for the needs of the new economy. This crisis assumes different forms for different reasons. Great areas of economic life elude the control of the different national Parliaments. From now on, the big agricultural decisions are being taken in Brussels; the same will soon apply to transport, finance, the coordination of the different sources of energy and soon also to the coordination of certain basic investments. Hence the need to transfer to a European Parliament (elected by universal suffrage) a certain number of controlling functions that can no longer be carried out at the national level. Technical transformations are also causing one traditional function of Parliament to disappear: that of being a sounding board, influencing public opinion, and a means of circulating information between the government and the electors. In former times, the government explained its policy to Parliament. The Members of Parliament then explained it to their constituencies and received their grievances, which provoked questions to the government. Today, when the government wants to explain its policy, the President or the Prime Minister addresses the electors direct, either on television or, in technical matters, by convening the representatives of the employers', workers' or farmers' organizations. These, in turn, tend increasingly to apply direct to the Administration, or the government, and even to exert pressure upon it, bypassing their parliamentary representatives. Over problems of general policy, the government makes increasing use of Gallup polls, which indicate what the majority of electors think about a particular question with more accuracy than consultation with Members of Parliament would give. France has gone even further; from time to time, it is the French people themselves who express their opinion on important problems and take the decision. Thus a tranformation is taking place, as a result of technical progress, that is clearly reducing the importance of Parliaments as intermediaries.

### Parliament and the Plan

Similarly, parliamentary initiative concerning legislation is fast disappearing in Europe. It is the government that now, nearly everywhere, takes the initiative for legislation; there is even a tendency to restrict the power of Members of Parliament to introduce Amendments. The Member of Parliament today, especially in France, is therefore expected to pay allegiance not to this or that temporary political vicissitude but to the progress made on public opinion through the Plan. In France we are now (March, 1965) working out the Fifth Plan; its essential principles were adopted two months ago by Parliament; namely, an over-all increase in production of 5 per cent per annum and of 4 per cent in consumption.

The basic decisions having been taken, the Plan is now being drawn up by several hundred modernization committees. Some of them cover a certain sector of industry and are composed of employers and workers. Others are regional (France is now divided into twenty-two regions) and are composed of representatives of employers, workers, farmers, universities and local electoral bodies; these are working out regional development plans. All the proposals are then presented to the *Commissariat au Plan*, which drafts the actual Plan; the draft is then submitted to the Economic and Social Council and is finally ratified by Parliament.

It is important to note that a new form of economic and social democracy is taking shape here—a democracy that consists, not in electing parliamentary representatives every five years, and occasionally expressing an opinion about their activities, but in preparing, and then regularly following up, the Plan for the economic and social development of the country. On these commissions (both sectional and regional), there are nearly a thousand delegates who are really the leaders of every economic and social activity in France. A decentralized regional democracy is taking shape.

As for Parliament, it is clear that all it can do is to approve the Plan and the budget (also on a five-year basis) for the Plan. It can no longer pass laws on its own, particularly where these would involve considerable expense, for that would upset the balance and would question the basic decisions adopted when the Plan was voted. Parliament is therefore tending to lose its intermediary function and its function of initiating legislation and is becoming essentially the body which adopts the Plan and which then, through questions in Parliament, controls its execution by the governmental institutions. If the government replies are inadequate, a parliamentary debate is held, which ends by passing a resolution to indicate what policy Parliament would like the government to pursue. And if the government does not pursue that policy, Parliament challenges it with a vote of "no confidence" and may even overthrow it. (The methods differ from country to country.) But it appears that it is this controlling function that needs to be examined, strengthened and organized, if the parliamentary institutions are to be adapted to the needs of this new world.

The crisis in parliamentary institutions is accompanied by a more serious crisis in the political parties. In France today, all the old parties have fallen into disrepute; the party that has the majority (at the time of writing), the *Gaullistes,* has no serious local organization and would certainly not survive without its leader. Throughout Europe, there is dissatisfaction with the political parties and a resulting political instability, which is extremely serious.

In Great Britain, the Labor Party, which came to power in 1964, obtained fewer votes than in the previous general election, in which it was defeated. It gained more seats this time because the Conservatives lost votes, mainly to the Liberals. Italy is on the verge of a grave political crisis; for the domination of certain parties in creating governments and taking decisions through "backroom" negotiations has completely destroyed the authority, the prestige and the workability of Parliament. In Germany, the crisis is perhaps less serious, although there, too, there are signs that people are losing confidence in the political parties, which are falling into disrepute. Most of the old political parties (with their outdated ideological associations) are incapable of solving the problems of the modern world. They were often based on ideological motives or were formed to solve past problems, and they date from the nineteenth century or the beginning of the twentieth. The problems that really concern the people—housing, education, land development, open spaces, improved hygienic conditions and the organization of holidays—are discussed outside the government and outside the central Administration and the political parties, within a local setting, or in the special societies set up for this purpose or in the clubs and discussion groups that organize "brain trusts" and debates.

A deep change seems to be taking place. In many of our European countries, there used to be a private sector of life, in which everyone did as he liked, as opposed to a public sector in the hands of a central authority, which operated on hierarchical lines. Today, society is becoming more socialized, private initiative being confined to the working out and joint discussion of a Plan. But, at the same time, life is becoming decentralized; all the functions of society now have to be undertaken by the citizens themselves. The state merely creates the rules, ensures a balance of forces and, if necessary, says the last word—but only after everyone has expressed his opinion and listened to others. What is emerging is a free, contractual society in which everyone feels responsible for everyone else, but in which everyone assumes his responsibilities within the framework of a common discipline. The new associations and groups that are forming and the studies that are being undertaken will give rise to new political forms that may, from the outset, be at a pan-European level. At this level, they will present a certain amount of political choice, and these new organizations will transcend (and perhaps absorb) the old, obsolete political parties.

## The Issues Before Us

We must now try to discuss the consequences of this economic and political evolution and the problems it raises. In the first place, the ideologies are finished—if by "ideology" is meant a systematic molding of history and a global view of it. People no longer believe in historical determinism; they no longer think it possible to deduce what *should be* from an analysis of what *is*. We are no longer presented with grandiose visions of the world based on a general philosophy and used as slogans for which men are urged to go to war. The military society is being steadily replaced by the industrial society, in which the problems are expressed in technical terms and are based on a general consensus. Today, there is no longer an unqualified Marxist dogma, nor is there any pure system of economic liberalism. There are pragmatic Socialists on one hand and enlightened Conservatives on the other, both refusing to accept an intellectual synthesis that is always authoritarian and totalitarian. They tackle the problems one after the other, trying to solve them through their empirical knowledge in the light of certain commonly accepted ethical values.

Some pessimists have drawn the conclusion that the world is moving toward a kind of domination by technocracy. This does not seem to be so. For one thing, the technicians, with some rivalry between them, do not always agree among themselves. They need to be divided politically when it comes to taking an immediate decision. Moreover, the higher-grade technicians are being increasingly recruited on a democratic basis; though we must recognize that, if we want to democratize the technicians, it is essential to technicize the democrats. Democratic liberty requires people to have thorough knowledge, which means that they must continue their education all their lives. Democratic liberty means that problems must be examined concretely and no longer in the form of generalizations inspired by an over-all philosophy.

What are the main problems which face us and which we have to solve today? These, I suggest, are the subjects on which study is needed.

A number of questions arise from the new effort to promote economic growth and social change.

1. We have seen that, in one way or another, all our countries have accepted a Plan—even if they avoid the word and prefer to use such terms as "concerted action" or "harmony of interests." Should this Plan be compulsory, should it operate as a stimulus, or simply as a kind of guidance? Or should it just be a center for statistical information, at the disposal of society, leaving the decisions and the responsibility in the hands of individuals? Should it result in orders, at least in certain basic sectors, and how should those orders be enforced?

In our economic life, should mass consumption be encouraged, in the form of what is called "American society"? Should personal consumption be encouraged to an unlimited extent? Or, on the contrary, should the Plan provide for a large proportion of the national wealth to be set aside for "collective consumption" in the form of education, scientific research, the provision of open spaces, the reduction of noise, the organization of holidays and leisure in all kinds of ways? This suggests a whole series of options, all of which involve the problem of the choice between authority and personal freedom, between the common good and individual egoism. Furthermore, we have seen that a large section of the working class is suffering from the military hierarchy that now exists in industry. Can we remedy this feeling of inferiority and distress by ensuring the permanent presence of the workers' trade union in the factory, by guaranteeing the workers a share in the undertaking and, in different ways, increased participation in its technical decisions? Here the experiments in several countries, where the workers share responsibility for the management, are particularly interesting.

And, in the development of the Plan, can we overcome tendencies toward the authoritarian state and encourage the pluralism of a responsible decentralized society?

2. We must also inquire whether this changing Europe (which is incapable of becoming a third military force in the world) could not venture on a *third course* in the social and political sphere, seeking to answer the basic questions: What kind of society do we want to create? What is our vocation to be? Since it is now within our power (thanks to technological progress) to forge our own destiny, for what purpose are we going to use that power? Here we encounter a number of problems. Will it be our purpose still to produce more and more goods, or to obtain more leisure in order to enable people to be themselves? As the possibility arises of gradually and moderately reducing the hours of work, shall we do so by cutting down the number of working hours per day, by advancing the retirement age, by increasing the annual vacation or by giving workers more time in which to take cultural vacations or time to enable them to reach a higher level of technical efficiency?

In this connection, there are special problems in the field of modern mass communication. Our lives today are dominated by radio and television, and we risk the distortion either of people's needs or of their ideas. Their needs are exposed to this danger if broadcasting is dominated by private interests that seek to find a market for the products of industry by artificial means; and their ideas are equally endangered if broadcasting is subject to government control. But broadcasting may, and certainly does, have an educational value. Can we not regard radio and television as public services, financed collectively, but managed by the representatives of the different economic, social and regional forces within the country and independent of political domination by different governments?

3. Europe cannnot live alone in the world. It cannot affirm its destiny in a kind of neonationalism at the Continental level. It has meaning only insofar as it works for a *universalism* that aims at benefiting the whole of man and all men. The first of these other men of whom we ought to think as our neighbors (even if they are far away) are the developing countries, which are still living in extreme poverty and which represent half the world. After ter-

rible conflicts and a long and painful period of transition, we have been decolonized, and they have their political independence. This does not yet mean that they have entered the modern world. Here a big effort is required. To begin with, we must stop exploiting them, as we are still doing. We must not forget that, during the last five years, these countries have lost more, through having to sell their produce at falling prices, than they have received in the form of international financial or technical aid. The first task therefore is to transform the functioning of the world market, which is today regulated entirely by the buying countries, who exercise a self-interested monopoly over it. We must recognize our responsibility toward these countries, and we must devote a minimum of our revenue (1 per cent was the amount asked for at the last World Conference in Geneva) to aiding the developing countries.

Such aid must be dissociated from political or military interests, and we should indeed aim at realizing the military neutrality of all the developing countries on the pattern of the international agreements achieved concerning the neutrality of Austria. We should agree not to send them arms from any source whatever and to let them pursue their political experiments without outside interference—not even on the pretext of defending the interests of the private capital invested in those countries. They have not yet reached a stage at which they can become involved in our problems, our conflicts and our organizational difficulties. It is therefore by respecting their neutrality and by giving them aid with no strings attached that we can best help them to solve some of the problems of their gradual integration into a modern economy.

4. What shall be the role of Europe in the ideological conflict? We can certainly see a tendency to *rapprochement,* owing to the profound changes in structure taking place in the Soviet Union and in the United States. The Soviet Union, which began as a model of centralized, authoritarian planning, has now discovered that this leads to bureaucracy and inefficiency. It is obliged to proceed to measures for decentralization. Some Soviet economists are advocating a restoration of the profit motive in the consumer industries as an indication of the trend of production, so that they can see what the needs of the consumers are. The Soviet Union is trying

to take its place in international commerce and to restore its connections with other countries.

In the United States, the change is of a different kind. For a long time, the United States was the only country to base its economy on the production of durable goods for mass consumption. Today, it is the first country to have passed that stage and to enter a new era, the form of which is not yet clear. For the last five years, most of the increased consumption in households has taken the form not of durable goods, but of a demand for *services*. The result is a permanent crisis in the industry that produces durable goods. Even during the present period of tremendous economic prosperity (partly due to military and other orders from the American government), there are nearly five million unemployed in the United States, a high proportion of the whole working population. It is too soon to see toward what final structures the Soviet Union and the United States are moving; but it seems as if the development of technology does not in itself necessarily involve adopting certain structures, though it does limit the political possibilities. Increased production does not of necessity mean an improvement in well-being, nor does prosperity mean greater liberty. Every phase of development and of technical opportunity is matched by a corresponding choice: to use the available resources either for the welfare of men or for the power of the state. This choice— between freedom and dictatorship—always has to be made.

In the face of all these problems, it is not the role of the churches to take sides with regard to a technical or a political plan. It is for them to help to clarify the problems, to encourage citizens to recognize their responsibilities and take them seriously and to express the problems in technical terms (no longer theoretically). Although today the world rejects systematic ideologies, in reality, as we have seen, all the problems that arise at the technical level concern human and social values.

In every instance, the real problem is *the role of man in society,* his future, his vocation, the ultimate meaning and purpose of human life. The essential function of the Christian Church is to lead men to realize what their vocation is and to translate into the transient techniques of social history the profound insistence on human freedom and human responsibility.

# 7

# NATION-BUILDING IN A POST-COLONIAL WORLD

by RICHARD ANDRIAMANJATO (Madagascar)

A MOVEMENT of emancipation has shaken the world during, and especially since, the Second World War, and as a result, numerous new states have arisen in Africa. This chapter will be concerned with the problems related to their establishment, functions and limits.

There is nothing to be gained by sweeping generalizations about the problems confronting the different African states. Though they have many geographical, historical and ethnological features in common, there are differences that cannot be ignored. These are to be found in the importance or extent of their territories, in developments during the colonial period, in the part played by the colonial masters and in their methods of exploitation and in the attitude of the new states toward the modern world. This last difference is largely governed by the degree to which industrialization has taken place, a factor that varies not only from country to country but from province to province within the same country. It is, nonetheless, still possible to discern certain common features that help us to understand the African situation today and to define the role of the state in our new nations.

The colonial system produced unnatural divisions, not likely to have resulted from a conflict between tribes and clans, or geographical or sociological factors rooted in the physical and ethnological structure of the continent. Colonialism was an external factor added to, and forcibly imposed upon, the conflicts and divergencies that already existed. It took little account of the human dignity of the black man and was interested only in exploitation, sources of income and all that could be converted into cash or exported, thus enriching the colonizing country. The Berlin Conference of 1884, at which the European powers defined their spheres of influence in Africa and signed a treaty that ensured the effective occupation of the entire coastlands, is confirmation enough —even though, at the same conference, they committed themselves to fight the slave traffic. The occupation and division of Africa were conceived, at best, with a view to the prosperity of European trade. Even the attack on slavery was included for the purpose of improving the long-term consequences of what could justly be called the wholesale exploitation of Africa; and the division and distribution of spheres of influence were based simply on money-making self-interest. When we speak of the new states in Africa, it is impossible to divorce them from their origins within the colonial system, with Europe as the exploiters and Africa as the exploited.

This division of Africa was accompanied by the elimination of all forms of activity that might interfere with colonial exploitation: the colonial powers made a concerted effort to destroy all aspects of culture and to eradicate all sense of membership within the human family. In short, they tried to inculcate into the African consciousness a principle of discrimination that put the white man on a superior plane and the black man at a stage halfway between man and beast. This destruction of traditional authority and culture sought only to uproot the African from his physical and sociological environment and to reduce him to a mere cog in the machine designed for production or exploitation. This purpose was accomplished by completely disorganizing African society so that it could be replaced by a system conceived by foreigners and designed to serve European peace and development. The Berlin Treaty itself was regarded as an important contributory factor to the peace of Europe. It was essential that Africa should not become the scene of conflicts between the civilized nations, but rather a source of revenue that they could share. To guarantee this peace, it became necessary to destroy the African himself and to make him accept whatever eased the way to his exploitation by the western powers.

Finally, we must add that this uprooting of the African has

affected not only relations between man and man, but relations between man and the supernatural and, more particularly, between man and God—or what the African believed to be God. Subsequent analyses of the process of colonization have tended either to decry religion, including the Christian religion, as one more factor in anesthetizing the African consciousness, or to look upon it as an aspect of the crisis in the African personality. Christianity especially is thought of as a religion that challenged all the values of African civilization. And it must be remembered that religion, including Christianity, which accommodated itself to colonialism and to all that we are accustomed to describe as the exploitation of one man by another, is regarded with deep suspicion in Africa.

All this is well known, but to recall it makes it easier to understand both the concept of the state that African leaders hold today and the efforts that they have made to build up nations. These facts also help us to assess the important place to which present-day Africa lays claim in the developing power structures of the world and in any future world civilization.

## The Presuppositions of National Independence in Africa

The great problem confronting all the peoples of Africa in the period immediately after the granting of independence (and notably since 1960, which has justly been called "Africa's year") has been that of building up a nation. In the French colonies, a period of preparation for independence was initiated in 1956 with the *loi-cadre* (the constitutional framework), which was to give the native people of a country a much greater share in its administration. This *loi-cadre* was acceptable to the majority of African leaders at that time and especially to those who were on the best terms with the colonial rulers. It allowed and encouraged a kind of apprenticeship in power and ensured that the transition from white domination of the Administration to the assumption of responsibility by the African would go smoothly.

The *loi-cadre* has been subject to some criticism. Its supporters, however, have replied with arguments based on the postulate that the African population cannot be entrusted with full authority without some prior cultural and economic development. It is the economic aspect that is emphasized, and it is repeatedly said that the colonial territories are still dependent on the economy of the mother country and that a thoroughgoing transformation must be effected before full independence is granted, if the state of independence is to be viable. Moreover, are there not certain responsibilities inherent in the future nation that cannot yet be usefully or effectively assumed by the local African leaders? It is therefore essential to plan and prepare for independence at all levels. Such a task cannot be carried out in one year, and those who worked out the *loi-cadre* naturally thought it should remain in force in the colonial territories for one or two decades. This opinion was shared by certain African leaders, who saw in Europe the only possible model of what a modern Administration should be and who built their evolutionary theories on the basis of the *loi-cadre*. I recall radio interviews at that time with certain African leaders who looked favorably upon the *loi-cadre*. They visualized that the system would be in operation for the next twenty years and that then only French North Africa and Madagascar would be ready for independence. In other words, it was scarcely possible for the colonial territories to set themselves up as sovereign states, because they lacked the general prerequisites for the maintenance of national sovereignty.

What, then, were these prerequisites, and were they satisfied in such a way as to make possible the sudden change that we witnessed in 1959–60? Or was the problem resolved in some other way? What are the characteristics of the states that have since then been established, and what is their status in the world?

The evolutionary theories of the supporters of the *loi-cadre* are based on the premise that, before any degree of genuine independence can be achieved, it is essential to have attained a certain minimum of economic independence, a minimum of competence at all levels of the Administration, a degree of the national cohesion that results from a prosperity in which all share and a common consciousness of belonging to the same nation, with all that the word implies in the historical, sociological, cultural and geographical sense. The black man, however, thought about colonialism on the lines set down by Aimé Cesaire in his "Discours sur le Colonialisme": [1]

The decisive motive here is that of the adventurer and the pirate, of the wholesale grocer and the privateer, of the gold prospector and the trader, of greed and force, while behind them is thrown the evil shadow of a form of civilization which at any moment in its history finds itself compelled from within to extend onto a world scale the competition between its conflicting economies. . . . No one colonizes innocently, or with impunity. . . . In the relationship between colonizer and colonized there is room only for forced labour, intimidation, press-ganging, police, taxation, robbery, violation, compulsory breeding, scorn, suspicion, arrogance, conceit, insensitivity, dissevered *élites* and debased masses. The absence of other human contact than that which results from domination and submission transforms the colonizer into a pawn, a sergeant-major, a convicts' warder, a rod of punishment, and the native-born into an instrument of production.

Thus the arguments on which the *loi-cadre* rested quickly became suspect, and some affirmed that it was only a new means of delaying the emancipation of the former colonies.

Another factor, and a decisive one, was the international political situation, which developed in such a way as to oblige the great powers to speed up the process of bringing to birth independent states in Africa and Asia. The historic Bandung Conference of April, 1955, where, for the first time, representatives of the colonial territories in Africa and Asia met to discuss their own problems without the supervision of the imperial powers, marked a turning point in the modern world. In fact, the African and Asian leaders reversed the western order of priority and introduced a new concept of the guarantees of sovereignty that could, in general, be applied in all countries under colonial rule. In reply to the argument that a certain standard of living and a certain degree of economic development are necessary before independence can really be achieved, they insisted on the primacy of the political question—the dignity of man as man. Looked at in this light, the political issue becomes a factor in economic development.

This attitude is fundamental. It governs all the subsequent stages of liberation from colonialism and embodies in itself the anticolonial revolution, for now the African leaders see the problem of

---

[1] Paris: *Présence Africaine*. 3rd ed., 1958.

the nation in political rather than in economic terms. Although there may be slight differences of approach, in essence it remains unchanged. Politics first, and economic questions second: This is the irreversible sequence.

### The Completion of the Process of Decolonization

We have now reached a point at which the colonial period is regarded as a parenthesis in the history of the nation. It must be closed, and the only problem is how best to close it. Two main theories on the process of decolonization have been put forward. The one holds that there are some features in the colonial structure that are worth retaining and from which profit may be derived (a theory found notably in those African countries that are especially friendly toward France). The other advocates a clean break with the colonial past and the building of a new world on the ruins of the old. While it is interesting to observe how the two theories have been historically conditioned, closer scrutiny reveals that they are manifestations of one fundamental phenomenon: the colored man's search to recover his true dimensions as a man. Here and there, different tactics may be employed, but always to the same end. After the annihilation of human values through colonialism, a new order must be created by and for a new man. The victim of the colonial system is called upon to break free from the restrictions that have been imposed upon him and to go on to discover the universal dimensions of his new vocation and action.

In "La Lutte du Parti démocratique de Guinée pour l'Émancipation africaine," [2] Sekou Touré defines decolonization as follows:

Decolonization is the fundamental and qualitative modification of all that remains of and was directly connected with the phenomenon of colonialism, and which from now on must be adapted to the exercise of our sovereignty and to the aims of our political revolution.

Everything must be re-thought in terms of this emancipation. Decolonization is not simply a matter of liberating ourselves from colonial domination, it must be completed by the total liberation of the spirit of those who were subject to the colonial system, from the evil consequences—moral, intellectual and cultural—of that system.

---

[2] *Du Ve Congrès du P.D.G. au discours devant les membres de l'ONU.* Vol. IV. 2nd ed. (République de Guinée, Imprimerie Nationale, Conakry.)

And in *Les Damnés de la Terre*,[3] Franz Fanon declares that in the process of decolonization "it is imperative to question the entire colonial situation." If this questioning cannot begin directly in the economic sphere, at least it can begin in that of human values. Thus, the leaders have directed their efforts toward reviving in some measure the "old man" who lies dormant within all the subjects of the colonial regime, so that a new man may rise up to found a new society.

But this is a process in which the African countries will encounter immense difficulties. The second phase of African and Asian emancipation is economic, and, to succeed in this sphere, it is essential to establish incontestable authorities. One cannot conceive of any effective economic planning or development in the countries of one third of the world (or elsewhere, for that matter) without a solid foundation of responsible organization of the state. And here the African and Asian countries immediately encounter factors that only increase their difficulties.

The first is the whole process of psychological and sociological damage occasioned by the colonial regime, from which recovery will be long and difficult. For example, the stability of traditional society was ensured by systems which were derived from long tradition and which imparted values similarly derived. But these ancient African systems were suppressed by the colonial system. The fundamental unity which forms the basis of the individual consciousness, tribal or popular, and which is rooted in a form of civilization that people have been obliged for some time to judge with greater objectivity, has been broken. It has been replaced by one sole condition—that of the victim of colonialism, of a man without dignity, without will, without direct responsibility, of a man who is a mere tool or instrument. It is certainly difficult to see how a mass of individuals living in a particular part of the world are to be welded into the organized unity of a state when they have not the slightest consciousness of any wider unity—racial, national, tribal, cultural, historical or geographical. It was a matter of discovering some center of common interest.

The colonial past itself forged a degree of unity; but it took a

---

[3] Paris: (Cahiers Libres, 27-28), 1961 (1962).

negative form. During the struggle for independence, people fought under the same banner against a common adversary: the imperial and reactionary forces. But once political emancipation had been achieved, this unity was no longer effective, and many countries soon ran into new crises. The government is overthrown by the forced resignation of the President of the republic; or the regime becomes increasingly a dictatorship and a police state, where the liberties so hardly won are once again undermined by forces that command a greater or lesser degree of justification. In a sense, crises of some kind are inevitable. The transition from an earlier condition of stability, maintained willy-nilly by the colonial power, to a stability based on a choice made within the framework of a social contract cannot be achieved without far-reaching changes.

Accordingly, the leaders of the new countries have been driven to dig deep into the past and to forge a myth to put before their people, so that some degree of national and collective consciousness, capable of withstanding the disillusionment and post-revolutionary pressures that always follow the wild enthusiasm of the early days of independence, may be achieved. In fact, a profound change has come about in the psychological and political motivation. The aim is no longer to throw off foreign domination, but to strike and hold a balance of the internal forces in each nation. This is the heart of a problem still to be resolved.

Yet such an attempt to revive the wisdom of earlier days in order to contend with the modern situation is bound to be inadequate, for research into the past means removing oneself from the present. And it is interesting to note that, when crises concerning the authority of the state arise in places where the uprooting and systematic depersonalization organized by the colonial powers has been the least destructive of individual personality, or where religion has acted as a refuge for traditional standards, far from furthering the development of human potential in order that man may fulfill his destiny in freedom and responsibility, these crises have proved, in fact, a curb on true development. The situation is further aggravated by the fact that, while the new states are unable to bypass the successive stages by which the world reached its present level of civilization, they are obliged to hold a concept of the state which has, in general, evolved over a long period and which has been accompanied in many countries by recurrent crises, troubles, revolts and revolution. The modern state is one that is built on a contractual foundation, in which those who govern are appointed by those who are governed. Such a state can function successfully only among peoples and in nations that have achieved, at least in principle, a degree of intellectual and moral evolution sufficient to provide the right climate in which to develop personal and collective discipline. The question is whether the traditional values are reliable for this purpose, and if not, what other standards and values can be put in their place.

The only independent states are thus driven to search in two different directions and to endeavor to reconcile two spiritual quests that are, in practice, so difficult to bring together. To dig into the past in order to build a better future, when that future is separated from the past by a great gulf, because of the radical and revolutionary changes that are taking place in the human spirit and in modern society, would seem an enterprise doomed to failure—if it were not imperative to revive the past simply in order to recover the human. In fact, the African's attempt to rediscover his former culture is only another manifestation of the struggle against the depersonalization that characterized the colonial era. He is concerned with rediscovering the past not in order to revive it but simply to ascertain what it means to be a man among men, with the consciousness and the potential of a man.

## The Basis of National Unity

If a way were to be found to emancipate the African from the inferiority complex deliberately fostered by the colonizing forces, the effect would be felt at all levels of the population—and particularly as regards the guidance and government of the state. For this is where the problem of those responsible for government in relation to the masses lies: On what does their authority really rest, when standards are no more than modes which change with each successive crisis, or which suffer a more gradual change in those societies that claim to be modern?

The best solution would be deliberately to mobilize the masses by systematically educating the whole population. If traditional standards have crumbled, despite the efforts of the nationalists to save them, and if the current trend toward world unity (in the large treaty organizations that are being formed today) continues to develop, it is essential to build up a new national consciousness that is capable of being adapted to new conditions at the national and the international level. This task is both long and hard; and for want of a revolutionary *mystique* (which a few exceptional rulers maintain at immense cost by judiciously timed economic measures such as nationalization and agrarian reform), most leaders have been content to adopt an easier course.

The second way consists of working out the cost of holding on to power, of falsifying the expression of popular opinion by "rigging" elections and pretending to hold plebiscites, of evading dialogue and thus suppressing at the outset all notion of coresponsibility. It even seems that those who hold the highest office in the various nations have made it a maxim of government that their people were not prepared for true democracy, and so have justified the imposition of arbitrary measures. Wherever the transition from the colonial era to independence has not been marked by a radical change in the team of leaders at the top, the sense of liberation experienced on the attainment of independence has been destroyed by the arbitrary action and injustices suffered under the new regime. Disturbances, the overthrow of governments, the dictatorial *Putsch* in answer to the growing opposition and the increasing dissatisfaction of the masses—these are the symptoms of the malady that plagues new states.

To solve their problems, some leaders have not hesitated to come to terms with the former colonial power, in order to facilitate the transfer of that psychological capital, the blind submission of the people to those in power. They demand financial aid and technical and military assistance. Others, fewer in number, prefer to exploit the capital of endurance and sacrifice required during the struggle for independence and to realize it now as a constructive force. Those who adopt this line are compelled to practice a certain purism and to keep as free as possible from the interference and tutelage of the former colonial power. A number of factors influence the choice of one or the other of these two tactically different positions. They include historical factors (whether the leaders were previously chosen and maintained by the colonial power or were leaders of the struggle for independence), considerations related to economic structures and international trade, cultural deficiencies (such as a shortage of technicians in all spheres), psychological factors and such strategic factors as the need for self-defense.

In short, the new states have to face limitations of all kinds, and they find themselves in even more of a cleft stick than during the colonial regime. Moreover, they have to play a dual role on the international stage—seeking to reconcile the internal position of the various governments with their external claims and, at the same time, looking for outside help to put the economy on its feet. They have to use their political liberty to solve acute economic problems. This accounts for the positive neutralism these countries adopt in world affairs.

## The Need for Regional Unity

Severely handicapped by their economic difficulties, the new states quickly realized how greatly their actions were limited by the existing structures. In isolation, they could scarcely hope to effect any change in the setup that the established powers had organized. By such indirect means, moreover, as bilateral or multilateral agreements, the former colonial territories have transformed their relations with the ex-colonial powers, and they have observed at close quarters the great powers that governed and, to a large extent, still govern the world.

They have discovered that international and regional organizations have been created to protect the interests of each member nation. For example, what is the European Economic Community but an agreement concerning the economic development of western countries and trade between them and certain African countries, in order to encourage economic growth and avoid certain economic conflicts? If such well-organized and highly industrialized countries find themselves obliged to establish groups and to submit to a common discipline in order to safeguard their standard of living, their purchasing power and their hegemonies, it is even more imperative for the small countries to think about grouping themselves together

—not simply on a local but on a Continental (or even larger) scale.

Such groups, however, should not have economic objectives only, but should be so constituted that they form a framework for the emancipation of the individual state from a system that has spent its force and must now give way to a new world. They must also show that "unity is strength," and that membership of a larger group implies, *ipso facto,* an increase in potential, security in the face of opposing forces, greater stability in the state and greater efficiency in action. For the individual states, these groups have a clear significance: They strengthen the existing authority, expand the bounds of action in order to satisfy the growing needs of an ever-expanding population and provide a means of combating those situations that bring a people to the verge of despair. In the place of an effective national *mystique,* the leaders have sought to find an international *mystique* with which to mobilize the masses. Their success has depended and still depends upon the choice they make. Some have chosen to proclaim their affiliation to the western countries and have stated their reasons for doing so; others have sought to justify their affiliation to a group of countries that profess revolutionary socialism. The majority, however, have succeeded in steering between Scylla and Charybdis and have advocated a neutralism to which the epithets "positive" and "active" are applied, or which is sometimes described as "nonengagement." The essence of success is to establish the prestige of those in power in the eyes of the world and to strengthen their effectiveness within their respective countries.

Groups such as the African and Malagasy Union, which still reflect the structure of the former colonial empires, are giving way to wider organizations. Regional conferences, like the African Conference in Addis Ababa, which led to the creation of the Organization for African Unity, are of primary importance. These organizations are working on the basis of a political agreement to change the economic order of the world. It is significant that, at the Geneva Conference on World Trade, the seventy-five countries that are most undeveloped economically adopted a common front vis-à-vis the great nations. Yet the motive of these groups is not simply self-preservation. They are meaningful only insofar as they encourage a world-wide revolution that will lead to a better world order.

For when we come to analyze the forms of bilateral aid granted by certain countries and to expose their underlying motives, and when we discover that the Cold War continues under another form, then the liberty of the new states remains questionable, and it is clear that the great nations have shown little real change of heart as regards their notion of political hegemony and domination. The colonialist spirit may change its form, but it is far from changing its basic character. It is not a matter of altering the world equilibrium in favor of the underdeveloped countries, but simply of patching up the differences by measures that have no deep significance. On the pretext of protocol, an attempt has been made to delay the progress toward true democratization; that is, the taking of decisions at the international level. It has also been proposed that a nation's importance should be assessed not simply according to the number of its citizens, but by taking into account a kind of coefficient, based on the nation's economic potential and its exercise of leadership. It is well known, for instance, that there are those who advocate a radical change in the structure of the United Nations on the ground that "it is scandalous that Nicaragua should have a say equal to that of the United States."

## The New Nations and the Search for a New World Order

In the face of this situation, the underdeveloped countries have become conscious of a new vocation—the vocation of overcoming, by sheer weight of numbers and by combined forces, the power and technique of the more advanced countries. The conflict that might well result could be disastrous for the world. In fact, the stability of our planet depends on preserving the balance between these two mighty forces, the one resting on forward-thrusting economic development and relying on technology, the other deriving its intensity from numbers and from the determination to have done with servitude and misery.

Within this framework, each state is searching for a better existence and a greater degree of prosperity and has to struggle against regional or international limitations. The emancipation of the new states will not be complete until they are able to harmonize their respective actions by adopting a united world outlook.

All this calls for a spiritual and cultural transformation that will promote the reconstruction of civilization—a civilization that will be both open to new developments and based on truly human values. All national cultures need to undergo both a deepening and a modification. They will be deepened by throwing into relief in each culture those elements that are rooted in the universally human institutions and modified in order to assimilate the attainments of different generations and to place these attainments at the service of man. But before initiating any movement toward the creation of a new order, it is essential to reconsider the ethical codes that are now in use.

The world in which we live is characterized by the threat of annihilation, by the pride of the great nations, which seek to become yet more powerful, by the instability of the underdeveloped nations, by trouble spots and recurrent wars in Africa, Europe and Asia. All these impose upon humanity a great burden of uncertainty and fear—the fear of a tomorrow without hope. If peace among the nations is to stand on a solid footing, concerted action on a world-wide scale is essential. At present, various groups of states exist that are all more or less egoistic, antagonistic and hostile. It seems impossible to develop these groups into any kind of federation or confederation, headed by a representative world government, unless their preconceptions, inhibitions and parochial, nationalistic myths are destroyed. All nations, and especially those that are rich and powerful, must be ready to accept some revision of their position and to transcend the stage of blind, chauvinistic nationalism. This is possible only if people from all areas and backgrounds can be brought together for dialogue.

This is the point at which the church can help to bring to birth a new world order. Insofar as it remains faithful to its vocation and to its witness, the church, which transcends all national and cultural frontiers, seems to be the place where a useful dialogue can be maintained. But, all too often in the past, the church has been conditioned by historical and sociological factors, so that it has simply reflected the divergencies and vicissitudes of the different nations and has been the accomplice of the great powers even in

their acts of oppression and massacre. Before it can become a setting for dialogue today, the church must free itself from such
historical and sociological conditioning. Its dialogue must begin
at home; it must converse with itself about its own past.

## The Church and the Ethical Issues of Decolonization

The church's true role is that of a liberator. Jesus Christ came
into the world to reconcile the world once and for all to God.
Henceforth, those who are reconciled may share in the work of
liberation, for Jesus himself said, "He who believes in me will
also do the works that I do; and greater works than these will he
do." These works are concerned with the total human situation,
in which spiritual and temporal are bound together, sharing the
same condemnation, but sharing also the same grace and the same
salvation. The liberation won through Jesus Christ reaches to the
very depths of human existence. But there are forces in the world
that oppose and resist this revolution that Jesus Christ began, and,
in dealing with them, the church has been tempted to distinguish
between the spiritual and the temporal. It has avoided the dialogue
with itself vis-à-vis the temporal order, and has often preferred
to take refuge in superficial solutions and in the preaching of a
gospel that accommodated itself to the weaknesses and excesses of
those in power. At critical moments in a nation's life, or in regard
to the destiny of the world, it has often remained silent.

Is not the church now urgently called to revise its own theology
and exegeses? Must it not have the courage, in fulfilling its prophetic mission, to do as the church of the first century did in the
face of the powers of the world, and pray, again, with the apostles:
"And now, Lord, behold their threatenings: and grant unto thy
servants, that with all boldness they may speak thy word" (Acts
4:29)?

Today, it is precisely the prophetic aspect of the church's mission that is the most clearly emphasized—to announce the will of
God to men, to teach them his ways and to recall them to the
way that he approves, a way of justice and peace. By so doing,
the church can contribute to the search for a better and more just
order and can hasten the dawn of a better world. If it is to play

an effective role, it must first take into account the temptations to which it has so often succumbed in the past. These temptations were of the same kind as those the devil offered Christ, and they always begin with: "If you are the Son of God . . ." Being the Son of God can never mean fleeing from responsibilities.

Some fundamental rethinking of theology is urgently necessary throughout the church, but especially in Africa.

It is as well to remember that in any eventual dialogue with the newly independent states, the church will be confronted with one outstanding demand on the part of its possible partners: to be, for them, an effective participant and spokesman. Developments in Europe seem to indicate that there is no difficulty in finding theologians who can fit their thinking into the context of the nation, and so deal with such controversial questions as the right concept of the state, the true nature of authority and the right relations between church and state. But this type of theological engagement and frank declaration of belief may still prove inadequate for the new states. For when the former mission territories (which are also ex-colonial territories) question the worth of western civilization as they saw it practiced during the colonial era, they also challenge the entire values of Christian civilization. What we need is a sufficient number of Africans who can reply to this challenge, who can realize the truths of the gospel and implant them in the particular sociological soil of the developing African continent.

There are two other directions in which the church in Africa is called to some rethinking. First, there is the question of the emancipation of national churches from the western missionary societies and churches. Is it not true that, in some churches, emancipation has not resulted in any real progress in understanding their responsibilities, but has been, rather, another manifestation of anti-colonialism that jeopardizes a right theological understanding of their role in world-wide Christian witness? Secondly, the churches need to ask themselves whether the phase of instability and disorder through which they are passing is not prejudicing the gospel they claim to preach. While we have no wish to stigmatize those churches that seek a biblical and theological justification for racial discrimination, we must acknowledge that the existing differences of view infect even the churches and expose them to the risk of enfeeblement.

Nevertheless, the very presence in Africa of the church, through which God acts for men, is immensely valuable and indicates in itself the limits beyond which powers and states cannot go. Amid the uncertainty and fear that favor abuses and disorders of all kinds, the church is called to proclaim the gospel of peace and salvation—a salvation God freely offers, without exception, to all men.

Among the many ethical questions confronting the new states today, the following seem to be the most urgent:

1. How far is nationalism a necessary evil at this stage in the development of the newly independent countries, as they struggle to mobilize the energies required to bring about the urgently necessary economic revolution?

2. Does not the harsh and bitter struggle for leadership in Africa, in the Arab lands, in Asia and in the Afro-Asian bloc afford yet another manifestation of the instability left by the colonial era? How far are heads of government in a position to act according to a universal perspective that takes into account the values and standards of all cultures and all nations? Can they avoid the temptations of power, covetousness, the use of force, sectarianism, corruption and falsehood? Can they avoid transforming their states into instruments of oppression instead of making them guarantors of the liberty and equality of every citizen? Have they passed the stage of trickery, of enforcing, in the name of the people and their wishes, a measure that in fact represents the will of a small minority?

3. In reviving old and forgotten standards, is it possible to detach and bring out the positive values that will help to develop the personality of the former colonial subject?

The church should be able to find the answer to some of these questions. In the universal effort to rediscover man beyond slavery, beyond the debasement of colonialism and beyond the different cultures, the church is bound to preach again its eternal message: that God wills to meet men with his love that he may set them free and that they may be found equal in his sight, loved with the same love, blessed with the same pardon and enjoying the same kind of existence. In this context, all organizations, whether national or international, are of value only insofar as they give all mankind access to that freedom from domination of every kind. But who, if not the church, is to tell the states and organizations what their functions and limits are? Who else will speak of man's true worth?

Our desire is to see the church at the center of life in the newly independent countries, addressing itself faithfully to a dual task —not only declaring to them that their salvation is accomplished, but calling them to share in the great reconciliation of all men everywhere.

# 8

# THE POLITICAL DYNAMICS OF LATIN AMERICAN SOCIETY TODAY

by Mauricio Lopez (Argentina)

The world has received two contradictory pictures of Latin America. The traditional image, drawn largely from the eighteenth century, is that of lands "flowing with milk and honey," rich in natural resources and precious metals. The Tower of Gold, on the banks of the Guadalquivir River in Seville, where the coveted metal made its first stop before getting into the hands of European kings, nobles and merchants, bore mute but eloquent testimony to that abundance. Two more ingredients completed the picture: the fact that here were educated peoples who had an unlimited capacity to assimilate European culture but who were unable to produce a stable political order for themselves, a rather surprising combination of a delicate cultivation of the spirit with a kind of civic irresponsibility that has been so well illustrated in an almost interminable series of comic-opera revolutions.

This traditional picture was not false; it was simply incomplete. Hidden behind the scenes was a continent impoverished by the continuing existence of structures and patterns of life that have kept two thirds of the population of more than 200 million in harrowing conditions of misery, injustice and cultural backwardness. What makes this situation different is the fact that the people have become aware of their condition. They are now conscious of being an irresistible political force, and, spurred on to action by politicians and intellectuals, they are ready to use any and all means to attain a fuller and more worthwhile life. The revolutionary ferment that has taken hold of this continent is nothing but the reflection of this impatience of the masses to put an end to an old social order, which has continued almost intact since the colonial period, and to share in the development of a more brotherly and just human society.

## The Slow Decline of the Colonial World

1. Those who undertook to subdue and rule the Americas from the end of the fifteenth century onward came upon sizable native populations which had in some instances—such as those of the Incas and Aztecs—a well-advanced social and political organization and which had succeeded in building up vast empires. Wielding the yardstick of European anthropology, the conquistadors regarded the Indians as "barbarians," to be liquidated, driven away or used, whichever was most convenient. In general, the Spaniards decided to make use of them as farm laborers, miners and artisans. To dispel any doubts that they were human beings, one of the popes decreed that they had souls and could therefore be evangelized. The Roman Catholic Church, in concerning itself with this task, did much to elevate the Indian's condition and to lighten the yoke imposed by the secular arm.

The conquistador brought with him the institutions, culture and forms of community life of a Spain that refused to move into the modern world and preferred to shut itself up in its medieval dream. This heritage was to make itself felt heavily all over the American continent. The colonial Administration created the *encomienda* system, turning over to the conquistador a large expanse of land—*latifundium*—and a certain number of Indians who would cultivate it in exchange for clothing, food, shelter and spiritual care. Obviously, there was thus established a feudal system of property and economy. The products of the land and the mines were sent off to the big city, and the fabulous profits that were obtained by their exploitation were not reinvested but were wasted away in a life of luxury or in erecting ostentatious churches. When the colonies broke off their political ties with Spain, economic practices were in no way changed. The economic liberalism that was brought in was to benefit the industrial nations of Europe and the tiny Latin American *bourgeoisie*. The feudal regime of agrarian property survived, as did the one-crop or one-product system, yielding coffee, bananas, sugar, cotton, copper and silver that were exported to Europe. Latin American economy continued to be complementary to that of Europe. To the latter went the products extracted from the ground and from under the ground; to the former went the manufactured products. When the economic interests of Britain or France were considered to be threatened, there was recourse to armed intervention or some other show of strength.

This tributary character of the Latin American economy was not altered when the United States assumed an imperialist role. During the colonial period, the two parts of the American continent lived in ignorance of each other; when independence arrived for both, the southern "Americans" felt inspired by the ideals of liberty of their northern brothers. The latter helped the South American patriots to break loose from their Spanish tutelage; and when the struggle against the colonial forces took shape, the enunciation of the Monroe Doctrine strengthened still further the solidarity between the two Americas. Together they were to work for the prosperity of the American peoples, for relations of common interest and for defense against any new European attempt to assume control. At that time, there were no points of friction in economic matters. The two had paralled systems, and both were providers of raw materials for Europe. It was a brief idyl, which began to fade as the United States emerged as a great world power. Having finished its march to the West, the United States established its borders by buying Florida from Spain and Louisiana from France and seizing half the territory of Mexico. It managed to disencumber itself from nearby competitors by snatching Puerto Rico from Spain and occupying Cuba. Continental solidarity was a vehicle no longer of friendship but of imperialist purposes. Especially since the First World War, United States commerce and capital has established the third colonization of Latin America in the name of democracy and free enterprise. They did so with the tacit consent of the Latin American oligarchies, whose herodian mentality caused them to live with their backs turned on their own country, unmindful of the privations of its people.

2. The crisis had a social dimension. Latin American society is far from homogeneous. Indians, whites, mestizos and Negroes make up, to a greater or smaller degree, the racial ingredients of society in the different parts of Latin America. The pure Indian has remained on the fringe of national life, neither participating in community affairs nor sharing in political decisions. There have been, it is true, a number of serious attempts to integrate him into society—some of them showing visible signs of progress, for instance in Bolivia. The Negro was brought as a slave from Africa, especially to the Caribbean regions and Brazil. Unlike the Indian, the Negro assimilated the habits, food and dress of the white man. In Brazil, he was recognized as a full-fledged citizen; and, although some social and economic discrimination exists, it has no legal sanction, nor is it supported by any idea that he is naturally inferior. The mestizo had very insecure beginnings. He steered between two worlds, with his father's Spanish culture and his mother's Indian mentality. Hence his first unsure steps; hence the ambiguity that harassed him; hence the lack of historical background to which he could attach himself. But, unlike the Indian, he was ambitious, and he steadily gained ground and social stature. Today, especially in Mexico, he constitutes a true lever for social and cultural advancement and is a decisive factor in political leadership.

Latin America's diverse racial origin forms in itself an invaluable contribution to the cultural and human wealth of the continent. The disquieting factor, therefore, is not the diversity, but the marked dualism to be seen in the social sectors. True, we can speak of an increasing rise of the middle classes, but these are not sufficiently large to counterbalance the extremes. This dualism has economic bases. A very small number of families monopolize most of the wealth, while the great mass of the population exists at a standard of living that borders on misery. At first sight, the statistics that indicate an average annual income of $370 per inhabitant would seem to indicate a substantial rise in the living standard of the whole population. Nothing is further from the facts. The inequality of income, national and individual, contradicts any expression of optimism. Actually, more than half the population—that is, more than 100 million people—have an average income of $120 a year. While there are countries, like Venezuela, that reach some $500 per inhabitant, others, like Haiti, do not exceed $55. A mere 5 per cent of the families has from 30 to 45 per cent of the national income. In every country, the oligarchies, which have become wealthy, chiefly in agriculture and cattle-raising or in foreign trade, have not reinvested their capital but have transferred it to bank accounts abroad. It is estimated that over $15 billion belonging to the Latin American capitalists have been sent to Europe and the United States. It is not surprising that the foreign companies should do the same, exporting their gains much more substantially than reinvesting them.

The most noteworthy demographic feature today is the phenomenal population increase. Human beings are multiplying in Latin America at a higher rate than in any other part of the world, and the demographists calculate that the population will be tripled by the end of this century. Two characteristics mark this rising human tide: its youth and its mobility. Children under fourteen years of age make up 40 per cent of the population. This is a great blessing for a developing continent, which needs the contribution of young blood fired with hope, but for the present it forms an onerous burden that weighs heavily upon the active population. Moreover, the poor conditions of farm life are causing a sizable internal migration from the country to the city. It is a phenomenon that is repeated everywhere—Buenos Aires, Mexico City, São Paulo, Santiago, Lima, Caracas, Bogotá; yet that generator of dreams, the city, becomes a place of disillusionment for new arrivals. They are kept on the outskirts and allowed to enter only to perform their daily work. When they return to their shacks at night, the meal is scanty, the single room a confused symbiosis of human beings and animals crowded together, and each morning brings the anxiety of uncertain employment. It is moving to see, only a few yards from the elegant beach of Copacabana in Rio de Janeiro, those pigsties of dwellings that hang like clusters of leaves on the hillsides. From the mountain top, the Christ of Corcovado looks down not only upon the city but upon thousands of poor, upturned faces, animated by feelings of rebellion against a rich society that forgets its obligations in respect to social justice. These belts of misery in our metropolises constitute an excellent broth-culture for social revolution.

3. The crisis has also a political aspect. In contrast to Africa and Asia, which began to free themselves from political colonialism at the time of the Second World War, the countries of Latin America obtained independence from Spain in the first quarter of the nineteenth century. The wars for independence, fought out locally at an impressive cost in lives and property, broke up the unity of the empire and subdivided national units to the point of exaggeration. Brazil was an exception. While other countries poured out their blood in internal struggles that retarded the establishment of order, Brazil was ruled by an enlightened and progressive monarch. Even the introduction of the republic did not cost a single drop of blood, for Pedro II, a liberal who abolished slavery at the cost of support from the oligarchy, finally packed his bags and abandoned Brazil for good.

When the Latin American countries severed their ties with the mother country, they looked to the Anglo-Saxon democracies for a constitutional model. Liberal democracy was introduced and "imposed" by the ruling classes, who thought that they had thereby found a political instrument with which to weld together their country's national unity and social life. Liberal politicians were so dazzled by the Anglo-Saxon democracies—indisputable examples of "political and social order," the importation of which would eliminate all problems of national organization—that they were blinded to the real needs of their countries. Democratic institutions could hardly function in countries where there was almost no middle class in which to establish them and where enormous sectors of the population could neither read nor write and were not even socially integrated into the nation's life. Accustomed to the authoritarian government of the Spanish crown, the masses tended toward the *caudillo* type of ruler, who governed with a strong arm and a paternalistic spirit. In such circumstances, democracy was more a name than a reality—a formal apparatus benefiting the privileged classes and utterly devoid of social content. This does not mean that there has been no opportunity to practice a genuinely democratic form of government. In the balance of accounts, the examples of Uruguay, Chile, Costa Rica and Mexico belong on the credit side, but it is also true that as long as the crude social dichotomy persists, democracy will be more of a slogan than a vital reality.

4. Ignorance and illiteracy are other evils that corrode society. Much has been done to promote education and to develop popular culture. Argentina, Uruguay and Cuba have literacy rates that compare well with those of many European countries; Mexico spends more on education than on arms. Nevertheless, that task remains gigantic. Generally, the illiteracy rate is alarming—as much as 90 per cent of the population in certain countries. Among people over fifteen years of age there are more than seventy million illiterates. It is easy to imagine the disadvantages that confront this enormous mass. Their participation in society and their chances of influencing it are reduced to a minimum. Incapable of giving thought beyond their own daily concerns, they are unable to assume by themselves any significant political role.

Furthermore, the bilateral relations of economic and political dependence with the United States constitute another symptom of their delayed development. Democracy and free enterprise, imposed utopias from abroad, have proved incapable of raising the living standard of the population and of laying the foundations for a constructive national political life. United States diplomacy —and sometimes the Marines—have always operated to protect economic interests and to blow away the spirit of revolt, thereby paralyzing popular recovery. To these ends, use was made of pseudodemocratic regimes as well as of dictatorships. The Organization of American States (OAS) appeared, with suspicious unanimity—the honorable exception being Mexico—to be dedicated to no other task than to serve those interests.

As the colonial world collapsed, it left a continent unsettled and adrift in its inner being. There was, on the one hand, a minority that possessed all the wealth, lived and thought à la Europea, was educated, cultured and democratic. On the other, there was the great mass of the urban and rural population—underfed, illiterate and ill-housed, which began to be aware of its condition and to be awakened to a revolutionary frame of mind that no one could check. This precarious economic, political, social and cultural development is today the source of one of the most explosive revolutionary situations in the world.

## The Awakening of Social Conscience

1. The attempts to end this colonial heritage can be fairly well identified from 1920 onward. About that time, a vast social and political process began that was directed toward achieving a more equitable and economically free society. There was a real mobilization of ideological forces and tendencies, an urgent desire to give the continent a modern face-lifting. The European model of community life appeared worn out and decadent; it no longer served as a guide for new paths and aspirations. The urban middle classes felt that their hour of history had come, and, undergirded by new political parties, they took over power. The small industrial *bourgeoisie* displaced the landholding oligarchy in determining the course of economic life. The working class began to organize, listening to the far-off echo of the Soviet Revolution and to the campaign cries of European socialism nearer at hand. Some of the Latin American countries have shown themselves able—albeit precariously—to practice democratic ways, but in general the political life has seesawed between constitutional governments and dictatorial regimes. Art and culture have sought for inspiration that is rooted in the soil and have tried out new ways of expressing the national ethos. The university "reform" movement has championed the democratization of academic life through the admission of students from all social strata; and in the ideological plane, "Aprism" has summoned the peoples of Latin America to fight for social justice, reintegrate the Indian population in national life and uproot economic imperialism.

The balance sheet of the four decades that have passed is far from satisfactory. Progress has been recorded here and there, but there has been no over-all development to set in motion all the forces of a country. Moreover, the resistance of the ruling classes, in connivance with foreign economic powers, has blocked the most promising undertakings. The land problem has received the attention of governments, and, in some places, plans for agrarian reform have been put into effect that would enable the peasant to work his own land. Farm work has been mechanized and steps have been taken to diversify the crops. But these have been partial attempts that have not noticeably modified the physiognomy of the countryside. Thus we have, side by side in the same country, zones of vast production with adequate agricultural technology and other zones with the most primitive farming methods, which barely serve to keep their inhabitants from starving. Josue de Castro expressed it in a moving way when he wrote of northeastern Brazil as the land of desolation and death. Buenos Aires, São Paulo and Mexico City are powerful industrial complexes, developed under a policy to protect the national capital. Labor unionism is awake and has managed to get its rights protected through measures of social legislation that in some cases, as in Uruguay, are truly progressive. But the rhythm of industrial expansion has slowed down, the withdrawal of capital resources hinders the creation of new enterprises and the policy of low salaries is inflicting a severe malaise upon the working class, which finds itself helpless and frustrated in the face of the violation of its rights and the constant threat of unemployment.

The middle class is today more numerous and more prosperous than it has been in the past. It has unquestionably succeeded in strengthening its position, but it is not very much open to initiative that would draw it closer to the working class. Jealous of the advances it has won, it fears that social effervescence may signify a temporary reversal in its living standard and it prefers to entrench itself behind the façade of an irresponsible liberalism. This amounts to a dangerous polarization of society that fails to find a way to combine interests and aspirations for the good of the national development.

2. All this shows how difficult it is to know whether Latin America should be included in the sphere of western countries or would fit better among the countries of the so-called "third world." Development is not wholly absent, but more in evidence in an underdevelopment that gnaws away at the continent's deepest entrails. The twenty countries of which Latin America is composed derive from a common conquest and colonization; they are related in Latin languages and cultures; they have maintained their distinctive ethos; and they have always spoken in favor of continental

solidarity. But this historical and cultural community begins to break up when we look at it from the ethnic, geographic, economic and political points of view. The limited value of generalizations is perceived when one has to deal with rich or poor countries, lands with high or low literacy rates, those with temperate or tropical climates and countries populated in varying proportions by American Indians, Caucasians and Negroes. But this Latin American ambivalence does not succeed in hiding the difficult conditions of population growth. Thus the central problem of Latin America is the radical transformation of its social patterns and institutions and of its way of life. A real political and social upgrading of the masses must be effected, for they are tired of living a marginal existence; they know, or at least instinctively feel, that technical advances have been attained that would give them access to material welfare and cultural life, and they are driven by a harsh revolutionary determination to achieve these ends. No one has described the situation better than did the Argentine economist, Raul Prebisch, when he said in his farewell speech upon leaving the Secretariat of the Economic Commission for Latin America in July 1963:

In Latin America, the systems of production and life must undergo deep changes, and something new must be built up. And if we do not succeed in doing it now with our own hands, if a resolute, firm, clear-sighted response is not made to this present imperious demand, the new generations with bold, fearless and perhaps irreverent hands will wipe the slate clean of the world that we have not known how to transform and will erect another that may not be what we would have desired for ourselves and for them.

3. That challenge had already been taken up several years earlier by those 'bold, fearless and perhaps irreverent hands" of which he spoke. The Cuban Revolution of 1959 constitutes, in the wide scope of its aims, the most important social and political event in Latin America in this century. A true mirror of a continent in ferment, it reflects all the problems, tendencies, aspirations and temptations of our time; it is a miniature world of destiny's threats and promises to a whole people in tension. Its rhythm is felt in every sphere of Cuban life, and its influence—though apparently becoming less resounding—extends everywhere. The first

fruits of a new society in formation, it offers itself as the most radical pattern on which to lead Latin Americans to break their remaining ties with their colonial past and to plunge into the still-confused and ambiguous domains of a society that is more brotherly, more progressive, more just.

The objectives of Castro's Revolution had been fixed in 1953 in the Moncada Program, which included agrarian reform, nationalization measures, urban reform and educational reform. The revolutionaries considered it impossible to carry out a revolution of the classical or bourgeois type that would be limited to the re-establishment of the formal freedoms of democracy without touching the capitalist structures of the national economy. If they had done so, they would not really have changed anything, and they would have sacrificed vigorous and decisive popular support to assure their position and gain their ends. The goals of the revolution, apart from any ideological definition, would inevitably go counter to the United States' interests. It is not surprising that, after a certain initial enchantment that the "romantic" aspect of Castro's action helped to encourage, the United States government showed an attitude of caution and hostility, followed by threats of economic sanctions. Faced with the danger of seeing his movement shipwrecked, Castro sought and obtained economic and military assistance from Soviet Russia and decided to give his revolution the ideological dress of Marxist Leninism. It is the task of impatient biographers to recount Fidel Castro's ideological history and to establish his supposed or actual Marxist affiliation before he started his movement. For better or worse, Castro introduced the first Latin American experiment with an economic, social and political regime in open rupture with liberal capitalism. Here is an economic revolution of a socialist kind, in which the benefits of agriculture and industry are put at the disposal of the centralized planning state; it is also a revolution against the economic colonialism exercised by the United States. Deep reforms in the system of land control and production, changes in urban property ownership, a decentralization (still at the planning stage) of the industrial centers and a vast plan of reforms in the realm of education (in the main already carried out) have all helped to raise the material and cultural living standard of the working masses and have done away with endemic unemployment of a structural kind. Gross errors committed in different sectors of the economy are being recognized and corrected. The Marxist dogmatism of the early days is giving way to an attitude that is more flexible and more mindful of Cuba's historical and social reality. The absence of rigid official instructions contributes to a more spontaneous and variegated cultural life. The state continues, as before, to be secular and neutral in religious matters, and there is no reason to suppose that the present government—which, incidentally, maintains diplomatic relations with the Vatican—will assimilate the militant atheism of some of the people's democracies of eastern Europe. There are also some shadows that could jeopardize the revolution itself. The lack of technical teams to advise and direct the social and economic development is still felt; an enlarged and barely competent bureaucracy constitutes a real short circuit between the government and the people, and there is an inevitable but costly distraction of energies and resources to assure the internal and external security of a country that still feels threatened by invasion. However, the effectiveness with which it has attacked the real problems of underdevelopment, and the way in which it has been able to stimulate and fill with hope the masses who have been raised to the status of essential components of the new society, should be counted to its credit.

As might be expected, a revolution of such a nature has had ample repercussions throughout Latin America, though "Castroism" does not express itself everywhere in the same form. There are groups inspired by the Cuban Revolution who have embarked on the course of guerrilla warfare, with the support of the peasant masses, in order to overthrow legal constitutional order. Other groups, made up of leftist intellectuals, some of them Christians, express their sympathy with the Cuban regime, criticize the policy of the United States and defend the principle of nonintervention in the affairs of other countries, but believe that the revolutionary struggle should be launched constitutionally.

The OAS has decreed the ostracism of Cuba; all the countries that form part of the OAS, and even Bolivia, which does not, have severed diplomatic relations with Cuba. Only Mexico has refused to take part in this "quarantine" or in any other joint action against the Castroist Revolution.

Nevertheless, the revolution has had its immediate catalytic effects. In the first place, it laid bare the widening gulf between Anglo-Saxon America and Latin America. Already, in 1958, the then President of Brazil, Juscelino Kubitschek, in what he called "Operation Panamericana," proposed a plan in which North and South Americans would commit themselves to the struggle against underdevelopment and its habitual train of evils. This scheme was left in the limbo of neglected dreams until action was needed to block the way to Cuban influence. President Kennedy, in the presence of the Latin American diplomatic corps, announced at the White House on March 13, 1961, his Alliance for Progress program to "end the dictatorship of misery in Latin America." This was a genuine economic and social charter for decisively embarking on the road of development within the framework of the liberal institutions of the West. The plan calls for grants totaling some $20 billion from public and private capital, for the most part by the United States, for a period of ten years.

In the four years since it was started, the Alliance has proved to be inadequate and ineffectual. The financial aid has not been used for the promised reforms—as was to be expected—in view of the fact that most of those governments are made up of representatives of the oligarchies and that private companies are the source of such investments. To initiate a structural reform would therefore mean acting against their own interests. Moreover, the Alliance as planned is insufficient. To foster a minimum required annual rise of 2.5 per cent per person, it would be necessary to double the proposed investments. Hitherto, it has been effective chiefly in the political sphere: It has checked the spread of Castroism and has shut the door to leftists, with the threat of economic sanctions on any government that shows any degree of sensitivity to the demands of the masses. It is handcuffed by a basic contradiction, namely, that of trying to bring about a social revolution with the cooperation of reactionary forces.

Relations between the United States and Latin America are today placed in the widest context of the division between rich and poor countries by the definition of a problem which is more exactly economic and ideological, but which also has its moral effects. The problem is to discover how world commercial relations can be changed in order to overcome the economic dictatorship of the wealthy countries—to which Russia "objectively" belongs—over the underprivileged countries and thus enable the latter to enter upon the road to development and progress. In this connection, the Conference on Trade and Development organized by the United Nations (Geneva, March-June, 1964) is a beginning that promises hope. It is a great opportunity for the "civilization of the privileged" to find here a way of involvement in a humanism that is less materialistic and more closely associated with a common cause.

### Ideological Choices, Political Spectrum and Christian Responsibility

1. The ideological dimension of the revolutionary ferment in Latin America covers a wide gamut of choices. It is evident here that we are no longer dealing with the abstract and universalist ideologies of the nineteenth century but with a collection of ideas and values which respond to a specific historical circumstance and which become more concrete upon being related to the economic and social development of the continent. Among those most commonly in practice are liberalism, authoritarianism with popular support, reformism and revolutionary socialism.

Liberalism is the ideology of a kind of industrial and commercial *bourgeoisie* which recognizes the need to modernize social patterns but which, in the face of social mobilization, is more closely concerned with preserving order than with assuring justice. Nothing, therefore, distinguishes it from conservatism, with which it comes to terms in matters of private property, free enterprise and liberal democracy. At present it lacks intellectual vigor, but it maintains its political and economic power almost intact, and its aggressive counter-revolutionary activities are evident everywhere.

Popular authoritarianism is the ideological pattern that seeks to give expression to the feelings and desires of the urban and rural laboring masses. It is colored with a strong nationalistic spirit, and its political authority assumes the form of a protective state. The nation is above any private interest and constitutes an organic whole in which the workers play a front-rank political role. It trusts to the people's struggle to obtain new social forms and to create a more just community. The people's movements in Latin America have been fostered especially by political leaders who have established charismatic relations with the masses. Among the most important are those that belong to "Varguism" in Brazil and "Peronism" in Argentina, two experiments in authoritarian democratization that have left deep impressions in the political sands of those countries. Popular authoritarianism is kept alive in our days by certain groups of young Army officers who gather round so-called socialist "Nasserism." They hold that the Army should enter the political struggle openly and become the vanguard of the nationalist people's revolution. They consider that the democracy so far practiced has been an exclusive privilege of the oligarchies and that the parties that have popular roots have been powerless to change the situation. They fight against capitalism because it is incurably linked to imperialism and against communism because it does not succeed in combining social justice with religious belief.

Reformism is the ideology that gives greater attention to the economic and social slant of development than to its political dimension. It favors a government in which technocrats hold key positions and which will make possible the launching of a full and harmonious development of the nation's economic resources, the application of more technology to agriculture, the fixing of a more rational position for the industrial forces and the promotion of education, especially for the training of professional workers and technicians. The reformists prefer to think in continental terms; they focus upon Latin America as a whole and advocate measures to coordinate the structural development of every nation with that of the others. Its chief exponents have been feeding their theories to public opinion through the Economic Commission for Latin America, a regional organism of the United Nations. They not only condemn economic imperialism, but dedicate themselves to creating the appropriate structural conditions that will enable each nation to emerge from its situation of dependence. In this, capital and foreign companies can play an important role as long as they identify themselves with the highest interests of the country.

Revolutionary socialism gathers together the tendencies toward the left and postulates a strong central government and a radical and complete change of the present patterns. It constitutes an important focus of attraction for the masses of workers and peasants and is a fertile laboratory of ideas for students and intellectuals. It shows a strong Marxist influence, which, along with other characteristics, distinguishes it clearly from the bourgeois-influenced democratic socialism—and the working people become the motive power and the nervous system of the revolution. There are those who choose the revolutionary war because within the present democratic system they see no prospect of a total renewal of Latin American life. Only the force of arms can knock down pillars of traditional society. Other leftist groups believe that peaceful life is still viable and think—at least in some countries—that within the present constitutional system bread and justice for all can be achieved.

2. The political prism of what has come to be called the "revolution of development and social justice" reflects this ideological panorama. There is a manifest loss of support for the traditional political organizations which developed out of the middle classes and which are instruments of the oligarchy. They have wasted themselves away by their use of power, and they have no new and imaginative program to offer. They stay in power by means of shady electoral machinations, or by regulations that hinder the illiterate masses in getting to the ballot boxes or by skillful divisive maneuvers in the area to the left.

People's parties have grown in importance, as would be expected, in the countries where trade unionism has developed the furthest, such as Chile, Argentina and Brazil. Peronism has achieved great electoral successes in Argentina, where it can claim more than half the voters. Its weak flank is its ideological vagueness. The Popular Action Front in Chile binds together Marxist leftists and has shown itself to be a disciplined force able to make itself significantly felt as an opposition party. Castroism, by its very nature, is forced to carry on underground and, in countries like Venezuela, Guatemala and Colombia, still watches for its opportunity. The armed forces are being trained in guerrilla warfare and have managed to limit the field of action of these revolutionary movements. In Brazil, Popular Action, a combination of Christian and Marxist elements, has achieved outstanding results in awakening the political conscience of the masses through a persistent campaign of education and promotion of popular culture.

The most important political event after the Cuban Revolution has been the vertiginous entrance on the scene of the Christian Democratic party. In some countries it remained a rather embryonic force, with a scanty, fluctuating number of voters. It has belatedly come to pick up the postwar triumphs of the European parties of the same name, after the maturing of a political point of view based on serious reflection about Latin America in a state of revolution. Credit should go here to the contribution of the *Centro Bellarmino* in Santiago, Chile, which provides the Christian Democratic party with the ideological platform that enabled it to define the lines of its political, social, economic and cultural activity. Depending on the color of the glasses through which one looks, it can appear as either rightist or leftist. To Latin America, it looks like a modern, dynamic, progressive party with a pinkish tinge if compared with traditional political bodies. Furthermore, it enjoys the sympathy of the Roman Catholic Church, which is unquestionably a formidable asset, giving it a badge of respectability and prestige that makes it palatable—although with a slightly bitter taste—to the conservative classes. Its anticommunist views—enlightened and not hysterical—make it trustworthy in the eyes of the great power to the north. In power today, in Chile and Peru, with vigorous activity in Venezuela and other countries, its goal for the future is to fulfill a desire to accomplish the "revolution in freedom."

According to its leaders, this revolution carried out by the Christian Democrats in Chile has a double meaning: on the one hand, to loosen the power of the privileged classes in the economic and political realms and, on the other, to restrict considerably the freedom of foreign capital to maneuver and to make it play a decisive role in the development of the country. The aim is therefore to do away with this double dependence—external and internal—which was suffocating the life of the masses. The government has drawn up a program of land reform and is striving for a decisive say in the exploitation of the copper mines, which are the main resources of the country and are, at the moment, in the hands of foreign enterprises. On the social level, the Christian Democrats are busily trying to carry out a thorough promotion of the rural and urban masses, avoiding any kind of class struggle. On the political level, the government will call, when necessary, a referendum to give the people an opportunity to express democratically their views on the crucial problems of nation-building. The private sector of the economy will not lose its initiative if and when it accepts the rules of the game of a policy of development.

This Christian Democrat Revolution is much more interested in political action and efficiency than in a carefully defined ideology. For this reason, it is eagerly seeking the support of a people renowned for its generosity, openmindedness and tested endurance. This is solid ground to start with, but it must be said that time is against any delayed and soft action. The Chilean masses still live in great poverty, and a greater material austerity than that to which they have so far been subjected cannot be imposed. The question is how to obtain a progressive and rapid improvement of their standard of living and how best to integrate them into a more just and dynamic community. If the government succeeds in doing this, it will then be the first significant achievement of a political movement that, throughout Latin America, is endeavoring to make compatible, from the very outset, economic development and political freedom.

3. The Christian Church in Latin America faces a challenging and difficult new period. Political and social change oblige it—whether it wants to or not—to revise its theology, its structure and the form of its presence. This is true for the Roman Catholic Church, which has been in the continent for more than four centuries, and for the Protestant Church, which has been there for about a hundred years.[1] The Roman Catholic Church is deeply rooted in the colonial world; it was the instrument of mass evangelization of the Indian—a task that never really reached his soul; it established the standards of thought and conduct of millions of people; and it remained closely bound up with the ruling classes. It approached the masses in a paternalistic manner and generally

---

[1] See GONZALO CASTILLO CÁRDENAS: "The Challenge of the Latin American Revolution," *Christian Social Ethics in a Changing World*. (Vol. I in this series.)

preached submission and respect toward those in high places. The winds of revolution are not blowing over it for the first time; it suffered a buffeting in the Mexican tempest of 1910, which stripped if of a great part of its material possessions, leaving intact its way of life and thought. Relations with the state were noticeably changed; the church remained confined to the "spiritual" sphere, and the secular state took care of politics, tolerating no interference. With time, this *modus vivendi* came to be firmly fixed, and it has not hindered the church from proceeding to recover its lost influence. The Bolivian Revolution of 1952 did not enter the religious sphere, and, although the socialist tinge of its social concerns annoyed the hierarchy, this did not seriously affect its influence on the Bolivian scene. It should be underlined that the Protestant Church experienced a notable upswing after the revolution.

The Cuban Revolution (1959), with its clear Marxist-Leninist accent, has raised the question of the relation between the church and the world in the most radical terms. This event brings to life, with almost brutal evidence, a new form of society, with all its promises and threats—a society that undertakes to revise aims and values, leaves behind all ideological or spiritual homogeneity and takes possession of technical resources for a better mastery of nature and city life, with a population in explosion, restless and, for the most part, secularized.

It is thus a critically difficult situation for the church. A new stage in human history is opening up, and Christians, who are involved along with other men in the world revolution, are summoned by God to pay attention to the signs of the times. What is occurring in Latin America is part of a revolution of worldwide dimensions. It is the elevation of humanity to the technological age, the passage of mankind from a dependent status to a kind of maturity that leads it to sever its ties with metaphysical or religious guardianships. It is a time in which man is discovering the realities of history as essential to his being, and technical skill as a fit instrument with which to construct a more just and brotherly community life.

The church has had to learn about this circumstance through a crucial experience: the Cuban Revolution. Cuba's abrupt mutation into the socialist world took the church by surprise; it felt excluded from this new world and concluded that it had nothing to do with it. The church fell into the trap of defining its relations with society more by its attitude toward communism than according to the profound significance of the changes. From there to its present eclipse was only a single step; all the efforts that the church is now making to come out again into the light show how long and hard the process of recovery will be. The same can be said of the Protestant Church in that country. Church attendance is increasing and religious practice is deeper, and yet the general atmosphere seems to make of the church a place of quiet refuge for disenchantment.

The social change has sharpened the conflict between the generations in the church. The older wing remains closely bound to the old order, pronounces anathemas against the dangers of communism and minimizes the need for changing patterns and forms of life. The younger wing looks at the revolution and, without being in unanimous agreement, encourages Christians to take part in it as the most responsible way to witness today. Someone has spoken of the "ghetto church," which erects a wall around itself and rests on its splendid past, and the "dialogue church," open and communicative, present in the struggle that man may be more humane and may live in a more responsible community.

Pastors, theologians and laymen feel summoned today to a task of reflection that will lead the church to a renewal of the form and fashion of its presence. On the basis of biblical revelation, they see the Lordship of Christ not only in the community of believers, but in society and in history. They feel that the signs of the times move God's people as such—and not only its members as individuals—to live in a new Diaspora, a dispersion whose environment is the post-Christian world. On the frontier of the dispersion, the *koinonia*—unification in Word, Sacrament and the bond of life —lives in the midst of men, shares in their problems and hopes and with them weaves the fabric of history. It does so in the steps of Christ—in a life of service among men—and not in order to implant a program dropped from heaven. And, in the midst of men, the witness of Christ also includes keeping the whole human enterprise on a plane of relativity; on that level of the penultimate where Christians participate in the struggle for economic development and social justice as a preparation for the coming of Grace.

The ecumenical movement (involving Roman Catholicism more and more) is of great significance for the renewal of Christ's Church in Latin America. Theological faculties, study centers, "church and society" organizations, student and youth movements and laymen's institutes are enabling the church to appear in a new light and are making of the Christian faith not an article from the past but a living and efficacious reality for our times. These are signs of hope in the midst of perplexities and confusions.

In the mind and feelings of the people, the Latin American social revolution is like a second War of Independence that will lead to the creation of basic conditions for a true and concrete democracy. A growing drive to do away with old structures of exploitation, to create new patterns of life for the benefit of everybody, is under way. This is not an easy task; multiple obstacles and suffering still lie ahead, but the hope that a more just and human society can be established is stronger than ever. The Latin American man seems to have his future and that of his fellow worker in his own hands; he sees himself as the decisive force for bringing about a new order and a new purpose in life. For him, the only alternative is injustice, submission and nonbeing. If the constitutional means to achieve this aim are blocked for him, the revolution will have to resort to violence and civil war.

Along with that, there is a general dissatisfaction with the traditional ties between the great power to the north. Pan-Americanism intended as relations between unequal partners does not make any sense today when the republics from the south are coming of age and are determined to have their own voice in the international arena. This does not mean a breaking of relations between the two Americas but the recognition that a new system of communication should be worked out whereby, through mutual respect, both the United States and Latin America might develop the kind of society more akin to their peculiar ethos and values.

It has been said that Latin America is on the threshold of a new way of life by the assimilation of technical progress and social planning and the natural vocation of its people to human freedom. Here is a continent with a wealth of humanity and opportunities. The earth's treasures are provided in quantitative balance—neither too little nor too much—just enough, as Dr. Arnold Toynbee would say, to shut out easy answers and sharpen the intelligence. The Christian Church is called to provide men of heart and thought to join in this challenging but promising enterprise, because it is a struggle of people to free themselves from beliefs that cripple the human spirit, and a struggle where men dare to oppose unjust laws and crippling social barriers.

# 9

# THE AFTERMATH OF
# COLONIALISM IN ASIA

by T. B. SIMATUPANG (Indonesia)

WHEN Hitler invaded Poland on September 1, 1939, and when, in the first week of December, 1941, the Imperial Japanese government decided to attack Pearl Harbor and invade Southeast Asia, little did they suspect that the war they started would accelerate the emancipation of so many nations from western colonial rule and, in the case of Korea and Taiwan (Formosa), from an eastern colonial power. That is not to say that the Second World War called the new nations into existence out of nothing. As early as the end of the First World War, two very different world leaders, President Woodrow Wilson and Vladimir Ilyich Ulyanov Lenin, advocated the right of self-determination for dependent nations.

The nationalist movements for independence in many colonial countries go back to the beginning of the twentieth century and, in some countries, even as far as the nineteenth. In fact, the urge to get rid of foreign rule has always preoccupied the dependent peoples, and the memory of some kind of precolonial Golden Age stimulated their struggle for liberation throughout the colonial period. But the Second World War helped to bring many new nations to birth.

The differences between the newly emancipated nations are bewildering. Each of them has had its own precolonial history, some going back to the early dawn of civilization. There are differences in the duration, the character and the intensity of western colonial rule. In each of the dependent nations, the national movements,

arising at a certain stage in the development of the colonial societies, had a different philosophical background and was dominated by a different mood. The methods and the circumstances during the final stage of the struggle also varied from country to country; some went through a long period of turbulence and armed
struggle before a settlement could be reached, while others emancipated themselves peacefully from colonial rule. Moreover, there
are differences in religious and cultural backgrounds, ethnic origin,
geographical location, climatic conditions, size, natural resources
and political orientation.

But the impact of the forces originating in the modern West is
apparently so strong that, even when they operated upon different
social, cultural and religious materials and, despite the differences
among the western countries themselves in their colonial policies,
the results, as seen in the newly liberated nations, show basic sim-
ilarities and are even comparable to basic phenomena of the modern history of western nations.

It has been a common experience of the colonial peoples that
all their efforts to liberate themselves from western colonialism,
often motivated by a spirit of genuine heroism, failed as long as they
faced the modern West with their traditional art of warfare and
with their traditional methods of organizing society. Only after
they had absorbed or borrowed enough elements of the spiritual,
scientific and material revolution that had transformed western man
and western society into modernity were the nonwestern nations
able to set themselves free.

For a few centuries after that mysterious transformation of the
West, western Europe, after narrowly escaping subjugation by the
Arabs and the Mongols during the Middle Ages, dominated the
whole world. Along with sufferings, oppression, exploitation and
discrimination, the world was unified and totally reshaped during
this era of western imperialism, and, as if at the touch of the magic
wand of the revolution that had already transformed the West, a
revolutionary process, comparable, though not similar, to the western modern revolution, was initiated among the nonwestern nations. The attainment of independence is only a milestone, though
a vital one, in this revolution.

After independence, the newly emancipated nations were caught up in the dynamics, the emotions, the expectations and the problems of an "unfinished revolution," with the triple aim of (1) liquidating anachronistic remnants of the era of western imperialism; (2) rapidly modernizing and industrializing toward a fully developed nationhood, while at the same time manifesting a country's own identity; and (3) participating fully in the shaping of the emergent world.

From the point of view of a newly emancipated nation, the postcolonial era is one of transition, in which the world of imperialism is being left behind as the new world emerges.

How can we begin to understand the staggering problems that will confront the newly emancipated nations in the coming decades? What will be the relations between the nations which constitute the majority of mankind and the nations which have gone through a comparable stage in their history earlier and which, during the next decades, will themselves proceed toward further stages of development? What responsibility does this imply for the Christian in the face of these problems, both in the newly emancipated countries and in the countries that directly or indirectly took part in shaping the world during the centuries of western imperialism?

## The Dynamics of the Unfinished Revolution

For a few centuries, when modern man and modern society were exclusively western phenomena, western imperialism controlled, unified and reshaped the whole world. In some parts—in the settlement colonies—a white population, sometimes along with colored slaves, was transplanted, while the indigenous inhabitants were virtually removed from the scene. For all practical purposes, these areas have become extensions of the western world. In other areas—the exploitive colonies—western political and economic control was imposed upon the population. In others, again —the mixed colonies—a significant number of white migrants settled among a colored indigenous majority. A number of countries, because of their inherent strength but more often because of rivalry between the imperial powers, remained independent in the formal sense, though here, too, the influence of western imperialism penetrated deeply into all sectors of the people's lives.

In the meantime, during the nineteenth century, western society, which had been modernized around the sixteenth century, was further transformed into an industrial society; and the zenith of this era of western imperialism may be located somewhere around the turn of the twentieth century.

Since then, western dominance has been receding, while the modern revolution has spread to the non-European peoples, in a way that implies that the phenomena of modern man and modern society were no longer western monopolies; and western dominance basically came to an end when the non-European peoples began to master modernity. A new world began to take shape.

What will this emerging world be like? Will it be a world of independent, modern, industrial nations, western and nonwestern alike? Will it be centered, structurally, on a number of superstates? What, as it emerges, will be the role of nationalism, ideologies, race, religion, cultures? Will modernity bring prosperity to all nations?

The birth of the new nations has strengthened significantly the forces of change, for the unfinished revolution is one of the strongest driving forces in that direction.

Since gaining independence, most of the new nations have thrown their weight into the struggle to achieve the first aim in their unfinished revolution—to liquidate the anachronistic remnants of imperialism.

As the new nations pursue the second aim—rapid modernization and industrialization—they perceive that emancipation not only leads to the necessity to modernize but also evokes a reassertion of the national culture, which became more or less submerged during the colonial period. They know that, unless they modernize and industrialize rapidly, they will not solve their internal and external problems, and their independence will be only a façade, hiding economic and political control by other nations. But they hope, at the same time, to preserve what they feel to be of abiding value in their basically premodern and preindustrial culture. This dual urge—for rapid modernization and industrialization—linked to a nostalgia for the past, may be a transient state of mind in the growth of newly emancipated nations, which will one day discover that modernization and industrialization are undermining every premodern and preindustrial culture. But, at present, they are seeking to fulfill both purposes, together with the third aim in the unfinished revolution—to play a vital part in the shaping of the world that is emerging.

But the newly emancipated nations are equally determined to participate more directly in all the deliberations that affect that shaping.

Let us imagine that, in a certain town, as in the old Greek cities, a minority of the inhabitants have full rights of citizenship, while the majority are more or less slaves. Recently, however, some of the slaves have become free, while others remain without the rights of citizenship. The newly emancipated slaves are working to liberate their friends and to liquidate other remnants of the former relationships. They are striving for education and wealth, since otherwise, despite their attainment of formal citizenship, the old oligarchy would remain in control. But the former slaves have a third aim for the future—to take part in full in the changing of the Constitution of the *polis*.

If that is an apt parallel, we can proceed to search for some insight into the internal and external problems that the newly emancipated nations are likely to face. Excessive hopes, disappointments, failures, frustrations and sufferings will not be unknown experiences in the next few decades. But we may expect the triple aim that has been described above to provide enough dynamic to continue the unfinished revolution—if necessary, by abandoning ways and means that have proved unsuccessful and by adopting others.

### Modernization, Industrialization and National Identity

No responsible leader of the new nations will challenge the need to modernize and industrialize. The rising demands of their own population cannot be met in any other way, nor can effective, as distinct from nominal, equality with the older states be won.

But how is it to be accomplished? And how, along with it, is a nation to maintain and develop its own identity? What are the foundations on which the newly emancipated nations will build their political, social, economic and cultural structures as they meet this double challenge?

No nation can ignore its history. In fact, being a nation presupposes awareness of a common history, a sense of solidarity in the fact of a common challenge and the vision of a common destiny. The national identity, that elusive phenomenon, is always there, providing a distinctive quality to every aspect of social life and culture.

Thus the newly emancipated nations ask themselves the old questions, which are nonetheless new every time: Who are we as a nation? How can we make sense of our past, our present and our destiny and understand them as one continuous story? This preoccupation is symptomatic of the modern spirit, aware of the possibility of change and progress, dynamic and active, politically and socially conscious, seeking for national self-assertion. This is proof that, within the nation, at least an influential small group, the revolutionary elite, have been drawn into the mainstream of modernity during the colonial period.

It is this group that writes in glowing terms about the precolonial past, teaching the masses to be proud of their history and to rid themselves of the sense of inferiority infused into their minds during the western dominance. This sense of history shows the modernizing elite that there is nothing inherently superior in western man, with his relatively recent emergence, in comparison with many of the non-European peoples, some of whose flourishing civilizations reach back into the earliest history of mankind. But how are they to explain the undeniable fact of European superiority for a few centuries after the European Middle Ages? And how are they to convince themselves and the masses that this period of western dominance is only temporary and that a great future lies ahead?

During the colonial period, a few generations after the last armed resistance had been convincingly crushed, the modern nationalist movements, generally under relatively young leaders with a western university education, began. These leaders have eaten freely of the tree of western knowledge, including those branches from which the Marxist fruits and the fruits of nationalism hang, as though ripened especially to feed them in their struggle for liberation.

Nationalism, Marxism and the idea of revolution are, in varying proportions, the main components in the development of nationalist thinking. It may be true that nationalism forms the basic ingredient and that Marxism, in many cases disconnected from its atheism, serves a secondary role in teaching the young leaders, in the face of an apparently invincible foe, how capitalism bred imperialism and colonialism, assuring them that, according to an iron law of history, they will be in at the death of the causes of their sufferings and will see a new and glorious era begin. Countries that saw no prospect of overcoming the colonial status by constitutional means were especially prone to persuasion by this doctrine that the privileged group would yield only to force.

While observing that the emerging national elite have drawn to some extent on non-Christian sources, we must also bear in mind that it was in this colonial period that the Christian Church was planted in many of these countries; but, on the whole, it would be true to state that, during the formative stages, the churches did not play an especially creative role. Leading nationalists have not seriously considered how modern society came to emerge in western Europe, whether there is any relation between this modern spirit and the Christian faith or what the long-range results of modernization will be for their national culture and its moral foundation. They were, and in general still are, preoccupied with the more practical question—how to utilize ideas from all sources in mobilizing all the forces in the nation, first to gain independence and then to transform the nation into a modern industrial society, while still manifesting their own character.

In the first place, they had to formulate some kind of synthesis, to be worked out in the minds of the people, and embracing explosive and sometimes contradictory elements: a nostalgia for the past and a sensitive pride in the national heritage, along with sometimes almost utopian hopes for the future, which are based upon an excessive faith in the power of science and technology to transform man and society; a clinging to religious and cultural traditions rooted in a premodern society, along with the urge to modernize as rapidly as possible; resentment against the industrial nations, especially the ex-colonial powers, along with the knowledge that their skill and money are needed. And with it all go the problems of how to secure the survival of the nation, how to maintain order and unity and to implement the transformation into modernity and industrialism while guaranteeing freedom and justice.

We might illustrate from an impromptu speech by President Sukarno of Indonesia, before the members of the American Embassy staff in Djakarta on October 9, 1963:

When I was in Washington in 1956 I told Congress that the Republic of Indonesia was proclaimed on the 17th [of] August, 1945, and that it is founded on five principles, the well-known Pantjasila Principles: first, belief in God. That is the first principle of the Republic of Indonesia: belief in God Almighty. Number two is the belief that the Indonesian people is one undivided nation: the Indonesian nation. Number three, humanitarianism: the belief that the Indonesian nation is just part of mankind or humanity; number four, democracy; number five, social justice. On these five principles Dr. Muhammad Hatta and I proclaimed the Independence of Indonesia, after domination by the Dutch colonialists for 350 years. On that date the Indonesian Revolution, the very well-known Indonesian Revolution, began. You have in history the American Revolution, the French Revolution and you have also the Indonesian Revolution, which pursues three aims: firstly to establish a humanitarian state, a republic stretching from Sabang to Merauke. (Sabang is the utmost north of Sumatra; Merauke the utmost east of West Irian.) The second aim is to establish in this republic, the Republic of Indonesia, a just and prosperous society; a society free from exploitation of man by man. I always say it in French, a society *sans exploitation de l'homme par l'homme.* The third aim is to contribute to the close friendship of all nations; to contribute to the brotherhood of man.

These sentences reflect the emotions and expectations, if not all the problems, in one of those nations that are living in the aftermath of colonialism.

During the centuries after the Renaissance, the western nations cherished sometimes excessive expectations that science would solve all the problems of man and society; they experienced intoxicating emotions of nationalism, they lived through the often painful transformations of western man and society into modernity and industrialism.

Basically, the new nations are passing through the same emotions and the same expectations; and they face the same problems, although telescoped into a few decades. But the problems are further complicated for them because, unlike the West, in these countries, as a whole, nationalism and modernization are not indigenous to their religion or their culture but are alien elements, which, as they transform man and society, shake the religious and cultural foundations.

Again, unlike the western nations, which had a free hand in exploiting their colonies and, to a lesser extent, the labor force in their own countries, the new nations have to accomplish their modernization and industrialization without colonies and in the face of highly organized labor movements, which rule out all possibility of "cheap labor." They have to modernize and industrialize in a world dominated by the power relations and ideological competition between these countries that have already been transformed into modernity and industrialism.

What will happen in the newly emancipated nations in the next decades? They have caught the vision of becoming modern industrial nations that will manifest their own identities. Failure to realize this vision will create frustrations and a mood of explosion.

Is a peaceful and stable world possible, when some two thirds of its population are in a continuous mood of frustration and aggressiveness and have no overriding awareness of their stake in maintaining world peace? And what will prevent these nations, if they succeed in modernizing and industrializing their societies, in what we may well regard as their years of adolescence, from repeating the nationalist follies which most of the western and at least one nonwestern nation have committed in the period, when the ongoing process of modernization and industrialization provided them, and especially their ruling circles, with a growing sense of power?

Whether these nations grow into well-adapted and balanced members of the community of modern industrial nations, or whether the frustrations of this decisive period will leave resentment and aggressiveness in their minds, depends on the international development within them and on the attitude of the industrial nations. It is here that the churches, both in newly emancipated and in the developed nations, bear a heavy responsibility.

## The New States and the World

The threefold aim outlined in this chapter will provide a basis for a measure of solidarity and cooperation between the developing nations of the world, in spite of the differences, and even the antagonisms, among them. The general mood in the world is not one of disagreement with this triple aim. No nation is in a position today to express open disagreement with anticolonialism and anti-imperialism, with rapid modernization and industrialization for the developing nations or with their full participation in the affairs of the world. And yet there are sources of possible irritation between the new and the older states.

There is, in the first place, the discrepancy between the formal equality between them and the fact that the older states sometimes still retain extensive economic, political, cultural and even military interests in the new states, whereas the new states have virtually none in the older; and there is the fact of the great and even widening gap between their respective prosperity and scientific and technological development. The fact that the new states need the "know how" and even the material assistance of the older nations in overcoming this inequality tends to feed their resentment and to strengthen the sense of superiority that still lingers on among the older states. The Cold War enabled many new states to obtain assistance from the industrial countries without becoming too rigidly tied to any of them, while others did so by becoming more or less protectorates of one of the older states.

Then there are secondary sources of irritation.

The established industrial nations, irrespective of ideological outlook, have a more intimate knowledge of the effects of war, at the present stage of science and technology, and a far greater stake in the preservation of peace. They therefore tend to dub as irresponsible the attitudes of many new states—their emphasis on anticolonialism and anti-imperialism; on the creation of international conditions favorable for their rapid modernization and industrialization; and their suspicion that the overemphasis on defense tends to freeze situations that need fundamental change or even tends to open the door to the re-establishment of foreign military, political and economic control.

These irritations cannot be eliminated or even reduced to harmonious surface relations as long as the new states have still not attained the minimum stage toward modernization which would give them a more real equality in their dealings with the older states.

The problem for the next decades may well be on the one hand to keep these irritations within bounds and to prevent a loss of patience, while on the other hand searching for entirely new solutions to the common problem of totally liquidating colonialism, imperialism and discriminations, and pooling the resources of the world so that a minimum stage of modernization and industrialization is extended to all.

Only then will we be able to say that the period of transition between the era of western imperialism and the emergence of the new world structure is over.

## Christian Responsibility

It happened to be in western Europe that modern man and modern society were born from a Christian cultural heritage. It happened to be Christian nations from the West that unified the globe and extended the modern revolution to all peoples. It happened to be in the era of western imperialism that churches were planted throughout the non-European and non-Christian world.

In the period of transition that we have discussed, the churches throughout the world, stronger in the industrial West and weaker in developing non-western countries, face the common responsibility of supporting the forces that are at work to make an end to the untenable division of mankind into an affluent minority and a starving, backward majority. They must, at the same time, serve as agents for conciliation between the new and the older states, working to overcome both resentment and the sense of superiority, and beginning within the Household of God.

# PART III

GROWTH OF GOVERNMENT
RESPONSIBILITY
AND POLITICAL POWER
AND THE CLAIMS
OF HUMAN FREEDOM

# 10

# THE NATURE OF GOVERNMENT IN A FREE SOCIETY

by JOHN H. HALLOWELL (United States)

## The State As a Servant of Justice

EVERY man is born into society. He is never asked whether he wants to live in society. The "social contract" theorists were wrong. Society is not the creation of men, but the condition in which men are born. Man's nature requires the fellowship and services of other men. He is not self-sufficient. Only in organized society can men live the kind of life that will help them to mature as human beings. We do not choose to assume the obligations of parents: these obligations are what we mean by parenthood. Our parental and filial obligations, though they can be ignored, are not a matter of choice but of fact. And just as we assume certain obligations by virtue of becoming parents, so we assume others by being born into society. We are born with obligations to our Creator, to ourselves, and to our neighbors. It is from these obligations that we derive our rights.

To live in an organized society requires submission to some authority, for we cannot live in society and be a law unto ourselves. That is the essence of anarchy, and anarchy is a "war of all against all." Government comes into being to provide the necessary authority. It is not an arbitrary, artificial creation of men, but a natural outgrowth of family life, of the need for the division of labor, of the dependence of man upon man. While we do not consent to the fact of government, we may consent to the form of government. But the fact of government, the need for its functions, arises from the social nature of man. Government is necessary to adjudicate rival claims and interests, to decide how the material and spiritual resources of the community are to be shared, to restrain individuals from harming other individuals, to defend the community from external attack, to promote the good of all. It is not only life that men desire, but the good life; and government comes into being to help men live that good life.

Christianity teaches us that men have not only the potentialities for leading a good life, but inclinations to evil as well. From the Christian perspective, the state has not only the function of helping to provide the social, economic and educational conditions conducive to the development of human potentialities but also the function of restraining the evil propensities of men, of preventing them as much as possible from doing harm to one another. The state has both positive and negative functions. These functions are inherent in the nature of government itself. While the *ends* of government are derived from the nature of man, the *form* of government is a matter of choice. This does not mean that some forms of government, tyranny for example, are not intrinsically bad, but it does mean that there are a variety of legitimate forms of government. Government may take the form of the rule of one, or of a few, or of many. Its legitimacy does not depend upon the number who participate in government, but upon whether it is government in the interest of all, or government in the interest of the rulers; whether it is a government restrained by law, or government by arbitrary decree. Some forms of government are more suitable to some circumstances than others. Many have thought that a mixed form of government, a form combining features of monarchy, aristocracy and democracy, was the most practicable form, but it is certainly not the only legitimate form.

It has been suggested that the state is as natural to man as the beehive is natural to the bee. But the state differs from the beehive just as man's nature differs from that of the bee. The hive is governed by laws, just as the state is; but the bees do not live a political life, because they do not understand the laws that govern them, nor is such understanding essential to the efficiency of those laws. The bees obey the laws of the hive by instinct, and have no freedom to do otherwise. Man is free to obey or to disobey. His understanding of the laws must be elicited, his cooperation solicited. Man's freedom, his capacity to choose between alternative ways of acting, is the source both of his greatness, when used well, and of his degradation, when abused. Only man is capable of deliberating over alternative ways of acting and of exercising freedom of choice—this capacity is the source both of his dignity and of his corruption.

As a consequence, politics is not a form of social engineering, but of moral endeavor. Good government is not a matter of providing the correct blueprint of a perfect society and of constructing, on the basis of that blueprint, a new society—rather, it is a matter of working with what are often recalcitrant individuals to secure that degree of order and of cooperation of which they are capable. The objects with which engineering deals are inanimate, material things, and the engineer is concerned with shaping or making those things into useful objects, such as buildings, highways, bridges. The materials are transformed by the engineer in conformity with some useful purpose that he has in mind. The purpose does not inhere in the things themselves but in the mind of the engineer. But the objects with which politics is concerned are not things but human beings, personalities. Human beings cannot be manipulated like material objects, and any attempt to do so will be destructive of their very essence. They are not like so many bricks or pieces of steel that have only to be laid in the right place according to a blueprint. They can cooperate or rebel. To enlist their cooperation is one of the principal tasks of politics.

Politics is unlike engineering in that it is a form not of technology but of moral endeavor. It is concerned not with *making* something but with *doing* something. As one writer put it: "We do not build the state to live *in* (as we live in a house)—we live the state. Our living state is an integral part of our lives. Here, the builders are what they build." Politics comes into being, moreover, to assist men in doing what they are already predisposed to do. Steel does not have to be made into bridges; it has no inherent predisposition to be anything—it can be manipulated and used in any fashion that the engineer decides is appropriate to his purpose. But human beings are predisposed to live in society and embody ends in themselves. Politics ministers to an end which is not of its own devising, but which is inherent in life itself. It comes into being in order to help men to live a good life in society. It does not invent that end, but finds that end inherent in all human striving. As a consequence, it is not productive knowledge that the statesman requires, but practical wisdom or prudence. The statesman is not concerned with making anything, but rather with inspiring right action; his ability to enlist the cooperation of others in taking right action is the test of his ability as a statesman.

Government comes into being in order to minister to human needs and aspirations, to help to provide the social conditions necessary to the fulfilment of human potentialities. Government is made for man, not man for government. For this reason, it has long been asserted, in the western political tradition, that there are principles of natural justice to which all governments should conform if they are to be legitimate. The classic statement of that conviction is found in the writings of Cicero when he wrote:

There is in fact a true law—namely, right reason—which is in accordance with nature, applies to all men, and is unchangeable and eternal. By its commands this law summons men to the performance of their duties; by its prohibitions it restrains them from doing wrong. Its commands and prohibitions always influence good men, but are without effect upon the bad. To invalidate this law by human legislation is never morally right, nor is it permissible ever to restrict its operation, and to annul it is wholly impossible. Neither the senate nor the people can absolve us from our obligation to obey this law. . . . It will not lay down one rule at Rome and another at Athens, nor will it be one rule today and another tomorrow. But there will be one law, eternal and unchangeable, binding at all times upon all peoples; and there will be, as it were, one common master and ruler of men, namely God, who is the author of this law, its interpreter and sponsor. The man who will not obey it will abandon his better self and, in denying the true nature of a man, will suffer thereby the severest of all penalties, though he has escaped all the other consequences which men call punishment.

This conviction that there is a law higher and more fundamental than any law enacted by men, principles of natural justice to which positive laws ought to conform, has given rise in the West to constitutional government. By that we mean effective and regularized restraints upon the powers and functions of government in terms of

a law more fundamental than that enacted by a legislature or decreed by an executive. As Cicero stated it: "We are servants of
the law in order to be free."

Constitutional government arises not only from the conviction
that there are principles of natural justice binding upon ruler and
citizen alike but also from the conviction introduced into the western world by Christianity that men have obligations to God as well
as to Caesar, that man has a dual loyalty and a dual citizenship.
The Christian is a citizen not only of the state in which he lives,
but potentially at least a citizen of the Kingdom of God. The allegiance the Christian can give to any government is necessarily
limited, for he can give absolute loyalty only to God and to God's
commandments. This is not to say that the Christian does not
have the same obligations as all other citizens, but that his allegiance must necessarily be a conditional one. This notion that man
has a dual citizenship and a dual loyalty was bound to create tension and even conflict, but it lies at the foundation of what we
call constitutional government. It is the loss of this tension that
creates a situation that makes the coming of totalitarian government almost inevitable. The principle has been violated on both
sides—by some Christians who sought to unite church and state
in a theocracy, and by some secularists who insist upon the absolute sovereignty and omnicompetence of the state. It is the recognition of a dual loyalty that gives freedom substantive meaning.

Those who have been anxious to assert the absolute sovereignty
of the state have always been critical of the Christian religion as a
divisive force in society. Thus, J. J. Rousseau complains:

Jesus came to establish on earth a spiritual kingdom. By separating the
theological system from the political system, he brought it about that
the state ceased to be one, and caused internal divisions which have
never ceased to agitate Christian peoples. From this twofold power
there has resulted a perpetual conflict of jurisdiction which has rendered all good politics impossible in Christian states. No one has ever
been able to know which one to obey, priest or political ruler.

And Thomas Hobbes registered his complaint by saying: "Temporal and spiritual government are but words brought into the
world to make men see double and mistake their sovereign which
is Leviathan, the Mortal God." The modern totalitarian state

claims, in effect to be both church and state; it acknowledges no limitations to its competence, and claims to be both the source of truth and the determiner of the purposes of society. It is part of both classical and Christian teaching that the purpose of the state derives from the nature of man; and that while men are free to choose the form of government under which they want to live, they are not free to alter the purposes of government. The state is not the source of what is true and good, but the servant of justice. While the state must promote the good of men, it is not competent to define that good. Though helpful to men in providing conditions conducive to a good social life, the state is not an instrument of spiritual salvation, nor can it bring into being the Kingdom of God.

## The Rule of Law and Individual Liberty

It is because men have responsibilities not only to their neighbors but to themselves and to God that they must have the freedom proportionate to those responsibilities. The claims that individuals rightly make to various kinds of freedom derive from their obligations. These obligations are both the ground upon which individuals claim to have certain natural, inalienable rights, and the limitations upon the use of these rights. Although certain rights are natural to man and inalienable, they are not absolute. Freedom is not an end in itself but a necessary means for the attainment of ends more ultimate than freedom. If freedom is conceived as freedom from all restraint, it is no longer freedom, but anarchy.

Because men have been endowed by their creator with the capacity to think about alternative ways of acting, they have the obligation to think as well as they can. This means that they have both an obligation and a right to cultivate their minds and to seek the truth wherever it can be found. An individual has both an obligation to secure an education, and a right to as much education as he can master. It means that the individuals can claim the right to freedom of speech, of press and assembly, for it is the existence of these kinds of freedom that makes possible a genuine search for truth and provides an opportunity for the dissemination of the truth when known. But the obligations that demand recognition of these rights also limit their use. Freedom of speech, of press and of assembly are not absolute rights. The individual has an obligation to use them in a responsible way. To use them knowingly for the purposes of deceiving others, to spread known falsehoods, bigotry and hatred, to pander to the lowest emotions and instincts is to abuse them. These freedoms are rightly used to promote rational discussion and deliberation, to air legitimate grievances, to organize opposition to injustice and irresponsible government. It is difficult to say when they are being used in a responsible way. What appears to be pornography to one person appears to be literature to another; what appears as bigotry to one appears as truth to another; what appears to be a legitimate appeal to correct an injustice to one appears as a call to violence and rebellion to another. But the difficulty of making such judgments should not obscure the necessity for making them. Governments differ in the way in which they make such judgments, but such judgments are inevitable if we are to have government and not anarchy. And it is upon the individual himself that the greatest obligation lies to understand the reason for the existence of these freedoms and to limit his use of them in accordance with their purpose.

It is because men are required to acknowledge their Creator that they must have the freedom to worship God as their conscience dictates. Freedom of worship is also necessary in order that men may have an opportunity to encounter different conceptions of God and different ways of praising and serving him. But rarely has this been conceived to be an absolute right in the sense that most advanced societies have not permitted men to perform immoral acts or acts of cruelty under the guise of worshiping "God." Western societies have sometimes erred in the past in imposing too great limitations upon freedom of worship, and they have learned from experience that genuine religious convictions can never be coerced. God wants our love freely given, for if it is not freely given, it is not love. Whether a society, however, can tolerate immoral practices, cruel treatment, or practices harmful to community health and safety is another question.

Although the Magna Charta (1215) very early proclaimed that "No freeman shall be arrested, or detained in prison, or deprived of his freehold, or outlawed, or in any way molested . . . unless by the lawful judgment of his peers and by the law of the land," it remained for the seventeenth and eighteenth centuries to draft more elaborate statements enumerating the rights of men. One of the earliest of these statements was the Massachusetts Body of Liberties adopted by the General Court of Massachusetts in 1641. The Preamble to this statement describes it as "The free fruition of such liberties, immunities, and privileges as humanity, civility, and Christianity call for as due to every man in his place and proportion. . . ." It promises to every man the equal and indiscriminatory protection of the laws. It guarantees to every man the right to petition the government, the right to trial by jury, protection against inhuman or barbarous punishment, the right to counsel when accused of a crime. It was followed by the English Bill of Rights in 1689, the Virginia Bill of Rights in 1776, the French Declaration of the Rights of Man and of the Citizen in 1789. Numerous bills of rights have been adopted since, including a United Nations Declaration of Human Rights. The recognition by government that individuals have by their nature a legitimate claim to the protection of their lives and liberties does not mean that government is the source of these rights. The rights do not derive from government, but from the nature of man. Nevertheless, the promulgation of written bills of rights by governments has been an important means by which governments have been limited in the exercise of their powers.

In the western world, one of the greatest safeguards of individual liberty has been the Rule of Law. In its narrowest sense it means that government must be government by laws as opposed to government by the arbitrary will of an individual or group of individuals. It means that there must be some formal, agreed upon way of making and proclaiming laws. Usually a Constitution, written or unwritten, prescribes this way. Frequently it means that laws should be the result of deliberation by elected representatives of the people. It is opposed to government by whim or chance, by preternatural forces, by consulting oracles or astrologers or by other irrational means. It presupposes some form of rational discussion and deliberation among those charged by the Constitution with the responsibility for making laws.

A second implication of the Rule of Law is the conviction that no one is superior to the law, that the law is binding upon the ruler as well as upon the ruled. A third implication is that the law must be impartially administered to all. Usually, provisions are made for the existence of an independent judiciary, the function of which is to administer the law fairly. Provisions are sometimes made for holding administrative officials accountable for their actions, especially when those actions are alleged to infringe basic human rights.

A fourth implication is that the content of the law should be reasonable and just. The law should not infringe any of the fundamental rights of the citizen, and the content of the law should be defensible in a forum of reasonable men. Indeed, it is one of the principles of the Rule of Law that those who make the law should be called upon to defend and justify it before the community for whom it is intended. In short, the Rule of Law imposes both procedural and substantive limitations, in the interest of individual liberty and justice, upon the lawmakers.

What will appear as reasonable in any particular community will depend in part upon the nature of the consensus prevailing in that community about the nature of man, the nature of justice, the rights and duties of individuals. These in turn will depend upon religious and cultural institutions and beliefs. The political process is concerned with attempting to reconcile rival claims and interests, with integrating the conflicting points of view and interests for the purpose of formulating some common policy. As such, the political process necessarily implies both the need for and the desirability of reaching compromises. But genuine compromises can take place only within the context of mutually shared interests and values. When there is no community of interests and values, there is no possibility of compromise and hence no possibility of politics. If a procedural way of doing things constitutes no limit to what is done, it is doubtful whether any procedure, as procedure, is a guarantee of the procedure itself. Individuals will adhere to a particular political procedure only as long as they recognize some good in it. And that good must, of necessity, be derived from something beyond the procedure itself. No government, in short, could be founded upon man's love of compromise. We make compromises, when we do, not because we love to compromise, but because we value some things more than the things we are asked to compromise. The possibility of compromise depends not only upon the availability of a mediating procedure, but upon the willingness of individuals to subordinate their subjective interests to the common good. Without an affirmation of a community of values and interests, without the willingness to give up some particular interest in the interest of the common good, mediation is an impossibility.

The Rule of Law is not to be interpreted, although it sometimes has been so interpreted, as a conservative defense of the *status quo*. The Rule of Law is not opposed to change, and may demand change when such change is essential to the realization of social justice. It is significant that the English Bill of Rights of 1689, the Virginia Bill of Rights of 1776, and the French Declaration of the Rights of Man and of the Citizen of 1789 were all products of revolution. Western societies have long recognized the legitimacy and even the necessity at times of revolutionary activity in order to obtain more just conditions. At the same time, the English and American Revolutions of the seventeenth and eighteenth centuries had as part of their objective the establishment of political institutions and processes that would hopefully replace the necessity for violent revolution with means of effecting revolutionary changes peacefully. It is one of the claims of those who defend modern constitutional government that it does in fact provide opportunities for peaceful revolutionary change in the realization of greater social justice. The British Labor Party has successfully secured a greater measure of social and economic justice for the citizens of Great Britain without resort to violent revolution, and within the framework of existing political institutions.

At the present time, the United States is experiencing a legitimate demand on the part of its Negro citizens for the recognition of equal rights and opportunities. It required acts of civil disobedience on the part of both white and Negro citizens to dramatize the legitimacy of these demands, to emphasize the injustice of prevailing practice. The response of the United States Congress in the form of the Civil Rights Act of 1964 and the earlier decision of the United States Supreme Court in the Brown case were attempts to effect peaceful change within the framework of existing political institutions. Whether the Negro citizen of the United States can, in fact, achieve substantial justice within the framework of existing political institutions will be a test of the claims put forth in behalf of democratic, constitutional government. At the same time, it is not within the power or capacity of any government to assure *perfect* justice to everyone—such justice is found only in the Kingdom of God. The love and justice of God stand always as a reminder to man of his own imperfection, as a goal to be prayed for and worked for, but always it is as much judgment as aspiration. This is never to be used as an excuse for condoning injustice or for inactivity in promoting and seeking love and justice, but it is a necessary lesson in humility if we are not to confuse the fallen creature with the perfect Creator. It is one thing to aspire with God's help to do his will here on earth; it is quite another to identify one's own will with that of God.

### The Free Society as Opposed to a Closed Society

What are some of the characteristics of a free society, and how does such a society differ from the totalitarian society?

In a free society, no effort is made to coerce or "manufacture" a consensus. The politician and the government are limited by the need to persuade the citizenry of the rightness, desirability and reasonableness of what they want to do. They are checked, in short, by "public opinion." They often can and must seek to lead public opinion, to change it, but they are limited in the methods they can employ to do so. Totalitarian regimes seek to manufacture a kind of consent for their rule by the extensive use of propaganda, and the government possesses a monopoly of all the means of mass communication. In a free society there is no such monopoly of control. While propaganda is not unknown in a free society, there are competing sources from which this propaganda emanates. It does not, moreover, all have the same message or purpose. When propaganda fails or falters, totalitarian regimes resort to terror, the secret police and the concentration camp. Free societies seek to protect their citizens from arbitrary arrests and imprisonment and generally have no category of crimes that can be labeled "political." Free societies do not employ secret police.

Totalitarian regimes are usually governed by a single political party, which claims a monopoly of political truth and justice. Free societies believe not only in the desirability but in the necessity of rival political parties. The British have institutionalized this necessity by officially recognizing and paying out of public funds a Leader of the Opposition, a position second only to that of the Prime Minister. It is thought that only by encouraging loyal opposition will the government in power be made responsible for its actions. Another function of rival political parties is to encourage public debate on questions of political policy, to formulate opposing political platforms and to present the voters with a genuine choice of representatives.

Through the party system, and by means of periodic elections, free societies seek to keep the representatives responsible to the people. This implies that no arbitrary barriers will be raised to holding office or to voting, that elections will be by secret ballot and that the ballots will be counted fairly. While totalitarian regimes frequently hold "elections," these tend to resemble plebiscites rather than genuine elections. Usually, only a slate of candidates is presented to the voters, and no genuine choice is possible. Opposition to the government in power is often labeled treason and dealt with as such.

Totalitarian regimes frequently espouse an official ideology with chiliastic claims—they depict themselves as embodying the "perfect" society of mankind. Thus they claim for themselves the functions of both church and state and tend to equate a particular political ideology with the "truth" about man and his destiny. They tend to view politics as a form of spiritual salvation. Free societies take a less exalted view of politics. While they think that government can help to provide the conditions necessary for the enjoyment of a good life for man, they do not think that governments can define that good. They do not expect the "perfect society" to be instituted by government. Rather, they look upon the task of government and politics as one of "finding proximate solutions to insoluble problems." While totalitarian governments claim to transcend policies, free societies recognize the perennial necessity for politics.

Free societies generally acknowledge the desirability of dividing and diffusing political power, while totalitarian regimes want to centralize it. Some free societies have embraced some form of federalism, while others have adopted means of developing power upon lower units of government. Totalitarian regimes sometimes have the form of federal government but not the spirit.

Totalitarian regimes cannot usually tolerate autonomous societies and activities within their orbit. Free societies are characteristically known for the large number of autonomous associations and activities that are found within them, for example: the family, independent schools, churches, labor unions, various kinds of youth groups, business associations, independent cultural groups, a wide variety of newspapers and periodicals. Totalitarian regimes seek to amalgamate all these kinds of associations and activities into one legitimate form. All human activities become, at least potentially, political activities in a totalitarian regime, subject, as a consequence, to political supervision and control. Thus, the question whether a particular kind of music, art or poetry is sound or not becomes a political question in a totalitarian regime.

While the free societies of the world rightly prize the safeguards of individual freedom that they have developed over many centuries, they are sometimes in danger of mistaking that freedom for an end in itself. They have sometimes been so absorbed in protecting individual freedom from governmental control that they have lost sight of the fact that freedom is not only a freedom from something, but a freedom for something more ultimate than freedom itself. It was one of the illusions of nineteenth-century liberalism that freedom could be an end in itself. We came very soon to see how unworkable this was in the economic sphere of life, and now we are called upon to discard the ideology of *laissez faire, laissez aller* in other realms of life as well. We have come, under the tutelage of experience, to understand that government is not necessarily a foe of freedom, but often its primary promoter and protector.

The principle of freedom alone cannot provide us with the necessary standards for evaluating public policies, for in the context of persons and interests, which is the heart of politics, we have inevitably to ask *whose* freedom shall we protect in order to do *what?* The word freedom is often invoked as a kind of incantation. The real problem emerges when we cease to invoke the abstraction and ask: Whose freedom to do what? Freedom justifies itself in just actions, in promoting a good way of life. It degenerates into license and anarchy when it is regarded as an end in itself.

Freedom must lead to creative activity, or perish. If freedom is interpreted simply to mean "Leave me in peace," if it cannot see beyond the defense of existing political boundaries and the preservation of the *status quo,* if it cannot enlist and support the energies of those peoples throughout the world who are determined upon revolutionary change in the interest of justice, it cannot long survive. Nikolai Berdyaev put the matter simply when he wrote: "Liberty will be saved by its union with Truth—it cannot be saved by indifference to Truth. Freedom means not only freedom of choice, but choice itself. . . ."

A prominent intellectual of the twentieth century speaks of man as one who is "condemned to be free," and no doubt he voices the anxious insecurity of many individuals in the free societies of the world for whom the responsibility of using their freedom is becoming increasingly an intolerable burden. In a meaningless universe without guideposts and goals, freedom is indeed an intolerable burden. But for the Christian, freedom is both a gift and an opportunity. Bishop Stephen Bayne has put it well:

The Incarnation is really an essay in freedom. . . . Mankind is too much given to weeping over the cross. He does not intend that we shall be flabby and precious in our devotion. This is the act of the strongest and freest of men, who freely chooses even this supreme obedience in choosing above all things that the Father's will should be done. This is the Christ of the gospels—this Person who from first to last shows no fear of freedom, asks no favours from it, accepts it, uses it, fulfils it. Whether he is alone in the wilderness choosing the manner of his obedience, or in Galilee teaching men how to live within the matrix of their freedom, or supremely acting out this freedom in the most final terms of life and death, the impact of Christ is the same. He is, for all humanity which will follow him, the supreme teacher and exemplar of what it is to be free.

# THE POWERS OF GOVERNMENT AND THE CLAIMS OF HUMAN FREEDOM

by Chandran D. S. Devanesen
and M. Abel (India)

*The Dynamic Role of the State in Promoting Human Freedom*

"No human life," says Hannah Arendt, "not even the life of the hermit in nature's wilderness, is possible without a world which directly or indirectly testifies to the presence of other human beings." This means in positive terms that man is a social being. He cannot live for long unto himself in isolation. He is not self-sufficient in satisfying his wants and material comforts, and he depends on others for the realization of his material and moral well-being. His intellectual curiosity craves the exchange of ideas, the enrichment of his personal experience by sharing in the experiences of others. Thus man's inclinations and desires—physical, intellectual and spiritual—irresistibly impel him to cooperate and associate with his fellow human beings and to join them to form a society.

This is not, however, the whole story. Man's cooperative social feelings and gregarious instincts are neutralized by his strong individualism and self-centeredness. He has his own desires, ambitions, appetites and, above all, his own will. Further, man's personal and individual interests and ambitions are so much stronger than his cooperative feelings and social affections that he often considers society as a means not only to develop his faculties and individual personality to the full, but also to impose his will on other members of society who are motivated by similar desires and aspirations.

The conflict between man's cooperative social feelings and his self-centered individualism gives rise to differences and rivalries between individuals as well as between groups of individuals. If these different and conflicting "pulls" are not to disrupt society and jeopardize the security and freedom of individuals, there must be some device by which they can be balanced and harmonized. As Professor Laski says, "Men move differently to the attainment of conflicting desires; a coercive authority is therefore necessary to define the terms on which the movement may legitimately proceed, to lay down the rules of permissible social behaviour."

Government is the device by which the conflicting individual wills and interests are harmonized and the social existence of the individuals rendered possible. It is expected to function as an umpire and to ensure that in the competition between individuals and groups in the pursuit of their own interests no one gets an unfair advantage. Thus, while man's social feelings and instincts make government desirable and possible, his selfishness, greed, ambition and avarice make it necessary and inevitable. So, to use the theological terminology of Alan Booth:

Government is in principle a good thing, and in biblical terms a high calling. If it exists because of human sin, then we have to understand sin in terms not simply of our criminal tendencies, but of our inbred desire to get our own way. Living together, we cannot entirely do so, and the only alternative to allowing the physically strongest to have everything he wishes is to establish some method of arbitration and authority, however imperfect, to make of a multitude of conflicting wills some pattern of coherence.[1]

Thus government must be regarded as a social organism, as the indispensable and beneficial means of human coordination and as a divinely ordained institution through which "God provides for all men to see a kind of justice which is a true image of the Righteousness of God."

In protecting and preserving and in functioning as a divinely

---

[1] *Christians and Power Politics*. London: SCM Press, 1961, p. 45.

ordained social institution to secure freedom, dignity and justice for all men, government possesses a monopoly of coercive power and the means to exercise it. But since this coercive power is ultimately exercised by sinful men, government is often vulnerable to the temptation to exploit its coercive power to idealize its imperfect notions, procedures and practices of justice and to claim complete sovereignty over the total life of men, which belongs only to God. It is often in danger of succumbing to the temptation to deify itself and to demand the total and absolute allegiance and loyalty of men exclusively to itself and to its ephemeral institutions and procedures. Whenever this happens, government, instead of functioning as God's instrument of justice and righteousness, degenerates into an engine of social injustice, oppression and tyranny, violating the dignity of the human being and denying the freedom and sanctity of the human spirit and personality.

So it should be realized that, while the government should not be denied its right and duty to utilize the power at its command in the cause of freedom and justice, it should be restrained from abusing that power to usurp the sovereignty and Lordship of God over all men and to liquidate the freedom and dignity of individual human beings by claiming and exercising absolute authority to direct the whole life of the individual and the community. In other words, the government should not only be enabled to control the governed but it should also be obliged to control itself, so that the freedom and dignity of men will not be in jeopardy. This means that the government should be neither too strong for the liberties of its own subjects nor too weak to maintain its own existence. How are the powers of government to be reconciled with the claims of human freedom?

So long as men believed in the divine origin of temporal power and tacitly acquiesced in authoritarian regimes, they were indifferent to the problem of drawing a line between state control and individual liberty. But ever since the rise of the secular view of life, an unending struggle for a just equilibrium between political authority and human freedom has been going on. The Protestant Reformation, surcharged with the spirit of the Renaissance, undermined the moral basis of authoritarianism and paved the way for the emergence of the self-conscious individual—an individual conscious of his distinctive personality and with a religious conscience free from servitude to Rome. But this self-conscious individual soon suffered an eclipse under the enlightened despotism of the autocratic monarchs of the national states of Europe in the seventeenth and eighteenth centuries. This monarchical absolutism of the nation-state resulted in religious intolerance and persecution, suppression of individual freedom and denial of justice to the vast majority of the people. However, the religious wars that were fought in the name of tolerance and freedom of worship, backed up by the secular nationalist theories of the constitutionalists and by the Lockean doctrine of the fundamental rights of man, succeeded in liberating the individual from the absolute authority of the state. Subsequently, the American War of Independence and the French Revolution, which were inspired by the political philosophy of Rousseau, Voltaire and other prophets of the eighteenth century Enlightenment, greatly helped in restoring to man his individuality, freedom and dignity. Finally, the liberal political philosophy of the nineteenth century accepted and confirmed the free and egalitarian individual as the primary and fundamental unit of the state.

Contrary to the widely prevalent misconception, the liberal doctrine of individual freedom does not imply an attitude of *laissez faire* on the part of the state. Even Mill, the most ardent champion of liberalism, recognized the need for state action "as soon as any part of a person's conduct affects prejudicially the interests of others." But vested interests in the capitalist societies of Europe twisted the doctrines of liberalism in such a way as to elevate the liberty of the individual to so high a pedestal that in its sacred name the capitalists exploited, sweated and starved the workers, the powerful oppressed the weak, the rich grew richer and the poor became poorer, while the state remained a passive spectator of this denial of justice and freedom to millions of individuals.

Today, as a consequence of technological developments and the progressive integration of social and economic life, power is becoming concentrated in fewer and smaller centers. Consequently, the obstacles to individual freedom have become all-pervasive and more formidable than in the nineteenth century. Therefore, state action, in the interests of liberty, especially of the weaker sections of the community, has become more necessary and on a larger scale now than Mill imagined. The problem in a modern society, therefore, is not merely one of defining the limits of the authority of the state or the powers of the government over the individual, as Mill formulated them. It includes the much more complex and difficult task of investing the state and the government with necessary and adequate powers to enable them to play a positive and dynamic role in creating the conditions in which liberty can flourish and in which an individual can develop and realize his personality in a given type of society.

## India's Struggle for an Open Society and Democratic Politics

In India and other new states of Asia and Africa, the solution to the problem of reconciling the powers of government with the claims of human freedom must be sought in the context of the historical needs and aspirations of their peoples and in the context of their peculiar social structures and cultural values.

The people of India are animated by a strong desire to build a dynamic, democratic, modern state on the basis of a well-integrated national community, with the newly emerging free and self-conscious individual as the fundamental and basic unit of all political and social institutions. The Constitution of the Republic of India in general and its Preamble in particular declare that independent India should aim at establishing a just, free and egalitarian society of free and equal individuals in the place of the caste-centered, status-ridden and hierarchically structured traditional society that denied the freedom and dignity of the individual and his personality. The Preamble to the Constitution clearly enjoins the Republic of India "to secure to all [its] citizens [a] Justice, social, economic and political; [b] Liberty of thought, expression, belief, faith and worship; and [c] Equality of status and opportunity"; and [d] to promote among all the citizens "Fraternity, assuring the dignity of the individual and unity of the nation." As a result of these constitutional injunctions and directives, much of the political process in India has come to pivot around the heroic effort to keep aligned two powerful but divergent motives—the desire for a strong, efficient, dynamic, modern state on the one hand and the demand of the individual citizen for justice, liberty, equality and dignity on the other.

However, beneath the surface of this apparent conflict of desires, there runs an undercurrent of intimate relationship and compatibility between the two. A powerful and positive government is neither incompatible with nor malignant to the self-consciousness and freedom of the individual as long as it respects the claims of the individual for personal significance and endeavors to create a congenial atmosphere in which the individual can realize social and economic progress, higher standards of living, a more effective political order and greater social justice. In fact, in the peculiar social and cultural context of India, the need for a strong and powerful government can hardly be exaggerated.

One of the major problems that make such a government necessary is that of national integration. The existence of only minimum governmental restraints on individual freedom in a country like Great Britain may be due to the fact that the British people are integrated into a national community and have become so well acclimatized to the requirements of a national community that social cooperation and social obedience have become almost national habits with them. In the words of A. D. Lindsay (Lord Lindsay of Birker):

England's social conformity is the spontaneous achievement of individuals. . . . The individual has been socialized in such a measure that in all essential manifestations he spontaneously reacts to society and the interests maintaining it. . . . The Englishman's dictator is installed in his heart. Authority does not need to put him in leading strings because it can depend on his using his freedom only to the extent that society can bear.

But such mutual good will, voluntary agreement and spontaneous cooperation and cohesion among different segments of the population do not obtain in India at present. The primordial sentiments and attachments of people based on race, religion, region or language are so strong that they are unwilling to surrender their narrow and parochial identifications and loyalties in favor of a spontaneous commitment and voluntary obedience to an overarching civil order. Such primordial attachments discourage people from identifying themselves with the larger national community but encourage them to assert their narrow, parochial group interests against the interests of the nation. Unlike civil discontent, which threatens only revolt against the existing government, disaffection fed by primordial urges threatens partition, irredentism or a redrawing of the very boundaries of the state. Primordial discontent often expresses itself in India in such extreme and unconstitutional forms as burning the national flag and copies of the Constitution, and in demanding the division of the country into several independent states. In such a situation, when people are unwilling to respond spontaneously to the demands of national integration, government has to "move them towards unity by force or mass psychology or a mixture between the two." Therefore, whenever fissiparous forces threaten the security and integrity of the nation, government should have necessary and adequate power to cut down the primordial sentiments to their right size and reduce them to civil order by invoking and enforcing measures like the Preventive Detention Act, Defence of India Rules, National Security Ordinances and Suspension of the Habeas Corpus Act, which impose restrictions on individual freedom.

A positive and powerful government is needed in India not only for maintaining the unity and integrity of the nation, but to enable the individual citizen to enjoy all those fundamental rights and liberties that are granted and guaranteed to him by the Constitution. The Constitution contains a chapter which affirms and guarantees the basic rights of the citizen. Most of the human rights enshrined in the Universal Declaration of Human Rights find a place in the Chapter on Fundamental Rights in the Indian Constitution. These rights are inalienable, and every human being is entitled to enjoy them in order to maintain his freedom and human dignity. They assure to each individual citizen equality before the law and equality of opportunity and nondiscrimination in matters of public employment, irrespective of religion, race, caste, sex or place of birth. They categorically declare that no person shall be deprived of his life or personal liberty except according to procedure established by law. Above all, they guarantee the right of freedom of speech and expression, the right to form associations or unions, to acquire, hold or dispose of property, to practice any profession or to carry on any occupation, trade or business, the right to freedom of conscience and freedom to profess, practice and propagate religion and the right to one's own culture and to study in any educational institution.

This declaration of fundamental rights embodied in the Constitution no doubt imposes severe restraints on the tendency of the government to encroach on the freedom of the individual. But it would be very naïve to assume that a mere declaration of fundamental rights, without striving to fulfill and create certain other necessary conditions, suffices to safeguard the freedom of the individual. Any serious concern for the liberty of the individual should be related to certain other larger questions, like equality, justice and economic well-being. It is rather ironical to speak of the freedom of a person who is constantly haunted by the fear of want and starvation, and who is reduced to a subhuman level of existence by an unjust social order based upon the caste system. Therefore, in order to make the rights and liberties enshrined in the Constitution meaningful and substantial to the average man, he must first of all be freed from the want and fear that are inherent in India's underdeveloped economy and oppressive social system. It means that the traditional social structures and cultural values of India, which are by and large inimical to the freedom of the individual and to the dignity of the human being, must be changed. The present underdeveloped economy should be developed to attain the "take-off stage" and self-sustaining growth by effecting the technological revolution of industrialization. In short, the reality and the substance of individual freedom depend on the successful implementation of a program for the modernization of society and of the economy of India. Modernization is a difficult and complex process, involving fundamental and far-reaching changes in the existing way of life. But to effect any real change, such as large-scale industrialization or land reform, especially in the face of resistance from the defenders of the *status quo,* a high degree of governmental control is necessary if society is not to disintegrate into anarchy. So, in India and other developing countries of Asia and Africa, government needs to be armed with adequate powers to enable it to remove all social and cultural obstacles to individual liberty and to play a positive and dynamic role in creating certain favorable social and economic conditions that are necessary if individual liberty is to flourish and to enable the individual to realize his best self, to develop his personality and to enjoy a greater measure of social justice and equality.

Accordingly, the rulers of independent India are endeavoring to create a welfare state based on economic and social planning, in order to remove glaring economic inequalities, to abolish privilege, to establish equality of opportunity, to raise standards of living and to provide social security to every citizen—all of which are necessary measures for the full enjoyment of individual freedom and the realization of human dignity. But by its very nature, the welfare state has to interfere with all aspects of the life of an individual. It has to interfere even with such intimate and private aspects as family relationships, marriage and inheritance, not to speak of its almost complete control over the economic life of the people. Such a development is necessary and unavoidable. However, constant vigilance is required on the part of the citizens of a welfare state in order to safeguard their personal freedom against the encroachments of a powerful and positive government. They must ensure that all the enormous and highly concentrated power of the government is utilized to promote social good and to enhance the opportunities for all the citizens of the state to realize freedom, equality and justice.

The liberal democratic tradition built up in India during the last hundred years, beginning with the Renaissance of the nineteenth century, has been so far quite resilient and resourceful in responding to the challenges of the positive and powerful government of a welfare state to the liberty of the individual. In many of the new states of Asia and Africa, excessive reliance on authority and charismatic leadership, indifference to the rights of the individual, dogmatic adherence to totalitarian political ideologies and the absence of a secular tradition of political thought have caused the collapse of open societies and democratic polities. But in India the story is different. A century of cultural contact with the West, faith in liberal values of life cultivated through western education, lessons learned through participation in the administration and the Rule of Law and the inspiration derived from the various social reform movements have all stood India in good stead in resisting the tempting appeals of totalitarianism from both the rightist and the leftist parties. Thanks to the existence of an independent judiciary, a free press, a middle class that is politically conscious and articulate and a network of voluntary agencies like opposition parties, trade unions, chambers of commerce, cooperative societies and minorities that are zealous in protecting their religious and cultural freedom, the democratic polity of India may claim to possess the necessary dynamism and potentialities to evolve into a genuinely open society.

It is, however, difficult to say anything confidently and categorically about the future of individual freedom in India. The legal protection available from the processes and procedures of parliamentary democracy is not sufficient to safeguard human freedom. Vigilance on the part of the public can alone check the tendency of the government to encroach upon the freedom and rights of the individual. But public interest in the maintenance of individual freedom and rights is somewhat lacking in India. Though the press is free, it rarely concerns itself with what Mill called "social tyranny more formidable than many kinds of political oppression." Trade unions and opposition parties are too much concerned with immediate gains to take an interest in fundamental issues of human freedom. Public opinion asserts itself only when issues touching deep-seated emotions are involved, as was evident in the agitations for linguistic states and during the period immediately after the *débâcle* in the North East Frontier Agency. But it is mute when the freedom and rights of an individual or of a weak section of the community are in jeopardy. Public protests against governmental restrictions on freedom of thought and expression in the form of the proscription and confiscation of the copies of "undesirable" books are conspicuous by their absence. For instance, when Aubrey Menen's book, *Rama Retold,* was proscribed by the government of India on grounds of public security and of the maintenance of law and order, the action of the government passed almost unnoticed and without criticism. Likewise, in 1957, when the agitation for Samyukta Maharashtra was at its height, a well-known Maratha historian, Professor N. R. Phatak, was forced by a mob to abandon his effort to deliver a public lecture on the Sepoy Mutiny of 1857, since his evaluation was offensive to "patriotic" sentiment. But nothing was said by way of protest against that mob violence either by the press or by public leaders. This kind of lack of public interest in safeguarding the fundamental rights of an individual or of a weak group does not augur well for the future of individual liberty. As J. S. Mill put it:

A people may prefer a free Government, but if from indolence, or carelessness, or cowardice, or want of public spirit, they are unequal to the exertions necessary for preserving it; if they will not fight for it when directly attacked; if they can be deluded by the artifices used to cheat them out of it; if by momentary discouragement, or temporary panic or a fit of enthusiasm for an individual, they can be induced to lay their liberties at the feet of even a great man, or trust him with powers which enable him to subvert their institutions—in all these cases they are unfit for liberty.

Besides an enlightened and assertive public opinion, the future of human freedom in a democratic welfare state requires that the individual citizen should participate intelligently and responsibly in the working of the state. Democracy in India has to struggle against the background of an apolitical tradition, political indifference and ignorance and civic unconsciousness. Dynasties came to power and perished, empires rose and fell, yet the common man was blissfully ignorant of all these changes. Such political apathy and indifference, though understandable in a monarchy or an oligarchy, expose democracy to the encroachments of dictatorships and totalitarian regimes. Therefore, the individual, in order to safeguard his freedom and rights, should not only be very diligent and zealous about his franchise and his participation in elections but must also contribute his mite to "the cooperative thinking" through voluntary organizations and must create the necessary background of ideas and policies for a democratic state. He must be supremely and actively concerned with the work of voluntary organizations like trade unions, chambers of commerce, research institutions and academic conferences, as well as with the work of specialized bodies that devote themselves to the examination of social, economic and political questions, and to the development and popularization of ideas. Only such concern for and responsible participation in the democratic process and in the work of academic, functional and voluntary agencies and organizations can render the freedom of the human spirit and the dignity of the individual invulnerable to the seductive appeals of totalitarian tendencies like the idealization of the nation-state, identification of the ruling political party with the state, the personality cult and fanatical political ideologies.

### Threats to Individual Liberty in Developing Nations

A more insidious danger lurks in the possibility of the government denying a minority the right to make its voice heard on public affairs. This danger arises whenever a person or the party in power identifies the nation and the state with himself or itself and equates unpopular opinions held by the minorities or by opposition parties with antistate and antinational activities. This tendency to deify the nation and to identify it with a particular leader or party is quite strong in the new states of Africa and Asia. For example, President Nkrumah of Ghana has written:

The Convention People's Party is Ghana and Ghana is the Convention People's Party.... There are some persons, both staff and students (of the University College of Ghana), who mistakenly believe that the words "academic freedom" carry with them a spirit of hostility to our Party and the Government.... The Convention People's Party cannot allow this confusion of academic freedom with disloyalty and anti-government ideas.

Likewise, Sekou Touré, of Guinea, has declared: "In our eyes there are no soldiers, no civil servants, no intellectuals; they are only supporters of the Party." The Guided Democracy of Indonesia and other single-party regimes are founded on this philosophy. In India, though there is not such real danger, the Indian National Congress has now and then tended to blur the line between the state and the party and to identify the nation with itself. The consequence of this dangerous tendency is that those who do not conform to the policies of the ruling party or toe the line of the leader are branded as traitors and outsiders. Further, the ruling party tries to exploit such a situation to create a state of emotional excitement and mass hysteria in which criticism can easily be stifled, public opinion bypassed, the press muzzled, enthusiasm for the party's regime manipulated, and all opposition liquidated.

It is unwise to deny freedom to express an opinion simply because it is not in tune with the belief or opinion held by the majority that happens to be in power. For such a denial amounts to the denial of the very personality of the individual and to reducing life to a dull, uncreative uniformity and rigid regimentation. In the words of Mahatma Gandhi:

No society can possibly be built on a denial of individual freedom. It is contrary to the nature of man. Just as a man will not grow horns or a tail, so he will not exist as a man if he has no mind of his own. In reality, even those who do not believe in the liberty of the individual believe in their own. . . . If the individual ceases to count, what is left of society?

Further, such a denial deprives the government of an opportunity to correct its errors and to bring its policies into closer accord with "what is permanently true." As Professor Laski put it: "Governments that are wise can always learn more from the criticism of their opponents than they can hope to discover in the eulogies of their friends. When they stifle that criticism, they prepare the way for their own destruction." Therefore, the true measure of individual liberty consists in the ability of the government or of the majority in power to tolerate, respect and accommodate (if necessary) a minority opinion opposed to its own. Therefore, it is essential not merely to emphasize freedom of speech but to uphold the right to express and maintain freely an unpopular opinion. Since a minority of today has every chance of becoming the majority of tomorrow, it should have freedom to convert itself into a majority by constitutional and peaceful methods of public debate and persuasion. It is undemocratic and contrary to the notion of individual freedom to suppress and silence the voice of a minority on the ground that it offends the feelings and beliefs of the majority.

In this context, the freedom of an individual to profess, practice and propagate his religion needs to be specially emphasized. The individual needs religious liberty and freedom of conscience in order to realize the work and love of God for him and to understand the destiny and purpose for which he is created. Therefore, to deny religious freedom to an individual, says Alan Booth, "is to truncate the true nature of man, and to deny the most fundamental and liberating of human rights. It is moreover to try to cut off at the source the means whereby God himself speaks to states and communities in judgment and mercy." [2]

The need to affirm and safeguard the individual's religious freedom can hardly be overestimated in the context of a multireligious society like that of India. Indian leaders, in government as well as outside, have often emphasized this need. The late Rajendra Prasad, as chairman of the Constituent Assembly, assured all the minorities that "they will receive fair and just treatment and there will be no discrimination in any form against them. Their religion, their culture and their language are safe and they will enjoy all the rights and privileges of citizenship, and will be expected in their turn to render loyalty to the country in which they live and to its Constitution." The Constitution, recognizing freedom of religion as one of the fundamental rights of the citizen, rightly affirms and guarantees to the individual freedom of conscience and the right freely to profess, practice and propagate religion. It also upholds the equality of all citizens before the law and their right to equal protection by the law, irrespective of their religious convictions and affiliations. Equality of opportunity in matters relating to employment or to appointment to any office under the state is also granted and guaranteed to all citizens irrespective of their religious professions and practices. Further, according to the provisions of the Constitution, every religious denomination has the right to establish and maintain its own institutions for religious and charitable purposes. All religious minorities "have the right to establish and administer educational institutions of their choice," and "the state shall not, in granting aid to educational institutions, discriminate against any educational institution on the ground that it is under the management of a minority, whether based on religion or language."

This is indeed an impressive array of safeguards for the religious liberty of the individual. But certain problems and difficulties have arisen with regard to the right to propagate religion. "Propagation of faith" forms an integral part of religions like Christianity and Islam. Because of its eclecticism and syncretism, some followers of Hinduism have been unable fully to appreciate and understand

---

[2] *Ibid.*, p. 49.

this right. As a result, adherents of missionary religions have been prevented on several occasions from preaching their faith to others. So, in order to enable those people who believe in the propagation of their faith to enjoy religious freedom fully, government and the majority communities in Asia should understand and practice the concept of religious liberty according to the letter and spirit of the Universal Declaration of Human Rights, which affirms that "Every one has the right to freedom of thought, conscience and religion; this right includes freedom to change his religion or belief either alone or in community with others, and in private or public, to manifest his religion or belief in teaching, practice, worship and observance." The missionary religions, in turn, should not employ any forms of evangelism that wound the feelings or violate the dignity and personal rights of others.

By far the most powerful threat to human freedom and dignity in India lies in her social system, which makes it extremely difficult for several millions of people to live as free and self-respecting human beings. No doubt, the Constitution, by declaring untouchability illegal and punishable under law, aims at removing the dead weight of caste and at demolishing artificial social barriers erected between man and man. But after all, the Constitution must be worked by men. As Professor Laski says: "It is the proud spirit of citizens, less than the letter of law, that is their most real safeguard." The constitutional provisions intended for the eradication of caste and untouchability may remain as ineffective as any doctrinal or theoretical safeguards, for two main reasons. First, the caste system has so greatly demoralized several millions of human beings that they lack the courage to feel that they are entitled to enjoy the fundamental rights granted and guaranteed to them by the Constitution. Second, because of their sentimental attachment to this traditional social system, caste Hindus, especially in the rural areas, still find it difficult to accept and move freely among men of lower castes.

Time alone can show whether the process of democratic liberalization will gain enough momentum to abolish caste and untouchability in the near future. But one thing is sure. Unless there is real penitence and an inward conversion of the heart on the part of the people who have to give effect to these constitutional provisions, the eradication of caste and untouchability is inconceivable. The situation requires men like Ram Mohan Roy, Ranade, Gandhi, Nehru and Vinoba, who could go about with a crusading zeal exhorting the downtrodden people to cultivate and develop the spirit of self-confidence and self-reliance. There must be a new evaluation of man as man, based upon the sanctity of his personality, which can shatter the sentimental standards and sunder the bonds of caste. Reason must revolt against irrational beliefs and customs. In order to effect such a psychological revolution and spiritual purification, the creative spirit and dynamism of the nineteenth century Asian Renaissance must be recaptured and should be made to animate the whole of India's cultural life. To that end, the church in India, which played such a creative and valuable role in the nineteenth century Renaissance movement in Asia, has a unique contribution to make.

# 12

# THE SEARCH FOR CONSENSUS DEMOCRACY IN THE NEW NATIONS

by PETER D. LATUIHAMALLO (Indonesia)

ONE of the major developments in Asia immediately after the Second World War was the emergence of a number of nation-states, which achieved their independence either by force or by a gradual transfer of the Administration from the colonial powers. This was accompanied by the withdrawal of the western powers from their former colonial territories in Asia, thus putting an end to the "Vasco da Gama" era of Asian history, which had lasted for 450 years.[1]

These newly independent states have to face new political problems, pertaining to the foundations of the state, the form of government, social welfare, international relations and the ultimate aim of the new nations. It must also be noted that, although the colonial powers have withdrawn from their territories in Asia, their return in various forms—intervention, subversion, new colonialism or military pacts—may endanger the peace, stability and integrity of the free Asian nations. The most pressing question for the new nations is how to achieve a stable and dynamic government. In what way should the country be ordered and governed so that freedom, justice and peace are guaranteed for all its citizens? What

---

[1] See K. M. PANIKKAR: *Asia and Western Dominance*. London: Hillary House, 1959.

role has it to play in safeguarding and promoting world peace and security?

In their search for a stable and dynamic government, the Asian people have made a number of choices. Some have adopted parliamentary democracy of the type that exists in most western countries. The communist countries have set up a people's democratic dictatorship. Pakistan is following what it calls "basic democracy" in preference to "liberal democracy" of the western type, while in Indonesia it is "guided democracy" that promises a stable government.

In the midst of these changes in Asia there stands the church of Jesus Christ. The church is part of the Asian world in which it lives and functions. Its task is to proclaim the Word of God, through unity, witness and service, for the salvation of mankind and of the world. While remaining obedient to its Lord, the church has to determine its relation to the state and to society, and to participate in the search for criteria by which to judge the various options of society.

### The Modern Asian Revolution: Its Nature and Goals

The Asian nations that have achieved independence since the Second World War are also seeking to transform their colonial society into a modern community. Such a change would require a revolution (*Umgestaltung von Grund aus*) unprecedented in history. That revolution and its objectives can be understood only in the light of capitalism, imperialism and nationalism.

The accumulation and concentration of capital in nineteenth-century Europe were achieved largely through the exploitation of Asian colonies. At the same time, capitalistic depressions have brought economic disorder and misery to Asians, the consequences of which are still felt today. The economic system of capitalism has thus raised the basic question of human survival, and has led to the alienation (*Verelendung*) of the masses in Asia.

Since it is the prime economic system of the colonial powers, capitalism has always been associated with imperialism, which is not only concerned with the forceful occupation of countries and the subjugation of their peoples, but is also inspired by mercantile motives. This was particularly true of British imperialism in India. Again, while the aim of the European conquest of Asia in the eighteenth century was trade, in the nineteenth and twentieth centuries it was mainly investment. Thus, imperialism also exports capital to the colonies.

All this had distressing effects upon the local people. In Indonesia, for example, indigenous middle-class enterprises were killed by the Dutch *Finanz-Kapital,* which set up an economic system that benefited only a small part of society, leaving the mass of the people in poverty. The regulations for land tenure drawn up by the colonial government were disadvantageous to the people because of the low rents; and labor on the land was cheap. Land thus became a means of exploitation, and the people the victims of exploitation.

As a result, relationships between westerners and Asians became unhealthy. Nationalist movements spread throughout Asia, to arouse the masses and involve them in the fight for justice and freedom. In this situation, the Christian conscience could not remain silent. When freedom, justice and human dignity are violated, the church is compelled to offer Christian witness and service. Yet the action of the church in the past was largely powerless, partly because the church was too much under the patronage of the colonial power.

Asian nationalism has both a positive and a negative aspect. Positively, it aims to achieve independence in order to build a new society based on freedom and justice. Negatively, this involves the complete abolition of colonial rule. This negative aspect is a necessary evil, since colonial powers do not easily grant independence of their own free will. It may therefore be said that nationalism has, in fact, an international orientation, emphasizing democratic principles. The national struggle is interpreted as part of an international problem, in that it is concerned with a new political, social and economic order. On the other hand, nationalism also emphasizes those aspects of national identity that are found in a nation's own cultural and spiritual heritage. Once independence is achieved, these nationalistic ideas and sentiments become the foundation for the building of a new future. In domestic affairs they give positive content to the search for freedom. In international relations they aim at the total destruction of imperialism and colonialism in all their forms. The ultimate aim is a new world, free of colonialism and imperialism. This would guarantee peace for all.

In general, then, the prime objective of the Asian Revolution is to establish a just and prosperous society, free from political, military, economic or cultural domination by other nations. For this enormous task, some countries have adopted western democracy; others follow communism. In this paper, however, we shall limit ourselves to Indonesia's experience, as an illustration of the need for dynamic government in order to achieve the objectives of this revolution.

## The Indonesian Experience

As an example of emerging Asian nationhood, Indonesia is both typical and unique. The social order is changing rapidly. Can the country produce the fundamental ideas and structures required for efficient nation-building?

In the first place, it should be noted that the social philosophy of Indonesia is based on the assumption of a genuine "Indonesian-ness." The nation's cultural heritage should be of first importance in the search for the philosophical foundation of the state and of Indonesian society. This quality of "Indonesian-ness" is the sum total of all that stems from Indonesia's spiritual heritage, and which is still alive today, despite the tremendous impact made on the country by western civilization and technology. At heart, modern Indonesian society embodies and continues traditional and cherished values. Though forms may be changed or modified, the basic ideas remain untouched.

This assumption of "Indonesian-ness" was proved during the years 1950–57, when the government sought to establish a liberal political and economic democracy. Liberal democracy did not help national reconstruction. Rather, it produced a situation in which people tended to be diverted from the original purpose of the revolution. They were used for selfish ends by political leaders, each seeking to collect votes for his party; and a complicated multiparty system evolved. People became mere tools of democracy, when democracy should be the instrument by which the people achieve their national objectives. Individuals and groups both sought their own advantage and lost sight of the welfare of society as a whole. The social consciousness of the people became poisoned by regionalism, group rivalries, a multiparty system and separate territorial policies, which disregarded the central government. In short, the importation of the western political tradition and of secularized western civilization proved a complete failure. The conditions under which liberal democracy can function successfully were also missing.

In this chaotic situation, President Sukarno was morally right when, on July 5, 1959, he issued the now famous decree in which, among other things, he called for a return to the 1945 Constitution —a Constitution that embodies the genuine "Indonesian-ness" that we have seen to be necessary. It was his duty as President to put an end to the chaos that was threatening the safety of the nation. Christians must prefer order to chaos, and need not be offended by his extraordinary action.

We shall now proceed to examine in detail the various aspects of democratic government in Indonesia today, and the opportunities thus provided for Christians to participate in nation-building and in the attainment of the objectives of the revolution.

## 1. *The Pantjasila*

The Pantjasila is a set of five principles enunciated by President Sukarno on June 1, 1945, by which the Preparatory Committee for Indonesian Independence defined the philosophical foundation upon which free Indonesia should be built. Historically, it preceded the drafting of the Constitution, which is animated throughout by the philosophy of the Pantjasila and cannot be understood apart from it.

In their original form, the five principles were: nationalism; internationalism or the principle of humanity; political and economic democracy; social justice or social welfare; and belief in God. They were later rearranged and laid down in the Preamble to the 1945 Constitution. The closing paragraph of the Preamble reads:

... the Indonesian State, which shall have the structural state-form of the Republic of Indonesia with the sovereignty of the people, and which shall be based upon: belief in God, just and civilized humanity, the unity of Indonesia, and democracy which is guided by the inner wisdom in the unanimity arising out of the deliberation among representatives, while creating a condition of social justice for the whole of the people of Indonesia.

The transfer of the principle of religion from fifth to first place is important. According to Dr. M. Hatta, formerly Vice President, this provided a solid moral basis for the state and government.[2] Dr. Hatta went on to say that the principle of belief in God has now become the guiding principle for the other four. It is not simply an indication of mutual respect among the religions: it is also a principle that promotes truth, justice, well-being, honesty and fraternity. Moreover, Article 29 of the Constitution expressly states that "the State is based upon belief in God. The State guarantees to every citizen freedom of religion and worship according to belief and conviction."

President Sukarno has expressed his own convictions as follows:

Not only should the people of Indonesia have belief in God, but every Indonesian should believe in his own particular God. The Christian should worship God according to the teachings of Jesus Christ; Muslims according to the teachings of the prophet Muhammad; Buddhists should discharge their religious rites according to their own books. But let us all have belief in God. The Indonesian State shall be a State where every person can worship God in freedom. The whole people should worship God in the cultural way, that is, without "religious egoism." And the State of Indonesia should be a State incorporating belief in God. Let us observe, let us practise religion, whether Islam or Christianity, in a civilized way. What is that civilized way? It is the way of mutual respect. The prophet Muhammad gave sufficient proof of tolerance and of respect for other religions. Jesus Christ also showed that tolerance.[3]

The principle of religion guarantees religious liberty and cooperation and dialogue between religions. It is an umbrella beneath which any existing religion in Indonesia can freely live and develop. In fact, since independence, no regions have been closed to the missionary work of the church. Indonesia as a whole has become a field of evangelism. Christian educational institutions and

---

[2] Lampau dan Datang, Nov. 27, 1956.
[3] *The Birth of Pantjasila*, 1945.

charitable work and a variety of other Christian activities are flourishing remarkably. It is not easy to find a parallel situation in other
Islamic countries where Christians are only a small group.[4]

The second principle of the Pantjasila is nationalism, or the unity
of the Indonesian people. This principle embraces all factions and
layers of society, all parties and diverse groups. The Republic of
Indonesia is neither a state for the upper classes and clergy, nor
a state for the proletariat. It is a state for the whole people. The
idea of nationalism presupposes the idea of oneness. The Indonesian people were united in their common will and desire to be
an independent nation, free from suppression and bondage. They
have had a common experience—three and a half centuries of
exploitation and pauperization by colonial rule—that has created
a common character. This makes for a unity that is, in essence,
revolutionary. The situation in Indonesia is parallel to the united
struggle of labor against the capitalist class in nineteenth-century
Europe. Questions of freedom, justice and human dignity have become every man's concern. They are also the concern of the
church. The Holy Scriptures tell us about freedom, about true
justice and love, about man as the creature of God, created in the
image of God. To give real content and meaning to the issues of
Indonesian nationalism and unity, the church has to enter into the
dialogue of our day and so help in the building of a new Indonesia,
which involves not only the creation of a new society, but also
the creation of a new type of man.

Closely connected with the principle of nationalism is that of
internationalism, "a just and civilized humanity." "Internationalism
cannot flourish if it is not rooted in the soil of nationalism. Nationalism cannot flourish if it does not grow within the garden of
internationalism." [5] The view of life emphasized in this principle
is that mankind is one. All men are God's creatures, and all
are equal before him. Without internationalism, nationalism could
easily develop into chauvinism or racialism (as Hitler showed).
Internationalism links together all members of the world society,
and stresses equality and brotherhood. Colonialism and imperial-

---

[4] In 1963, the population of Indonesia was 103 million. Christians number only 6 million.
[5] SUKARNO: *op. cit.*, p. 24.

ism, on the other hand, are inhuman and unjust, socially, economically and culturally, because of their irresponsible exercise of power over other human beings, and their assumption that the suppressed nations are inferior and should remain so. That is why the church in Indonesia fully supports the principle of internationalism expounded in the philosophy of the state. The world should be a community of free and strong nations, conscious of their responsibilities. In this connection, the resolution concerning Malaysia passed on May 14, 1964, by the Fifth General Assembly of the National Council of Churches in Indonesia is an interesting illustration of the thirty-six member churches of the council, and of their witness in international affairs:

The General Assembly declares its conviction that God, who created man as a free and responsible creature, wills that all nations determine their fate in full freedom and responsibility. Therefore, we must greet with joy and gratitude the double process which at this moment is taking place in South-East Asia; namely, the liquidation of the remnants of colonialism and the appearance of Maphilindo as a form of joint responsibility for developments in this part of the world.

The Fifth General Assembly of the National Council of Churches in Indonesia furthermore prays that the hindrances to negotiations between the statesmen of the countries in South-East Asia may be overcome, and that, when they take place, God may bestow the greatest wisdom on the negotiating statesmen, so that the negotiations may bear fruits which guarantee that the nations in South-East Asia may live in peace and friendship, free from imperialism and colonialism from whatever side and in whatever form, and work to establish justice and welfare each in his own country and for the safety and stability of this whole region.

At the same time, we are disturbed by the unchristian role of some western countries, which, directly or indirectly, seek to continue the old policy of colonialism. They do not render a Christian service to nations in this part of the world, and they weaken the Christian movement in Southeast Asia. For instance, Indonesians know that one of the life lines of Great Britain lies in Southeast Asia; namely, in Malaysia. They know also that the British have a firm hold on the economy of that region: 75 per cent of the industrial estates and mines are owned and controlled by Great Britain and other European countries, and 25 per cent by the Chinese. Moreover, the British armed forces, under the Far East

Unified Command, which has its headquarters in Singapore, together with other Commonwealth forces, have claimed "the right to continue to maintain the bases and other facilities at present occupied by their services within the State of Singapore, and [Malaysia] will permit the Government of the United Kingdom to make such use of these bases and facilities as that Government may consider necessary for the purpose of assisting in the defence of Malaysia, and for Commonwealth defence and for the preservation of peace in South-East Asia" (Article 6, Defence Agreement).

This Article may lead to serious misunderstanding. It is as though the United Kingdom wished to inform the nations of Southeast Asia that she is called to establish peace and security in this part of the world. Indonesia, however, interprets it as a prolongation of economic dominance and imperialism, maintained by military force. In their resolution, the churches in Indonesia showed their concern for justice, freedom and peace among the nations of Southeast Asia. They believe that colonialism and imperialism have returned in another form. Though the people of Malaysia may be unaware of the actual situation, Indonesia is determined to do its best to prevent the return of these inhuman systems.

The fourth principle—that of guided democracy—emphasizes the obligation of every individual to serve the public interest, as well as his right to a proper living. The procedure of trying to reach unanimous agreement through the deliberations of representatives of the community is in harmony with this principle. The deliberations (*Mushawarah*) must be wisely guided in order to reach a unanimous agreement (*Mufakat*). Every person and every group should have the opportunity of being heard, yet the ultimate goal remains *Mufakat*. There is no question of an Opposition in the technical sense. But opposition that contributes sane, reasonable and creative statements is indispensable in guided democracy.

The representation is as comprehensive as possible. The political parties are represented, of course, but also regions (in the People's Consultative Congress) and "functional groups"—farmers, peasants, laborers, civil servants, businessmen, the armed forces, veterans, priests (Muslim, Protestant, Roman Catholic, Hindu), teachers, youth, women; in short, all actual and potential forces within society. Guided democracy presupposes the broad representation and participation of the people, and is thus genuine democracy. The procedure is fundamentally different from that of liberal democracy, yet it is not a one-party dictatorship. It is based upon the idea of *gotong-rojong*—mutual cooperation for harmony. It is, in fact, the modern equivalent of a traditional Indonesian system. In former times, the principles of the Pantjasila did not form a systematic unit. Nevertheless, they originated from the same outlook and emotions and still have a strong hold on the Indonesian people. This is particularly the case in rural areas where changes have been less radical and where tradition plays an important role. Guided democracy has long been a factor in Indonesian society, and even during the colonial period it continued at the village level. It has always been averse both to dictatorship and to individualism. The old system of government was based upon *Mushawarah* and *Mufakat,* with the leadership of a single central authority in the hands of a *Sesepuh,* or elder, who was not a dictator, but a leader and protector. In the modern system of guided democracy, the guidance is given not by a person, but rather by the Pantjasila, the ideals upon which the state is founded. The Pantjasila is not only the philosophical basis of the state, but is also the actual guide for the Indonesian people in achieving the objectives of the revolution—a just and prosperous society, free from imperialism and colonialism. Its role is both static and dynamic, for it animates political as well as social and economic life.

Within this system, the church is represented both directly and indirectly. As a religious community, and thus a real force in society, the church has direct representation. It is also involved in the daily life of the entire nation. The problems of society should also be the problems of the church, and the church cannot refrain from participating in the search for standards and contributing to the total well-being of the nation—always bearing in mind the coming Kingdom of God.

There are, however, certain problems that arise in the encounter between the church and the world. The state is a powerful organization; it is a "power aspect" of the world, and power has often been irresponsibly used. It must also be recognized that the state has a different function from the church. As the Body of Christ, the church's function is to proclaim the Word of God, by word and deed, with a view to the salvation of the world. The state, on the other hand, is an organ existing in the world by the will of God to create and maintain peace and order, and for that purpose it is endowed by him with power to be used in the service of man and society. A problem arises when church pastors are also the political representatives of their religious community, and are thus called to exercise a dual function. Some churches find it impossible to reconcile these two separate functions. Some feel that such a minister should continue to be a minister, but that he should not have the pastoral care of a congregation while giving Christian service in the field of politics. Others feel that he should resign as a church pastor and participate fully in politics as a theologian or an expert on religion and morals.

The fifth principle of the Pantjasila is social justice, which has been a strong motive force in the struggle for independence. It was felt that political freedom would help to promote social justice and prosperity for all, and it is widely believed that guided democracy is able to bring this about.

Indonesian socialism is essentially religious. The establishment of a society in which social and economic equality is guaranteed for all is motivated by a concern for a new humanity and therefore a new society in Indonesia. The pillars of colonial society were partly the Indonesian feudalist class and partly the *bourgeoisie,* consisting mainly of Dutch, Chinese and other Orientals. The mass of the people had no part in the Dutch empire-building. The abolition of colonial rule will lead to the disappearance of the middle class (mainly non-Indonesian) and ultimately of the feudalist class also. The masses, with their bitter experience of colonialism, will certainly not repeat the errors of a bygone society.

If Indonesia is to develop a socialist society based on the Pantjasila, Indonesian socialism must be socialism in which belief in God is an essential element. This has been accepted by the nation, represented in the highest council of the Indonesian people.[6] The Eight-Year National Development Plan (1961–69) aims at the building of an Indonesian socialist society.

---

[6] See Act No. II, 1960, of the People's Consultative Congress.

Socialism is the only answer to many questions, including population growth, agrarian problems and the growth of small industries. It is also the answer to challenges at the international level. There is an alarming lack of balance in world trade between the developing countries and the industrial nations. Recent studies by Dr. Prebisch of the United Nations show that from 1950 to 1960 the Asian, African and Latin American share of world trade dropped from 30 to 20 per cent, and their imports increased much more rapidly than their exports. Moreover, a world commodity glut kept down the prices of their exports, while prices rose for the increasingly complex machinery that they import. At the same time, because of the switch to synthetic materials and new manufacturing techniques, the industrial nations are buying relatively few raw materials. The commodity-producing countries are trying to industrialize, but, in their inefficient new industries, production costs are high; and where they are competitive, many of the industrial nations have begun to raise their tariffs and to fix import quotas against them. If this tendency continues, it could cause serious harm to the developing countries and lead to a deterioration of international relations. The countries of Asia, Africa and Latin America therefore want the industrial powers not only to lower their restrictions on imports of manufactured goods from the developing nations, but also to give them preferential tariff treatment and to subsidize their national industrialization programs, particularly by grants in aid.

In Indonesia, attempts are being made to solve the problem of economic inequality by the introduction of modern technology and by increasing industries. In a society that has for centuries been mainly agrarian and feudalistic, the change is undoubtedly creating a number of problems, but there is no alternative. Indonesians have learned from the West that liberalism and capitalism result in conflicts that lead to exploitation. Such conflicts should be avoided by the application of the principle of *gotong-rojong;* that is, by the close cooperation of government and people in working toward the objectives of the revolution. Indonesia has also taken warning from the experience of communist countries, where one group dominates the rest, to the virtual exclusion of human freedom. Both extremes should be avoided.

Economic planning requires a "guided economy," as outlined by President Sukarno in his Economic Declaration of 1963. This is not economic dictatorship, but rather the orderly planning of the national economy on the basis of mutual cooperation. There is ample room for private enterprise, as well as for state or national enterprise. Both state and private enterprise must cooperate to establish a healthy economy, in which social and economic justice is guaranteed to all citizens. Naturally, private enterprise should give top priority to the objectives of the revolution, and private economic activities must be controlled by means of state laws, regulations and other methods. The people are also able to exercise some control over economic enterprises, both public and private, through the Parliament and the People's Consultative Congress.

The church of Christ must be concerned with and contribute to the establishment of a just and responsible society. Yet the church recognizes that even the best planning is not free from the influence of evil forces; for example, corruption. At a meeting in May, 1964, the General Assembly of the National Council of Churches in Indonesia made the following statement:

The General Assembly calls upon the churches to advise their members in sermons and by pastoral guidance concerning the great temptations that come to Christians in the present situation. The General Assembly furthermore calls upon Christians to maintain a sober way of life.

It expresses the need for:

1. Education towards responsible citizenship.
2. The creation of political, social, [and] economic circumstances in which there will not be such great temptations to corruption; a situation in which it is possible to live a sober and honest life; in which there are no prodigality and no great differences between the rich and the poor; in which there is continuous control, so that each man knows that no corruption can be done without punishment.

The church is called to fight against evil, and by her warnings, words and actions to express her solidarity with the people who are struggling for justice.

## 2. *The Constitution*

In accordance with the President's Decree of July 5, 1959, the 1945 Constitution is now in force. Both ideologically and structurally it provides a strong basis for the state and for the attainment of the objectives of the revolution. The ideological basis is the Pantjasila, set down in the Preamble, and the structural basis for stable government is contained in the thirty-seven Articles and the provisions for the interregnum.

The system of government defined in the Constitution is as follows:

a. Indonesia is a state based upon law (*Rechtsstaat*), not exclusively upon power (*Machtstaat*).

b. The executive power is vested in the Presidency (including the Cabinet) and is discharged in accordance with the Constitution.

c. The supreme power is vested in the People's Consultative Congress (Madjelis Permusjawaratan Rakjat). The Congress is responsible for drafting the Constitution and for determining the broad lines of national policy. It also elects the President and Vice-President, who are to put into effect the national policy outlined by the Congress. Under Congress, therefore, power and responsibility are concentrated in the President. The President is in no sense responsible to Parliament, but he must obtain the approval of Parliament for legislation and, in particular, for the State Budget. Cabinet ministers are responsible only to the President, but, like him, they must take into consideration the decisions of Parliament. Since Members of Parliament are also members of the People's Consultative Congress, Parliament is always in a position to check the actions of the President and to report to Congress. It should be noted, however, that Cabinet ministers are also members of the Congress, which thus includes members of the legislative and executive bodies, as well as of the judiciary.

While the supreme power is in the hands of the People's Consultative Congress, the President is the Chief Executive, responsible only to this Congress, and the "government" is virtually the President himself, assisted by the Vice President and a number of ministers. He is also the Supreme Commander of the Armed Forces, and is entitled to declare war, make peace and conclude treaties, with the concurrence of Parliament. He alone may proclaim martial law in times of emergency. He is responsible for appointments to diplomatic posts, and may also grant pardons, amnesties and rehabilitation. He is also the undisputed leader of the National Front, which aims to stimulate public action and to organize and direct the masses to the attainment of the objectives of the revolution.

In the exercise of his powers, the President may seek the help of the Supreme Advisory Council (*Dewan Pertimbangan Agung*), which, in accordance with the Constitution, is responsible for advising the President on matters that he submits to it. It also has the right to make proposals to the government.

The Presidential Decree of July 5, 1959, which dissolved the Constituent Assembly and reinstituted the 1945 Constitution, reaffirmed the concentration of power in the person of President Sukarno; for Section IV of the Constitution, "Provisions Concerning the Interregnum," states: "Before the period of election of the People's Consultative Congress, the Parliament and the Supreme Advisory Council, in accordance with the Constitution, their competence shall be exercised by the President." Until the next general election, therefore, all power is in the hands of the President.

At this stage of the revolution, the Indonesian people are convinced that leadership should remain with President Sukarno, and that he, as the revolutionary leader with the greatest personal authority and popular appeal, should also exercise the greatest constitutional authority, thus promising a strong and united leadership. In view of the supreme power that he wields on behalf of the revolution, and his tremendous prestige, the People's Consultative Congress, acting on behalf of the whole Indonesian people, has made him President for life (MPRS Act No. III, 1963).

In terms of structure, one may question the solidarity and workability of the Constitution. Yet it is a fact that, in its initial period at least, it has proved its value. It has worked well at all levels, and order has been restored after the tumultuous conditions of 1959. The Constitution is short and flexible, yet it contains all that is necessary for a country like Indonesia: democracy of an Indonesian type, guarantees of freedom and justice and the principle of *gotong-rojong*.

The Christian concern for peace, order, freedom and justice may find here ample opportunity for expression. Christians in Indonesia who are actively cooperating in the search for the criteria for life in a pluralist society can enter the struggle for a responsible society, since the 1945 Constitution provides for the participation of Christian pastors and laymen in the various state councils and institutions, and thus gives the church an opportunity unique in its history in Indonesia. At the same time, in view of the evils that may corrupt the best Constitution and the best statesmen, the church must be prepared for a spiritual struggle in public life.

### 3. *The Political Elite*

Political parties no longer have the position and influence that they had before the Decree of July 5, 1959. To qualify for legal recognition, they must accept the Pantjasila as the only ideological basis of the state and the Political Manifesto of the Republic of Indonesia as defining the broad lines of state policy, and this acceptance must be made clear in the Constitution of the party.

A problem arises in connection with the ideologies of the various parties, particularly of the Communist and Muslim parties. For the sake of unity, President Sukarno has suggested close cooperation in NASAKOM. ("NAS" stands for nationalist, "A" for *Agama* (religion) and "KOM" for Communist.) NASAKOM thus reflects the three mainstreams in Indonesian political life. All groups accept the Pantjasila and the Political Manifesto. There is no room for an ideological struggle, which is likely to result only in a struggle for power.

The role of NASAKOM is reflected in the leadership of state institutions, including the People's Consultative Congress, the Parliament, the National Front and local Parliaments. The addition in each case of military representatives completes the leadership. Such recognition of the inherent strength, qualitative as well as quantitative, of existing political parties is an act of political realism.

### 4. *The Military Elite*

Although constitutionally under the supreme command of the President, the Army has developed a significant role in the nation's political structure. Never a passive body, its actions against domestic political rebellions since 1948 have made its officers fully politically conscious. In particular, the Decree of July 5, 1959, provided an opportunity for Army officers to become openly involved in politics.

The development of the armed forces into a semipolitical organization is largely the result of general discontent throughout the country, caused partly by the failure of the 1955 elections to clear up the political situation, reduce the number of political parties and put an end to political and ideological strife and corruption. The Central Command in Djakarta and most of the officers believe that these problems could be handled only by the Army. When, in 1957, Army commanders led rebellions in Sumatra and Sulawesi in protest against the economic policy of the central government, the President and his government proclaimed martial law throughout the country. This gave immense authority to the Army commanders in each district. The civil administration was subordinate to the military, and everywhere except in Djakarta it became possible for military officers to exercise paramount influence in government affairs.

It may be said, then, that martial law became the Army's political charter. All the armed forces, including the police force, have fully entered into Indonesian political life, as well as into various other aspects of life. Their officers have been appointed to sit alongside civilian business managers and to participate in social and religious affairs, and they have been appointed governors and mayors. As a functional group, they are members of government and of such bodies as Parliament, the People's Consultative Congress, the Supreme Advisory Council, the National Front and the National Planning Council. They have also held diplomatic posts. Even after the end of martial law, they remained in their positions. In some instances, their role has become a legitimate one. Often they have done their job well, putting great emphasis on national unity, obedience and discipline. They have contributed a political outlook colored by their military experience, and as a well-organized and disciplined unit, loyal to the government, the Pantjasila and the Political Manifesto of the republic, they have done much to help in steering the course of the revolution.

Clearly, the elite of the armed forces have been integrated into the political, economic, social, religious and cultural life and structure of the nation. It is not to be expected that they will easily relinquish the authority they now hold. They feel that they have as much as civilians to contribute to national development. They made a great contribution to the fight for independence, and feel that they can also help the country to achieve the objectives of the revolution.

The position of the Indonesian Army is unique. It is not to be compared with the politically active military of South America, nor with the "passive instrument" forces of western Europe. Its role is likely to be in between the two. Ways and means have still to be found of determining how the Army can play a productive role in the political system. But it is clear that in Indonesia's rapid change from a backward and exploited country to a modern dynamic nation, the "military factor" must be wisely integrated into the total structure of government and society.

## Conclusion

Christians have a concern to encourage the development of dynamic government in Indonesia for a number of reasons.

First, in view of the coming Kingdom of God, already inaugurated in Christ, historical events must be taken seriously. In other words, history should be seen and understood from the viewpoint of eschatology. The social change and the struggle for a just and prosperous society taking place in Indonesia are matters of special concern to the church, and Christians must share fully in the search for solutions to the manifold problems. The problems of society are also the problems of the church; *tua res agitur*.

Second, the founding of a state upon its own authentic spiritual heritage, still a living reality despite the penetration of western culture, is the only possibility for a developing country such as Indonesia. It promises a firm basis (the Pantjasila) upon which a dynamic government can be built and holds out hope for the future.

Third, the determination to found a socialist society based on the Pantjasila does not at the moment present any obstacle to the church, which lives according to its calling and task in the world. At the same time, the church must be aware of the abuses and corruption that appear in all societies. In a guided democracy,

Christians share in the search for social criteria, and they do so with the understanding that their attitude must be a critical one and their only standard of judgment the Word of God.

Finally, the geographical situation of the Archipelago is such that separatism and insularism are real dangers. Only a charismatic leadership is in a position to unite the entire country on the basis of the Pantjasila, a doctrine which has great popular appeal and which makes life in Indonesia possible and tolerable.

# 13

# RELIGIOUS LIBERTY, HUMAN FREEDOM AND RESPONSIBLE GOVERNMENT

by A. F. Carrillo de Albornoz (Spain)

## The Links Between Religious Liberty and Other Human Freedoms

Religious liberty is a freedom *sui generis,* and the criterion applicable to it is not exactly the same as that which is applied to the rest of the human rights. These others all essentially concern purely human relations or the relationship of man to society, while the Christian notion of religious liberty concerns essentially divine-human relations, or the relationship of God to humanity, thus introducing a transcendent element that radically changes the essence of the right in question.[1]

The Christian insights, moreover, that constitute the foundations of religious liberty go deeper than those concerning other freedoms. For instance, religious liberty is demanded, even more than by the dignity of the human person, by the biblical imperative to obey God rather than men.[2] The absolute respect due to the highest loyalties of man, which is implied in the notion of religious liberty, shows the necessity to pay particular attention to the spe-

---

[1] A. F. Carrillo de Albornoz: *The Basis of Religious Liberty.* New York: Association Press, 1963, p. 38.
[2] Acts 5:29.

cific theological problems of religious freedom and to regard religious liberty as a *distinctive* human right.[3]

But the Christian theologians who rightly underlined this "distinctiveness" of religious liberty seem, in some instances, to have exaggerated this *difference* and to have been partly responsible for a wrong *separation* of the particular problem of religious liberty from the general question of human freedoms. In fact, it was a regrettable mistake to remove religious liberty from the whole context of human freedoms and to regard it as a world apart, without any essential and intimate connection with the main problem of free man in a responsible society.

These essential links are demanded in the first place by the very idea of religious freedom. With the sole exception of the freedom concerning our intimate and personal religious convictions ("freedom of conscience"), the exercise of religious liberty presupposes by definition the exercise of other human rights, in such a way that there is a dynamic interaction between them, as we see, for instance, when the freedom of religious witness presupposes both our religious liberty and our fundamental right of social expression.[4]

Second, this interrelation takes place not only between religious freedom and *each* of the single human rights but also between religious liberty and all other freedoms generally, or *considered as a whole*. It has been said that Christian thought has to proclaim "the rights of God" (in the sense of his absolute sovereignty) as the foundation and perfection of "the rights of man." [5] This doubtless means that, consistent with the need for human community, society must respect the prior and highest ends of man and God's Lordship over mankind. This being so, religious liberty and all other human liberties are, in principle and in experience, inevitably interlocked. This is probably what the World Council of Churches meant by saying that "religious freedom is the condition and guardian of all true freedom." [6]

---

[3] Third Assembly of the World Council of Churches, Statement on Religious Liberty: "Although freedoms of every kind are interrelated, religious liberty may be considered as a distinctive human right."

[4] CARRILLO DE ALBORNOZ: *op. cit.*, p. 39.

[5] *Ibid*. pp. 24, 39.

[6] Central Committee of the World Council of Churches, Chichester, 1949, Statement on Religious Liberty, *Minutes and Reports,* p. 15.

## The Present Situation in the World

We referred above to "experience." In this connection, we submit that sufficient evidence of the intimate relationship between religious freedom and human freedom generally is practically provided by all the different situations in the various areas of the world today. Present experience shows us in fact that the problem of religious freedom is always and everywhere inextricably entangled with the general problem of human freedom.

This not only means that, in general, where fundamental human rights are oppressed or endangered, religious liberty, too, is more or less denied, and vice versa but that, in the present social and political structure and whatever the theological and theoretical distinctions, a truly practical and real distinction between religious freedoms and other human freedoms is becoming increasingly difficult each day. For instance, current distinctions between "freedom of conscience" and the general "freedom of thought"; between "freedom of religious witness" and the fundamental right of "free expression"; between "freedom of public worship" and "freedom of assembly" or between the "freedom of religious groups" and the general "freedom of association," although perfectly correct at the level of theoretical categories, are becoming virtually irrelevant in the practical life of the civil society. Both kinds of freedoms—religious and other—generally rise or fall together with little or no distinction; and the common consciousness of the citizens regards them as a compact whole.

This is why in many countries today the practical problem, even from a religious point of view, is not that of knowing whether there is *religious* freedom, but of knowing whether there is *freedom*.

The acuteness of this problem appears particularly relevant in those newly independent countries of Asia and Africa, in which a peculiar notion of the "secular" state is taking shape. According to this conception, to be "secular" means that the public powers, knowing nothing about the relationship between man and God, declare themselves entirely incompetent in matters that *strictly* concern "religions" or "religious beliefs." Consequently, the state recognizes and guarantees to the citizen freedom of conscience and to the religious groups freedom of worship; and, from this point of view, the situation may be considered satisfactory. On the other hand, however, such a state considers itself uniquely competent *in the shaping of the whole structure of human society,* including all kinds of economic, social, cultural and spiritual values, and it denies to the "religions" the right to interfere in these matters. Now Christians have always seen as an essential part of religious freedom the right to express in word or deed the implications of belief in social, economic and political matters, both domestic and international.[7] Here the tension is unavoidable, and religious liberty can be fully exercised in such states only if citizens possess *the other human and political rights,* which will allow them, *as citizens,* and in the field of a democratic political community, to express the implications they cannot proclaim *as believers.* Thus we can clearly see that today the problem of religious liberty is no longer that of freedom of conscience or freedom of worship, but mainly that of *the implication of religious insights for questions of the whole human community,* and that, consequently, religious freedom and other human freedoms are coming to depend more and more upon each other. Therefore, it would not be an over-statement to say that religious freedom has ceased to be a marginal question and has become *the* question in the general framework of human rights and of the relationship: religion-society.

## The Tension Between Religion and Society

We have referred to "religion-society," and we have deliberately avoided the term "church-state"—an important distinction, imposed by the present circumstances of the rapidly changing world. If we are not mistaken, the center of interest for religious freedom (and, therefore, for its essential links with the other human rights) has completely changed or is at least in the process of changing. *Instead of the traditional tension church-state, we are beginning to register the increasing tension religion-society.*

For many centuries, in the old order (or disorder) of society, the subjects of tension—the church and the state—were very much

---

[7] Third Assembly of the World Council of Churches, New Delhi, 1961, Statement on Religious Liberty.

*concrete* issues, or rather, persons; and their tension was also a very concrete struggle for real power. The state in its different forms was in reality embodied and represented by what was then called "the Prince," and the church was factually embodied in the ecclesiastical authorities, many of whom had civil power as well, and were therefore some kind of "Princes." This "personalization" and "materialization" of the forces in tension made the conflict very hard, but also very simple. Relics of this situation still linger in those countries—like Spain—in which the "regalistic" conception of the binomial "church-state" is still more or less in force, although perhaps not for much longer.

The situation is quite different and far more complicated in many other countries. The institutional, personal and concrete powers of yesterday are undergoing a rapid change; and the personal consciousness and responsibility of the "citizen" and of the "believer" is increasing all the time, with the result that the binomial church-state is being taken over by religion-society; and that the tension of conflicting institutional powers is becoming *the tension of conflicting ideologies.* The main problem is no longer that of knowing how far churches and religious groups may be free within the state, but *how far religious insights may be received and incorporated into the developing ideology of the whole human community in the various countries.* In our opinion, this change originates in the different and changing conceptions of civil society and of the religious institutions. These modern conceptions are worth studying in detail.

## State and Human Community

The form and the structure of the state are nowadays so different in the various countries of the world that we cannot submit them to a common pattern. But, in spite of many different and, in some cases, opposing characteristics, the state is commonly conceived today as "the government of the people by the people." Some "democracies" may, of course, be more, or less, "democratic" than others; but generally there is no longer a "Prince" (or "Princes") who is regarded as the "father" of the people and whose will is the law; rather, the "Prince" is now the people themselves. It is the whole human community which has grown up, which has become conscious of its civic responsibilities and of its social and political rights and duties, and which therefore intends to take charge of the shaping of this precise community. Here, incidentally, we also see that the distinction between *state* and *society,* which was so clear when the state was the king (*"L'État, c'est moi"*) and society his subjects, has now become somewhat blurred. When the state is precisely the whole human community as it is juridically organized, it becomes much more difficult to draw exact frontiers between these two realities.

The main factual consequence of this new conception is that the interest of such a state automatically extends to everything that can be of interest to the human community, for society as such. Hence the increasing concern of the state for welfare in general, and for the social, educational and even spiritual needs of the people. It is obvious that we are here very far from the old liberal *"État gendarme."*

In this particular context, and for the purpose of defending religious freedom against every undue interference of the public powers, it is difficult to take the religious interests out of the whole bulk of the interests of society and to tell the state to keep its hands off, because this realm is taboo for it. If we were to put the problem in this form, the state would justifiably reply that everything that interests the welfare of the human community interests it, too. And then, without any particular conflict of power between *institutions,* between churches and governments, an ideological conflict might arise between society's conception of the basic structure of the human community and a particular religious conception. Here again we see the necessity for the "people of God,"—the believers—inasmuch as they are also citizens, to be able to exercise their civic democratic rights and their freedom to participate in choosing the desired form of government and in shaping the whole civil structure according to their religious and spiritual insights.[8] This shows too that the exercise of religious freedom and of the other liberties can in no way be disconnected.

---

[8] Third Assembly of the World Council of Churches, New Delhi, 1961, Statement on Religious Liberty: "The exercise of religious liberty involves other human rights: ... freedom to participate in choosing the desired form of government and in freely electing officials. ..."

## The Church and the People of God

Second, and as another aspect of the same problem, we must register a similar change in the present reality and conception of the church or, indeed, of every other religious organization. In theory as well as in practice, the church is increasingly coming to be regarded as *the people of God,* i.e. the community of the believers, rather than an "ecclesiastical authority" or a "power." It is precisely that community of men, with their faith, their religious life within society, their hope and their love, which is, as we look at the church, coming increasingly to the fore.

Here, too, we must remark that the main concern of this community of believers is no longer "the institutional power." In spite of some sporadic and deplorable attempts to gain temporal power and social audience, religious groups today generally have another main interest, which is at the same time greater and smaller than the former one. It is smaller because the believers now no longer deem it so important for their church, inasmuch as it is a "social power," to exercise any kind of pressure on the civil society. On the contrary, there is evidence of the growing feeling that the task of the church in the world is not to domineer but to serve. This new concern, however, is greater than the interest in exercising institutional power, because the believers, individually and in common, will always try to realize in their own life and in their surroundings the religious ideal they profess. And it is obvious that, at least for Christians, this religious ideal has social, economic, cultural and political implications.

## The Ideological Tension

As a consequence of these new trends, institutional tensions and struggles for power between churches and governments are gradually disappearing; whereas ideological tensions are increasing every day.

These tensions have one origin: namely, the presence of specifically different religious (or antireligious) insights, represented and promoted by various groups of citizens, individually and collectively, within the human civil society. But they have also two main points of impact, which, although intimately related, are, in themselves, different.

The first of these centers of concern is, as we have suggested, to understand the implications of religious ideologies for the shaping of the human community. In all countries today (whether they are predominantly Islamic, Buddhist, Socialist, Roman Catholic or Protestant) the most important problem is that of recognizing the right of believers to proclaim their own convictions, based on religious insights, on matters concerning public life, and thus to contribute to the structure of society without endangering the freedom of others and without exercising any undue pressure on the civil community.

The second point of tension refers to the impact of the universally recognized principle of religious liberty on the whole problem of human and civil freedoms; and the possibility of freedom of religion having a disrupting and revolutionary effect on the general question of the powers of government and of the coercive character of the civil society. Precisely because of the intimate links that in principle unite religious freedom and the other freedoms, (all the more so in our current experience), the question arises whether the Christian understanding of man as created for freedom means only *religious* freedom, or human freedom generally. It would seem that religious liberty as such (at least in a Christian perspective) should make an impact on the general consideration of all human rights. Religious liberty necessarily implies a clearer and broader recognition of all other rights and therefore a gradual diminution of the coercive element within civil society. The emergence of noncoercive organs of social and political action (such as the United Nations and its agencies) should be studied in this connection.

These points of tension cannot, we suggest, be avoided by trying to solve the problem of religious liberty with the help of an exaggerated distinction and separation between the "secular" and the "religious" elements in human society, for this separation is not in accordance with the present world reality. If we accept, as we do, the principle of the proclamation of religious insights that bear on public life, it becomes impossible to separate religion and civil society and to put them out of communication with each other.

## A Way of Solution

It looks as if these tensions can be overcome and reduced to a fruitful "dialogue," to a constructive confrontation, only in the general context of all human freedoms. Religious liberty alone, independently of the whole framework of civic freedoms, cannot provide the necessary conditions for this constructive dialogue between citizens, which may lead to the harmonious building of a common society. There will always be ideological pluralism among men, religious, philosophical and others, and even more so when people become better informed. What can be improved is the manner of bringing opposing ideologies face to face; and there is only one civilized way of doing this: the full mutual respect of fundamental human rights.

Here we should emphasize the precarious nature of guarantees given *only* for religious freedom (in the old sense of freedom of conscience and freedom of worship), while other basic human rights are crushed or denied. We could admit that, at least theoretically, it is possible to think of a situation in which some kind of religious liberty is recognized within a totalitarian regime. But, as long as the other human rights are not fully recognized and observed, the easing of ideological tensions between groups that profess different religious beliefs or convictions and the building of a truly peaceful community will always be impossible.

In spite of the many difficulties that must arise from this necessary confrontation, which is specific to the modern world, one great advantage could lead to the solution of the problem. Unlike the two conflicting powers of old (church and state), which were very different and distinct, today it is *the same person* who, at one and the same time, is both a citizen and has religious insights. The same individual is a member of the "people of God" and a member of the civil community. This means, first of all, that the ideological tensions do not necessarily imply a conflict between two opposing powers, but simply the peaceful and juridical process of the faithful obtaining, *as citizens* and through the democratic channels proper to the citizens, the rights and freedoms that they should enjoy as believers, and making dialogue and ideological confrontation with the other citizens possible. Second, this fact simplifies the whole problem, inasmuch as it is no longer a conflict between two powers, but only a question of human understanding *within* the same community.

The solution, therefore, to the problem of religious liberty should surely not be sought by basing it on the *total* incompetence of the national community in religious matters and on the complete separation between religion and civil life. On the contrary, religious freedom should be incorporated, for practical and legal purposes, into the whole question of human freedoms and within the whole framework of a responsible government that respects fundamental rights. In this matter, a regrettable confusion has been introduced between *institutions* and *human interests*. In view of so many unhappy experiences in this field, it is only too easy to understand why many people demand a real separation of *church* and *state*. *Institutions*—political and religious—can and should be separated; but not paramount *human interests* within the same man or within the same community. This is why the right way to reduce and indeed to remove the present ideological tensions should preferably be found in the full respect and observance of all human rights of freedom of thought, conscience, expression, assembly and association, so that every citizen may contribute freely (whether on a basis of religious insights or not) to the whole national community. In the normal development of a true democracy, founded on human rights, ideological and religious tensions will become constructive dialogue, and finally the spiritual values generally accepted by the people will constitute the common treasure of the human community, without endangering any particular freedom.

## *The Action of the People of God in Modern Political Life*

I should not mind labeling this paragraph "The Action of the Church" as long as the term "church" were not understood in the old and wrong sense of an institutional and worldly power unduly exercising pressure on the civil society. The church, in this sense, has no concern in the sphere of politics; and it was in this connection that we acknowledged above the justification for separating church and state.

The problem is presented in quite a different light if we consider the church (as we should) as *the people of God*. The church, inasmuch as it is the community of the believers, has much to say in the field of political life, and in two different ways. First, because religious insights frequently imply the necessity of making a choice in many political questions. Think, for instance, of the right to make war or to use atomic weapons; of the racial equality among men and their equal right to human freedoms; of the right of all countries to their independence and to govern themselves freely; of the fundamental human freedoms of thought, opinion, expression, association and circulation; of the rights of parents in the education of their children. In these cases, and in many others, the church has both the duty and the right to express its insights, based on the revealed Word of God, which the church must proclaim.

Second, the people of God may and should intervene in political life, inasmuch as their members are also citizens and therefore possess, individually and collectively, the right to participate in the political activities of their country and to proclaim their own convictions in political matters, whether they are founded on religious beliefs or not.

These principles are, of course, universally valid, but they become of paramount practical importance in the numerous new nations and modern societies that are dominated by a strong ideological force, which, as we have seen, intends to be solely competent to shape the whole human community in every respect. In all those countries, the role of the church, of the people of God, in proclaiming the implications of beliefs for public life and in maintaining freedom, not just religious freedom, seems to be a momentous and almost tragic necessity. And this is because of two particular circumstances, which it is worth our while to investigate.

To begin with, in many of these new nations, all the other general organs of public opinion that normally secure the correct development of a democratic *processus* gradually give way to the ever-increasing power and influence of an omnipotent and omnipresent state. The press, the university, the trade unions, even the political parties, other than that which is in power, must day after day submit to the pressure and to the *Weltanschauung* of the state, so that in the end they become governmental "instruments" rather than democratic organs of public opinion. In this event, the church (the people of God) remains the only independent voice, able fearlessly to proclaim fundamental principles for the human community, regardless of whether these principles are agreeable to the people in power or not. It can thus happen that, in extreme cases, the church becomes the last stronghold of freedom. The faithful, while remaining loyal citizens, will nevertheless have a healthy influence in preserving the basic presuppositions of a truly democratic society.

Then, again, even in situations where a large measure of freedom still prevails, the church is often the only social movement which sees clearly the importance of the secular society and which gives thought to the moral and political assumptions on which that society rests. Other political or social movements, deeply engaged as they are in the day-to-day events of public life, are often unable to preserve the right perspective and the necessary impartiality to judge those events in the light of fundamental principles; they cannot, as the saying goes, see the wood for the trees. The church, however, precisely because it is not engaged or implicated in the details of daily political life, is generally able to maintain a convenient distance and perspective, and, because it is not hindered by many incidental matters, it does not lose sight of the essentials. Free from the cumbersome technicalities of political life, the church may better lead the way and indicate the fundamental principles that should guide the normal development of a human community. It should always be part of the *service* of the people of God, who are the church, to help civil society in its task of safeguarding and transmitting the highest values which society is capable of recognizing.

If the churches, in their constitutional embodiments, have, in their past history, often lost sight of the principle of freedom, it is high time for them to renew their concern, if only to make their right contribution to the growth of a free world society. This is, doubtless, the meaning of the World Council of Churches' statement at the New Delhi assembly: "It is for the churches in their own life and witness, recognizing their own past failures in this regard, to play their indispensable role in promoting the realization of religious liberty for all men."

# 14

# THE RULE OF LAW:
# A BASIS OF RESPONSIBLE
# SOCIETY

## by Seán MacBride (Ireland)

It is a paradox of our world that the more progress humanity makes in the scientific and material field, the more difficult it becomes to prevent men from hurling themselves toward self-destruction. In a world in which there are no frontiers to thought and ideologies, and in which distances have ceased to count, the causes of wars are varied and complex. They range from the right of people to choose their own political system to the survival of the individual human personality in the face of increasing state control.

There have been repeated attempts to devise legal systems and to organize the family of nations in such a way as to set up a stable framework in which the rapidly growing population of the world could peacefully devote itself to the betterment of its material and spiritual life.

Over the past twenty years, two major efforts have aimed, on the one hand, at the proclamation and implementation of human rights, and on the other, at the understanding and the observance of the Rule of Law. The following analysis of these two parallel and related trends will review the problems involved and state the function of the Rule of Law as a basis of responsible society.

### Protection of Human Rights Through the United Nations and the Council of Europe

The unprecedented devastations and cruelties of the Second World War shook the peoples of the world and prompted their leaders to establish a comprehensive legal framework in which mankind could live and prosper peacefully. In 1945, the United Nations organization was founded "to save succeeding generations from the scourge of war ... and to promote social progress and better standards of life in larger freedom," as the Preamble of its Charter put it. Its purpose, as stated in Article I of the Charter, is threefold:

A. To maintain international peace and security, and to that end to take effective collective measures for the prevention and removal of threats to peace ...

B. To achieve international cooperation in solving international problems of an economic, social, cultural or humanitarian character ...

C. To promote and encourage respect for human rights and fundamental freedoms for all.

The first two objectives are prerequisites of the third, with which we are here mainly concerned. This third aim of promoting human rights was entrusted to a special commission of the United Nations, which elaborated the Universal Declaration of Human Rights, a charter of basic human rights and freedoms. It did so confident that it would thereby promote "the advent of a world in which human beings shall enjoy freedom of speech and belief and freedom from fear and want which has been proclaimed as the highest aspiration of the common people."

"The Declaration," commented René Cassin, one of its chief architects, "passed by acclamation by the representatives of forty-eight countries with eight abstentions and no opposing vote, continues to draw strength from the great spiritual, rationalist and materialist currents leading twentieth-century humanity away from the paths of violence, racialism and contempt of mankind. Each time, when a new State is admitted to the United Nations ... the authorities of this State go on record in their Constitution or in other legal instruments as adhering to the principles of the Declaration." [1]

The importance of the Universal Declaration is far-reaching indeed. "Just as 'Magna Carta,' the American Declaration of Independence and the French Declaration of the Rights of Man were important milestones in the struggle for human liberty, so was the adoption by the General Assembly of the United Nations of the Universal Declaration of Human Rights on December 10, 1948, an historical event."

The Universal Declaration is a categorical statement of the minimum protection that all states undertake to afford their nationals and of the orderly international behavior of states. To that extent, the Universal Declaration is more far-reaching in its implications than earlier national proclamations guaranteeing human liberty. It may well be regarded as a statement of the law which should be universally applicable to all human beings, and which should form part of the *corpus* of international law.

The Council of Europe was first to respond to the challenge of putting into effect the provisions of the Universal Declaration. Governments of European countries, inspired by a common heritage of political traditions, ideals, freedom and the Rule of Law, agreed to take the first steps toward the collective enforcement of certain rights stated in the Universal Declaration. On September 8, 1949, the Consultative Assembly of the Council of Europe recommended that the Committee of Ministers draw up a Convention on the Protection of Human Rights and Fundamental Freedoms. On November 4, 1950, the convention was signed in Rome and entered into force on September 3, 1953. To date it has been signed by sixteen countries, ratified by fifteen and strengthened by the right of application by individuals in ten countries, eight of which have recognized the compulsory jurisdiction of its court. To enforce respect for the obligations undertaken in the convention, the high contracting parties have, in the first place, constituted a European Human Rights Commission, which is a fact-finding body designed to give assistance in reaching settlement and to present a report to the Committee of Ministers, the execu-

---

[1] "Reflections on the Rule of Law." *Journal* of the International Commission of Jurists. Vol. IV, No. 2, Summer, 1963, p. 226.

tive organ of the Council of Europe. An even more important step was the setting up of a European Court of Human Rights composed of elected judges, to whom a case may be referred after the commission has noted the failure of direct negotiations. This unique system of international jurisdiction is now functioning. The court has given judgment in two cases, the Committee of Ministers has ruled on five, and the commission has registered some two thousand applications; moreover, there are innumerable references to the convention before national courts. Four of the member states have modified their domestic legislation to comply with the convention; in six states, domestic courts have applied the convention. In this way, the principle of the Universal Declaration of the United Nations has been put into practice by the European Convention.

The European Court of Human Rights constitutes a revolution in international law. For the first time in history, states have agreed to account to an international tribunal for their behavior toward their own citizens. In this way, international control has been established over a limited but important part of national administration. Unfortunately differences in ideology and the continued insistence on state sovereignty have so far prevented other regions from following the example set by the European Convention. However, promising steps have been taken in Central and South America toward the adoption of regional conventions inspired by the European experience. The International Commission of Jurists has recommended that similar instruments be drafted for Africa (1961) and Southeast Asia (1965).

Efforts to move forward were also made in the United Nations. Once the Universal Declaration was adopted in 1948, the Commission on Human Rights concentrated on drafting international covenants, designed to give binding force to its provisions. By 1954, the preliminary text of two covenants had been elaborated: a Draft Covenant on Civil and Political Rights and a Draft Covenant on Social, Economic and Cultural Rights. These were taken up by the General Assembly, which has, however, been unable to adopt them in their entirety. Above all, no agreement could be reached on means of implementation. As a result, there is as yet no effective United Nations machinery for the protection of human rights. Only a system of reporting has been introduced. Governments are supposed to report every three years on the status of human rights in their jurisdiction. In many cases these triennial reports are quite illusory; as they are kept secret, there is no possibility of questioning any omissions or distortions. This procedure has the additional drawback of enabling delinquent governments to say sanctimoniously that they report regularly to the United Nations on the position of human rights and that they cooperate actively in the work of the United Nations Commission on Human Rights.

All failures and disappointments notwithstanding, far-reaching results have been achieved in the last twenty years in the protection of human rights: the Universal Declaration proclaimed the basic rules of conduct for individuals, states and international organizations. The states of the Council of Europe have provided inspiring proof that these rules can be safeguarded and guaranteed by supranational legal institutions. However, the long years of vain efforts to achieve effective international protection of human rights on a world level point to the significance of another approach to this imperative task: the promotion of the Rule of Law.

### Protection of Human Rights by the Rule of Law

To work for the universal recognition of the Rule of Law is tantamount to enhancing the maintenance of fundamental rights and freedoms. This identity of the two concepts has been recognized in the Preamble of the Universal Declaration:

It is essential, if man is not to be compelled to have recourse, as a last resort, to rebellion against tyranny and oppression, that human rights should be protected by the Rule of Law.

The idea of the Rule of Law, as a system of legal institutions conducive to the protection of fundamental freedoms, has been taken up by an international nongovernmental organization, the International Commission of Jurists, founded in 1952 "to promote the understanding and observance of the Rule of Law throughout the world."

The strengthening of *respect for the Rule of Law* requires the active cooperation of the world legal community. As a nongovernmental organization, the commission moves within a frame of reference more flexible than that of a government body affected by political considerations. The Rule of Law can be upheld and its universal appeal enhanced only if lawyers everywhere become deeply conscious of their responsibilities and acquire the freedom to act as a world fraternity in accordance with their professional and moral conscience.

## The Modern Concept of the Rule of Law

The commission has held a number of international meetings, which have contributed decisively to the analysis and elaboration of the concept of the Rule of Law in accordance with the needs of contemporary society. The ten-year enterprise started in 1955 at the Congress of Athens, which took stock of violations and threats to the Rule and laid the groundwork for a comprehensive statement on the principles underlying it. The commission devoted two years to an international inquiry introduced by a questionnaire prepared by Norman Marsh, then its Secretary-General, and sent in 1957 to practicing lawyers, law faculties and legal institutions throughout the world. Using the unprecedented response of a wide cross section of the legal profession, the International Congress of Jurists, held by the commission in January, 1959, in New Delhi, undertook to draw a clear picture of what the Rule of Law means today in terms of working institutions, law and procedures.

The task was far from easy. In the legal terminology of other countries, the equivalents of the English term "Rule of Law," as first expounded by Dicey in his *Law of the Constitution* (1885), are apt to acquire different connotations. Moreover, the legal systems based on western concepts differ fundamentally from the idea of "socialist legality," although the growing recognition in communist countries of the position of the individual in society suggests the possibility of a common denominator.

The Congress of New Delhi took into account these different definitions of the Rule of Law, and undertook to give them a universal modern meaning. It conceived the Rule of Law as:

The principles, institutions and procedures, not always identical but broadly similar, which the experience and traditions of lawyers in different countries of the world, often having themselves varying political structures and economic backgrounds, have shown to be important to protect the individual from arbitrary government and to enable him to enjoy the dignity of man.

No conception of the Rule of Law and of legality that has secured any measure of support is entirely without substantive content. It was therefore necessary to state clearly that the concept of the Rule of Law is based on the values of a free or open society, by which is understood a society within which the free spirit of each member may find fullest expression. A free society is one that recognizes the supreme value of human personality and conceives all social institutions, and in particular the state, as the servants rather than the masters of the people.

Among the legal institutions, procedures and traditions that lawyers have generally found to be important in giving practical effect to the ideals underlying the Rule of Law, four were singled out for discussion. These were the *legislature,* the *executive,* the *administration of criminal law,* and the *courts and the legal profession.*[2]

The conclusions of the Congress can be summed up as follows:

• The function of *legislature* in a free society under the Rule of Law is to create and maintain the conditions that will uphold the dignity of the individual. This dignity requires not only the recognition of his civil and political rights but also the establishment of the social, economic, educational and cultural conditions essential to the full development of his personality.

In the field of constitutional law the principles of the Rule of Law may be strengthened by a written Constitution guaranteeing civil and political rights and limiting legislative power; or by the observance of unwritten established standards of behavior based on universal respect for old traditions of a democratic exercise of legislative power. In either case, fundamental human rights must be implemented and protected by effective procedural measures.

• The Rule of Law depends not only on the provision of adequate safeguards against the abuse of power by the *executive*—safe-

---

[2] A report on the Congress of New Delhi entitled "The Rule of Law in a Free Society," was published, and included a full account of its proceedings.

guards that have been listed in detail—but also on the existence of government capable of maintaining law and order and of ensuring adequate social and economic conditions. Therefore, the *executive* should be invested with sufficient power and resources to discharge its functions with efficiency and integrity. The existence of a freely elected legislature and an independent judiciary are the ultimate legal safeguards for the proper functioning of the *executive*.

• Reasonable certainty with regard to the citizen's rights and duties is an essential element of the Rule of Law. This is particularly important in relation to the definition and interpretation of offenses in the *criminal law* where the citizen's life or liberty may be at stake. Such certainty cannot exist where retroactive legislation makes criminally punishable acts or omissions, which at the time they took place were not punishable, or involved a less serious penalty. A person accused of a crime is entitled to a presumption of innocence, adequate legal advice, a fair trial and readily available legal remedies. None of these rights should be affected by the character of the offense or by the political, social or economic status of the accused. Though the Rule of Law is not bound to any particular penal theory, it does necessarily condemn cruel, inhuman or excessive punishment.

• An independent *judiciary* and a strong *bar*, free to manage its own affairs, are indispensable requisites of a society under the Rule of Law. The duty of the judge is to interpret the law and the fundamental principles and assumptions underlying it. In fulfilling his task, the judge should be guided by his conscience and remain free from any outside influence. The lawyer should be at liberty to accept any case offered to him and to press upon the court any proper argument without fear of the consequences. At the same time, it is his professional duty to accept also unpopular cases. Equal access to law for rich and poor alike is essential to the maintenance of the Rule of Law. Adequate legal advice and representation through some form of legal aid should be provided to those unable to pay for it.

The Congress of Delhi recognized that the lawyer, no less than the economist and social scientist, must be concerned with economic and social issues. The Declaration of Delhi did not limit the modern, supranational concept of the Rule of Law to its classical application to civil and political rights and freedoms. It emphasized rather its dynamic aspect, which includes concern for adequate social, economic and cultural conditions as a necessary corollary to the protection of civil and political rights. The outcome of the Congress revealed that "the Rule of Law is not tied to any nineteenth-century *laissez-faire* theory of the proper role of the state, particularly in regard to economic, social and cultural matters; but on the contrary that the Rule of Law, far from being opposed to the Welfare State, is an essential instrument of its purposes." [3]

Two subsequent international meetings, the Regional Conference of Lagos, in 1961, and the Congress of Rio de Janeiro, in 1962, elaborated further the classical tenets of the Rule of Law. But it was the Southeast Asian and Pacific Conference held in Bangkok in February, 1965, that dealt in depth with its economic and social aspects. Some 120 jurists of fourteen Southeast Asian countries, Australia and New Zealand were fully aware that the operation of the Rule of Law is endangered by continued hunger, poverty and unemployment, which tend to make truly representative government impossible. Consequently, they reaffirmed their dedication to promote, in consonance with the Universal Declaration of Human Rights, the economic, social and cultural rights of the individual. These rights were defined by the Conference as the right to work, to free choice of employment, to just and favorable conditions of work and remuneration that will ensure the worker and his family of an existence worthy of human dignity, of security and social protection and of the satisfaction and enrichment of intellectual and cultural faculties. Believing that these social and economic goals are to be reached by methods and procedures conforming to the principles of the Rule of Law, the conference formulated a series of conclusions:

• There is a need in each country to enact appropriate *legislation* and to develop legal institutions and procedures conducive to the achievement and maintenance of desirable economic, social and

---

[3] NORMAN S. MARSH: "The Rule of Law: New Delhi—Lagos—Rio de Janeiro." *Journal* of the International Commission of Jurists. Vol. IV, No. 2, Summer, 1963, p. 259.

cultural standards within the Rule of Law. These institutions and procedures should overcome inequalities of opportunity arising from birth or wealth as well as all kinds of intolerance.

• It was recognized at Bangkok that, in order to achieve greater economic and social benefits for the individual, some intervention in *property rights* may become necessary; those measures mentioned were land reform, nationalization, price control, control of private and state trade, and antitrust legislation. The scope of such measures should be limited by public interest, and they should be subjected to adequate safeguards afforded by the Rule of Law.

• It was further agreed that, in developing countries, sound *economic planning* is essential to social and economic development, but that the Rule of Law requires that both the ends and the means of such planning derive from and reflect the ideas, the need and the aspirations of the people concerned.

• Since an *efficient Administration* constitutes the basis for the smooth operation of the Rule of Law, a number of recommendations were made concerning the conditions of public service and the elimination of corruption. Recalling the experiences of Scandinavia and New Zealand, the conference recommended the examination of the possibility of adopting the *Ombudsman* concept as a means of correcting administrative errors and minimizing the possibility of maladministration.

Through the work done at congresses and conferences of the International Commission of Jurists, and through the literature that has sprouted in response to them in all parts of the world, the concept of the Rule of Law has received a truly universal meaning. It embodies all human rights listed in the Universal Declaration of Human Rights—political and civil as well as economic, social and cultural. The application of the Rule of Law and of the Universal Declaration are thus complementary tasks.

## Observance of the Rule of Law and Protection of Human Rights

The Rule of Law as conceived by the International Commission of Jurists refers primarily to national states and their legal systems within which action on behalf of fundamental human rights has so far been pursued. However, the importance of the Rule of Law transcends the frontiers of states. International law has as yet been only partially recognized, and, as pointed out above, international practice has been slow in developing machinery to protect the rights of the individual. Accordingly, congresses of the International Commission of Jurists expressed in their conclusions the expectation that governments of the world would maintain and further the Rule of Law through international or regional agreements patterned on the European Convention of the Protection of Human Rights and Fundamental Freedoms. Such agreements should provide individuals with an opportunity to appeal to an international body for a remedy against a denial of their rights. The 1965 Bangkok Conference added a practical proposal: it urged the lawyers of the Southeast Asian and Pacific regions to request their governments to support the establishment of an office of United Nations High Commissioner for Human Rights, as an immediate measure to safeguard effectively human rights throughout the world.

In all its activities, the commission lays the main emphasis on direct involvement of the individual lawyer in the promotion of international consideration of human rights legislation. The lawyer should not content himself with his practice and with the formal aspects of justice. His skill and knowledge are not to be employed solely for the benefit of his clients, but should be regarded as held in trust for society. Only thus can he rise to the challenge of responsible leadership in his community and contribute what the World Council of Churches understands by responsible government and responsible society.

# PART IV

## THE NATION-STATE:
## ITS VALUES AND LIMITS
## IN THE CONTEMPORARY WORLD

# 15

# NATIONALISM AND THE NATIONAL STATE

by HENRI BURGELIN (France)

## The Chief Aspects of European Nationalism

WE can speak of "nationalism" with reference to any human society, if by it we mean that any community tends almost inevitably to make its primary aim its own survival, and to put after that the realization of such aims or aspirations as are not only those of the individual members of the community but also those of the community as a whole; the community is indeed often personified and given far greater importance than that of the individuals who compose it. In one way or another, the group takes charge of the children, defines the rights and duties of all, determines the relationship between individuals, buries the dead. In exchange, the community demands a high degree of submission from individuals, and a devotion to the common cause that is reflected throughout history by a feeling of attachment to the group.

The essential object of religion is to justify, assure and manifest this attachment of the individual or the family to a wider community, and in this sense all religion is rationalistic: This certainly applies to all the religions of the state or the clan known to antiquity. It also applies to the religion of Israel, which in the Old Testament claimed to be the religion of a nation, in spite of the universal character of the truth that it proclaimed. The universal, revealed religions like Christianity and Islam have always compromised with "national" religions. Throughout history, the wars between Christians and Muslims seem very much like "national" wars on both sides, while schisms and heresies have succeeded only insofar as they have received national backing. It is unlikely, for example, that Lutheranism would have succeeded in forming new churches if it had not been supported by a strong feeling of German solidarity; and Anglicanism owes its existence to the existence of an English state and society.

Of course, it would be ridiculous to reduce the content of the different religious faiths to the national aspirations that they have supported. But, on the other hand, the content of the faith cannot be divorced from the historical circumstances in which it was expressed and developed, i.e. from its social and national incarnation. Nor can we ignore all the distortions undergone by the Christian revelation as a result of its being made use of by the national societies. In this way, nationalism aids and abets heresies and distortions of the truth. But, inasmuch as man belongs to a collectivity, it is not possible for him to perceive the truth of the gospel except through a national language, in national categories.

So far we have given the terms "nation" and "nationalism" a vague and general sense, denoting any organized society that has become conscious of itself, its existence and its needs; thus we have put at the same level widely differing human groups from primitive societies to the nations of today. In what follows we will restrict the meaning of "nation" to present-day society and essentially to European society, where states with powerful and developed political structures more or less coincide with nations. That is to say, the human groups show certain characteristics of race, religion, economic activity and, above all, language that distinguish them from others and give them a cohesion that is translated at the political level by the existence of the state. Certainly there remain multinational states—Belgium, perhaps, is an example—and nations separated between several states—such as the two German states today—or national minorities like the Germans in South Tyrol. But these are the exceptions in Europe, where, today, speaking generally, states and nations coincide.

Most of the concepts used in the sciences of human society are concerned with realities that are difficult to define, since the extent and the understanding of them differ according to place, time and situation; but the concept of nationalism—even if limited to society in our day—seems particularly difficult to grasp and to define. It has acquired a polemical value that is not easy to get rid of, and it is used with reference to widely differing realities. It has not exactly the same meaning in all the European languages, nor, probably, in other languages either. Outstanding authors have been unable to define nationalism satisfactorily. Rather, then, than try to give my own definition, which would certainly be as bad as all the rest, I prefer to attempt to describe what this extremely ambiguous term suggests.

First of all, nationalism refers to doctrines that can be classified in three groups.

1. Democratic nationalism: This was expressed with the greatest force at the time of the French Revolution, and affirmed that the source of political power lay in the "nation"—that is, the community of citizens. This revolutionary nationalism opposed the political conceptions of the *ancien régime,* according to which a "divine right" conferred power on kings. This version of nationalism emphasizes the political liberation of men and the democratic and secular character of institutions. It declares that the nation is not a fact of nature, but a result of human volition. A man whose language was German or whose origin was English could become a French citizen in 1792 just because he was a "patriot." The foreign policy of this nationalism was both universalistic and belligerent: It aimed at liberating all peoples from "tyranny" and believed that universal peace would be established the day that mankind was finally freed. If this doctrine was never transposed into pure politics unadulterated by personal interests, it was expressed and notably defended by the political refugees welcomed by revolutionary France; and Anacharsis Cloots pushed it to the limits of absurdity by claiming to organize Europe and the world in accordance with the institutions created by the French Constitution of 1791.

2. Territorial nationalism: This rests on a foundation absolutely opposed to that of revolutionary nationalism. Far from admitting the universality of the human race, this doctrine sees the individual as profoundly rooted in his native land, in his history, in his cultural, religious and linguistic milieu. It endeavors to preserve the

individual from that uprooting that would be fatal to any true civilization. This is, above all, a conservative doctrine, and can be found in different forms in many regions. It is not so much the "doctrine" of philosophers as the theme of literary and poetic works. German romantic literature is doubtless the best example, but we come across it everywhere, in France with Maurras and Barrès, in all the countries of central Europe, in Russia, Africa, India. Its political content is often very slight. Sometimes it is concerned with defending a human group against foreign domination by affirming the originality of a conquered people or of a threatened civilization: Good examples are found in the Polish literature of the nineteenth century or in Algerian literature today. Sometimes it is concerned with preserving or restoring an obsolete social and political order: It is not by chance that in France it was, above all, the Monarchists who developed these themes and that the Vichy government was the only one to practice this kind of nationalism. Finally, it is not interested in relationships between states. Certainly it claims national independence and tends toward xenophobia, but it is not necessarily out for war and conquest.

3. With this territorial nationalism may be associated another form of nationalism, founded upon the idea of the superiority of one group of people over others: sometimes it is the racial superiority of a group of individuals, sometimes an intellectual, scientific, economic or technical superiority. Here again, few true philosophers have defended the idea of the superiority of one human group over others, but at certain moments of flourishing civilization, of especially brilliant successes, whole peoples have become convinced that these results were due to their own natural superiority. Doubtless this idea was not foreign to the French at the time of Napoleon; it also dominated British "Jingoism" at the end of the nineteenth century, the time of the greatest success of the colonial empire; it fed German thought after their great economic expansion, even before Hitler made it the official doctrine of national socialism; and it is certainly not unknown among the peoples, Russian or American, who dominate the world today. It plays an outstanding role in the life of some countries, such as South Africa.

Although this kind of doctrine does not imply any particular internal regime, it plays a decisive role in international relations. The people who think themselves "superior" inevitably try to get this superiority recognized by others, who are usually unwilling to accept it. They also seek to derive advantage from this alleged superiority by spreading its influence beyond their own frontiers, i.e. by practicing what may be called "imperialism."

But the term "nationalism" is not limited to these doctrines; it applies also to a certain moral attitude and political program that usually have a doctrinaire basis. First of all, an ethic: This maintains that the rules applying to the state are not of the same kind as those to which the individual must submit. No individual choice, liberty or guarantee can prevail against "reasons of state"—that is to say the interest of the collectivity (according to this view). Conflicts between a liberal ethic and a national ethic occur all through the European history of the past two centuries. The Dreyfus case reveals the conflict in particularly sharp outline. And, quite recently, the struggles that spring from decolonization have again raised, in many European countries, the problem to what extent the individual should obey the state, just as Nazism raised it in Germany, and the modern dictatorships raise it in many other parts of the world. This question of the limitations of "reasons of state" also comes up in international relationships: Nationalism recognizes no limit to the right of war, and is skeptical about all forms of international collaboration, only accepting them insofar as they serve the immediate interests of the state.

At the political level, nationalism considers first and foremost the power and efficiency of the national state. It does not desire the Separation of Powers but rather their concentration; it is easily attracted to an authoritarian regime and has been the main support of the different forms of fascism. Similarly, it is attracted to centralization and suspicious of federalism and is fully prepared to subordinate the economy to political imperatives and to neglect social welfare.

Finally, nationalism includes a certain emotional content, sometimes even assuming a quasi-religious aspect. It is nourished by remembrance of the dead, by patriotic ceremonies, flags and fanfares, all of which easily develops into militarism, and colors religious practices with national overtones. The Christian churches have not always resisted the exploitation of the truth of Christ for national ends; both in the colonial wars and in the European wars the "Christian nations" have been far too prone to proclaim that "God is with us" and that the cause for which they took up arms was that of Jesus Christ.

## The Ethics of Nationalism: An Appraisal

This brief description of what seem to me the chief aspects of nationalism suggests at once a difficulty that we cannot evade when we attempt to evaluate the ethics of nationalism: If the word itself has so many different meanings, it is bound to refer to very different sets of values, and we can neither completely approve nor completely condemn realities that have varied so much according to time, place and situation.

From this point of view, it would be interesting to study the history of nationalism and to examine why this phenomenon, revolutionary at the beginning of the nineteenth century, developed into a movement that was essentially reactionary and conservative, at any rate in Europe, toward the end of that century. Here it must suffice to note that the whole of political Europe today has sprung from that movement of nationalism, for all the political systems that were not founded upon a sufficiently strong national will disintegrated—the Ottoman empire, for instance, or the Austro-Hungarian empire—while new national powers appeared and took their places in Europe beside the older states, which had succeeded in basing themselves upon a true national consciousness. Besides Italy and Germany, all the states that we know today in central and southern Europe came to birth between 1820 and 1920 and were the fruits of a specific national will.

Compared with the powers of the *ancien régime* these national states present certain advantages: They are better at arousing the energies of their citizens for their defense, for their economic development and for their cultural life and influence. Since they are based upon the consent of all, they are also better equipped to organize themselves according to democratic principles. Yet the Europe of nationalities also shows great weaknesses. On the one hand, questions about territory, frontiers and national minorities took on an extremely serious aspect once the principle was admitted that it was normal and right for each individual to live in the state that incarnated his own nation. Thus occasions for conflict and the gravity of such conflicts were multiplied. International cooperation became more difficult, especially in the economic field, where, after the First World War, nationalism was the source of real catastrophe, for national states that were really capable of preserving true economic independence were very few.

Thus some of the criticisms that can be leveled against the European nationalism of the late nineteenth century still apply today. Apart from those criticisms—however serious—which many economists directed to a system that destroyed economic ecumenism and hindered the healthy functioning of economic mechanisms, we must, I think, consider four very strong arguments advanced against nationalism at the end of the nineteenth century.

1. First, there was a social argument, found in the thought of many Socialists, and not only Marxists: According to them, social realities go much deeper than national realities. Nationalism has been an instrument in the hands of the ruling classes to divert the proletariat from the real struggle, the struggle between the classes, in order to serve the particular interests of those who control the state. Thus, for a long time, the Socialists proclaimed themselves antipatriotic; and they opposed to nationalism an internationalism —that of the aspirations of the working classes all over the world. Nobody has denounced more strongly than the Socialists the abuses of nationalism and the dangers that it contains.

2. A political argument was often put forward by the liberals of the nineteenth century, who, in countries where the national state had triumphed, soon separated themselves from the nationalists: In France, for example, there was the struggle of the Orleanists against the Bonapartists, and in Britain that of Gladstone against Disraeli. The liberals feared above all the triumph of "reasons of state" over "the rights of man," the mobilization of individuals and of the economy for the defense of the community, the loss of "essential liberties" for the benefit of the state.

3. An argument that affected international relations was that nationalism was the real cause of most of the armed conflicts in

Europe and outside it. Opposition to nationalism therefore seemed like a contribution to peace.

4. An argument that contained and surpassed all the others was that the idea of the equality of all men and the universality of the human race meant a radical condemnation of nationalism, the very nature of which constituted an element of division, of incomprehension and hostility between men.

These criticisms remain as valid in 1965 as they were a century ago; they still apply to our civilization, impregnated as it is with nationalism, so that future historians will probably think of it as the era of nationalism.

## *The Resurgence and Limiting Factors of Nationalism*

One might have thought, at the beginning of the century, that nationalism was nearing its end. The communist revolution, first of all in Russia and then in other parts of the world, might have given the impression that henceforth other ideologies were going to dominate the world; and, after 1930, European conflicts seemed more like struggles between ideologies than struggles between nations. The Spanish Civil War brought this feeling to a climax; and it is certain that during the Second World War other considerations than nationalism inspired the great alliance against Nazism out of which the United Nations grew. And most of the bodies born since 1945 that stood for international cooperation seemed to mark the end of nationalism.

Today it is difficult to support this point of view. Since the war, we have seen the resurgence of nationalism to the detriment of policies of a more doctrinal character. Increasingly, the rivalry between the Soviet Union and the United States seems to be developing into a conflict between two great national powers rather than a struggle between a liberal ideology and a communist ideology. The rivalries within the two blocs are much less ideological debates than rivalries between leaders who are apt to confuse their national aspirations with the interests of the community they claim to govern. Usually they are mediocre persons who hope thus to raise themselves to the level of the great. Finally, the smallest powers are still struggling for limited national aspirations; and it is only the overwhelming ascendancy of the great that prevents these struggles from degenerating into real catastrophes. Thus, although the effects of certain nationalisms remain limited, it is mainly because the preponderance of a few big states restrains the ambitions of the small ones, not because there has been any decline in nationalism.

Yet there is no doubt that nationalism is limited today by some new factors. The first and most important of these is the growing conviction of world solidarity. An ethic that takes account only of the interests of a limited group of men seems increasingly outdated by the progress of science and technology and by the increase in personal production and consumption. The national framework of the big European countries sufficed to supply the needs of their peoples at the beginning of the nineteenth century; but today not even the largest territories and populations or the most abundant riches can satisfy the aspirations of men.

There are increasing numbers of international groups of all kinds that nourish this sense of solidarity. As everyone knows, it is at the international level that many economic questions vital to the national groups find their solution. The increase in leisure time has diversified personal occupations and multiplied international groupings; many associations exist that band together people all over the world who are alpinists or admirers of Shakespeare, historians or makers of beer, trade unionists or devotees of Yoga. It is true that these elements of international solidarity are still weak in comparison with national cohesion, and are almost powerless compared with national states. However, the European of today is less exclusively engaged in a national society than the European of the beginning of this century, and is thus less dominated by nationalism.

Finally, at the political level, our time has seen a number of efforts and achievements that aim at dividing and therefore reducing the power of the national state and at entrusting certain responsibilities to supranational political organisms. Chief among them, or at any rate the one that has gone furthest in the disarmament of the states for the benefit of a larger community, is that constituted in western Europe by the European Economic Community. By placing economic responsibility upon a complex larger than the national states, its founders sought to disarm the European nationalisms by setting up, over and against individual and group aspirations, a more extensive authority, which would soon accept political as well as economic responsibilities. From the day when the responsibilities now assumed by the state are divided between the national states and a supranational power, especially when the Army and foreign affairs give up their national character, the irrational passions that form national sentiment will lose their influence and much of their intensity. Indeed, in Europe, where—except in Germany—most of the national problems are solved today by the present political geography, nationalism is no longer a force for progress or liberation. On the contrary, it is an obstacle to the rational exploitation of wealth, to human emancipation and to the defense of European society. Certainly this is not true of those parts of the world where the nations have not yet formed stable, rich and democratic states. The problem is whether these regions can be saved from nationalism and its dangers.

It seems to us, therefore, that we must distinguish carefully between nationalisms.

1. There are doctrines that deny the human race's universality in the name of an overabsolute concept of the nation. Neither race, nor religion, nor language, nor the imperatives of geography nor the facts of economy explain by themselves the existence of a nation that is the product of history and of human volition, and so has no value except insofar as it helps to preserve the liberty of the individual and order in the world. Such doctrines are based on inadequate knowledge and on a heretical theology.

2. The appeal to "reasons of state" in the face of the rights of the individual and the rights of other peoples is justified only in relation to certain particularly urgent needs and on a provisional basis. A kind of Roman dictatorship may be provided for in the most democratic Constitutions, but nationalism often tends to make it into a permanent and extremely dangerous institution.

3. The protest of oppressed nations: Here nationalism expresses the will to be free and to participate in wealth. However, this liberating nationalism can quickly turn into an oppressive nationalism as soon as its essential aspirations are fulfilled. The history of the ex-colonial countries swarms with illustrations of this kind.

4. Some political programs do not consider interests except that of the national group, and they scorn all attempts at international cooperation and organization, necessary to maintain peace, to achieve an equitable distribution of wealth and to secure human liberty in the world.

It is clear that according to situation and circumstances, our churches will have to give different interpretations to the nationalisms they encounter—particularly political interpretations, since nationalism belongs to the political order.

## Prospects of the National State

Having admitted this, let us try to see what forces are represented in the world today by the political system identified with the national state, and to weigh up the prospects that the future seems to offer to this system, which, as we have seen, is almost inevitably linked up with passions, the effects of which, on the individual, the state and the international order, are incontestable. At the same time we must ask what this prospect represents in the economic context and amid the social evolution that seems to be taking place in the world today. Decolonization and the effects of the Second World War mean that today there are few territories that do not enjoy the attributes of a state: There are still a few colonies, like those of Portugal, and a few regions the standing of which is contested, like Berlin. There are still many peoples who do not accept, or not without reservation, their integration into a state that does not allow them the full exercise of their liberties, particularly in the cultural field. Even countries with a national unity as strong as that of France or Switzerland have the problem of minorities. Yet we can say that, on the whole, the national state is the political system dominating the world today. Even international organizations, and the United Nations first of all, are founded solely on recognition of the sovereignty of national states.

Yet the term "national state" covers realities that differ somewhat according to the part of the globe each state is in and especially to the history of each state. I think we can distinguish four types of national states, the importance and value of which differ considerably.

1. There are the old national states, the existence of which is scarcely contested and where the state system, formed over a long period of history, easily wins the allegiance of a population that cannot imagine itself outside the framework of this national state. Even if the state existed before the nation, as in France and England, the Frenchmen and the Englishmen of today live in the national community as a fact of nature and regard the national state as an unquestionable reality. In Germany or Italy, where the state has really emerged from a pre-existing nation, the right of the nation to found a state is claimed no less vigorously. The present partition of Germany into two mutually hostile states does not prevent the Germans from enduring the imposed situation as a purely temporary one nor from affirming that the first aim of the policy of both the German Republics is to reconstitute a united Germany.

It is evident that the existence of this kind of national consciousness is a strength, an essential factor in the smooth running of political and economic institutions. It restricts the corruption of leaders; it means that political struggles are only struggles to acquire power within the norms of law and tradition, that governments are obeyed even by their political opponents and that the normal development of democratic institutions is made possible. Yet even in countries where the national consciousness is most unanimous, the devotion of the individual to the community is far from complete: Fiscal fraud, for example, is found in various forms in all western European countries. The law establishes a balance between the rights of the individual and the demands of the community, and it is more or less respected by both sides.

The existence of national states of this kind goes with a certain level of economic development. The formation of the state and the development of an industrial society went together, the national state giving capitalism the liberties, guarantees and protection that it needed. We may instance the heavy tariffs on imports at a time when industrial development required substantial autofinancing and therefore high prices; legislation referring to mines and to railways, which enabled industry to expand sufficiently; and armed protection against the claims of the working classes. A state that was not founded upon a sufficiently wide consensus could not have provided this aid to capitalism at its early stages—as is proved by the relative underdevelopment of Italy before its unification and of Austria-Hungary until the First World War. Conversely, the industrial economy furnished the national state with considerable resources—with money, first of all, which enabled the European countries to provide themselves with equipment and technology that permitted a better Administration and a more effective foreign policy.

We have seen above that once a certain level of expansion was achieved, the economy had less need of state protection, and the frontiers of the national state became hindrances to the normal development of economic activity. Unnecessary customs protection becomes useless or harmful, while a fairer distribution of wealth reduces class conflict. The need is felt for wider horizons, allowing greater specialization and more concentration of industry. A certain decline of the national state becomes necessary. But this decline came up against that national consciousness which is a heritage of the past, and it has taken the horrors of two World Wars and many conflicts to bring certain regions of western Europe seriously to consider transferring some of the responsibilities of the state to larger organisms that have no national character. Less elaborate institutions than the EEC, already referred to, bring together European states for many and varied activities: atomic research, the manufacture of planes and rockets, military organizations.

Thus we may say that today the national state has been superseded in those regions where this political system has attained its highest degree of development, and it seems probable (and in any event desirable, both for international order and for internal order within these countries) that more and more powers should be taken away from these national political systems.

2. Certain countries where national existence is of more recent date have developed a different kind of state, which seems better adapted to the needs of the present-day world; this applies to a few countries in the New World, like the United States and Canada, and, to a smaller extent, Argentina and Brazil and, also, in the

Old World, to the Soviet Union. Australia and South Africa also possess some of the characteristics of this type of national state.

All these states have vast territories, often populations of differing national origins, generally a high level of economic development and, in all cases, a political regime that leaves considerable autonomy to the regions of which they are composed. These states seem, in many ways, the best adapted to the world today. Their inhabitants generally have a sense of twofold allegiance—to the regional state and to the federal state—which possesses its authority only because it respects the rights and customs of each region.

This division of national feeling and political organization presents many advantages: in the economic field, it extends the market; at the political level it gives better guarantees that the rights of the individual will be respected; in the military sphere, it ensures a relative isolation, which shelters these states from serious territorial conflicts.

Yet recent developments in economics, technology and armaments have raised problems for these states that they can no longer solve alone. The decline of American isolationism suggests an awareness that the national state is insufficient to preserve security and prosperity. It is therefore by no means certain that in the future these countries will furnish a model of adaptation to the needs of the modern world; it seems increasingly evident that this twofold loyalty within the national state is no longer adequate to ensure the progress and survival of these peoples.

3. Some ex-colonial countries, or countries that suffer from serious economic and technological underdevelopment have not yet achieved more than an embryonic national consciousness and an inadequate political organization. The instance of Congo-Leopoldville is doubtless the most typical; but Africa, Asia and Latin America provide many other examples of the insufficiency of the national state.

Very often a national consciousness exists that has grown out of the struggle against foreign oppression; but once the struggle was over, this national consciousness proved incapable of providing the basis of a modern economy and of a sufficiently powerful state. There is not enough agreement about the territorial limits, the language, the religion, or the economic and social policy of these states, and their institutions are continually being questioned in the name of an economic and social program, as in Indo-China, or in the name of liberty and independence from external powers, as in Africa or Latin America.

If national consciousness exists, and even if people gladly claim to be "nationalists" in these countries, the content of this national feeling is less precise and clear than in the case of older states; the same individual feels that he belongs to several different superimposed communities. Neither the linguistic community, the ethnic community, the religious community nor the political community represents the same human group, the same territory, the same force of sentiment. In the past, under colonization, the struggle for existence blurred these problems, and people of different groups united against people of another race, another language, another religion and another civilization. The ex-colonial powers are often blamed for having created artificial states, the frontiers of which are still those of the old colonial empires, instead of following natural boundaries. In fact, it was difficult to do anything else in view of the political and economic situations and because of the weakness of any national feeling. The fact that regroupings of new states have been rare and often unsuccessful after decolonization seems to bear this out.

The plurality of loyalties presents serious disadvantages: There is less devotion to the state and therefore more risk of corruption on the part of state employees. The state is weaker and can only with the greatest difficulty demand of its citizens the sacrifices necessary for economic development. It is sometimes tempted to take dangerous steps in foreign policy to try to restore national unity and to avoid having to face dangerous internal opposition, which would threaten the state's very existence. Such steps, and the internal troubles from which many countries of this type suffer, often seriously upset the international order; this is so today in the Congo and in Vietnam, and it has several times been true of certain states in the Middle East, and in other countries of Southeast Asia.

In fact, the essential problem these countries face is how to remedy economic underdevelopment and the poverty of their people by transforming their economy into lines that will increase the national revenue and provide work (especially through industrialization but also by improving techniques and introducing a more varied kind of agriculture). The question arises whether industrialization must necessarily be accompanied (as it was in Europe) by the constitution of national states in the full sense of the term; or whether it is possible to bypass this stage (the dangers and perversions of which we have seen) and to pass on speedily to the stage of larger, multinational groups.

There is clearly no one answer that will fit all situations; it must vary according to the cohesion and age of the states already constituted and according to their level and their possibilities in the field of scientific, technological and economic development. Nevertheless, we must avoid taking the European model as the only possible or only good one, because the new states need not go through all the stages of economic development that Europe experienced in the nineteenth century. The age of coal and iron-smelting has very largely passed, and it is, in all probability, by adopting the most modern forms of technology, for example, by using atomic energy, that the new states will find means of rapid economic development. In fact, the most recent discoveries and inventions, which Europe had to acquire one by one, are available to them. China, again, proves that it is not necessary to become an industrial power of the first rank in order to master atomic energy. In these conditions the access to industrial civilization ought to be much less costly, less slow and less difficult for the new states than for the old; and the existence of a powerful and respected national state should be less necessary.

On the other hand, the mastery of new technology implies increased international cooperation. For a long time to come, for example, no African state will be able to furnish alone the financial, technological and scientific means needed to establish an atomic industry. A pooling of the resources of each, and cooperation with countries that are economically more highly developed are indispensable to the transformations required by the situation in Africa; but pooling and cooperation of that kind are possible only in an atmosphere of order and peace—and this would be destroyed by the constitution and strengthening of national states.

4. Finally, there are countries combining the characteristics of

two or three of the preceding groups; these are the countries that have elements both of highly developed and of underdeveloped countries, where a national state exists, but where the whole population does not feel that it has a real place in that state. Examples of this can be found again in South Africa, Asia and Latin America. There, also, the problem of underdevelopment is crucial, although it assumes different forms in different regions or social groups. There, also, the nation is insufficiently formed, but formed enough to give birth to a state that, in the name of the national interest, imposes (often by dictatorial methods) a political regime likely to preserve the position of the dominant element.

It is possible that, in these cases, the enlarging of the national society is indispensable for the stability that alone would make economic development possible; but for these states, too, international cooperation is indispensable, and if, in going through a period of political nationalism, they leave it out, the consequences for them may be disastrous.

It seems to us, therefore, that the national state belonged to a certain age, a particular stage in the economic development of the West, but that this stage is over and is not indispensable for those countries that are developing today. On the contrary, the nationalism implied in this type of state is a factor, even for the underdeveloped countries, that contributes to stagnation and economic underdevelopment. At the political level, its disadvantages are considerable, and nothing justifies them unless they are imposed by economic necessity.

In any event, the regroupings of national states in larger unities must not eventuate in a new nationalism, a tendency that is often seen, particularly in western Europe. The reason is to be found in the juxtaposition of large and powerful national states like the United States, with small and relatively weak national states in Europe, within the Atlantic Alliance. But if international cooperation is to lead to peace, progress and economic development, it is essential that nationalism shall not spring up again on a larger scale, where it is now tending to decline, and that it shall not triumph in those regions that do not yet know all its evils; it must also realize its limits in those states which seem best adapted to the industrial situation and which, therefore, dominate the world today. From this point of view, it is in the United States and in the Soviet Union that the fate of European nationalisms is being decided, as is the question whether the rest of the world is to pass through the stage of national statehood.

But we live, and shall probably continue to do so for several generations, in a period of tension between an old international order, founded upon the national state, and a new order, founded upon multiple systems of international cooperation. The triumph of the best is not a foregone conclusion, all the less so, since any return to "reasons of state" on the part of one member of the international community would provoke nationalistic reactions among all the others. For example, when France had recourse to her rights in preventing Britain's entry into the Common Market in January, 1963, to avoid the formation of a Europe that would be too open toward the United States, whether or not this was justified by an American threat to the independence of Europe, it undoubtedly provoked a series of reactions in all the countries of Europe and in the United States and a series of crises in the Europe of the communities. It may also have led to favorable repercussions in those countries that approved this manifestation of independence over and against the United States.

Thus any reversion to the national state is dangerous, any recourse to nationalism has consequences that cannot be foreseen, and the churches must be on the watch and ready to denounce any recourse to political actions that might jeopardize all the work so painfully achieved in Europe over the past twenty years, hinder a solution to the great problems of the developing countries and provoke catastrophe in international relationships.

# 16

# AFRICAN NATIONALISM: THE AFTERMATH OF COLONIALISM

by JOHN KAREFA-SMART (Sierra Leone)

WHEN Sir Winston Churchill made his "famous last words" remark that he had not been appointed His Majesty's first minister in order that he should preside over the dissolution of the British Empire, little did he guess that in actual fact he would live to see all of the territories under British colonial rule—except the smallest dependencies in the Pacific—attain self-governing status, if not complete independence.

The process of decolonization, which began at the end of the Second World War with the granting of independence to India and Pakistan, gained momentum in Asia, Africa and the Caribbean, with the result that one new country after another was added to the list of free, sovereign and independent states, thus qualifying for membership in the United Nations. It was no longer possible to hold back the forces of liberation, or to prevent the revolutionary effects of what another British Prime Minister, Harold Macmillan, so aptly described as "this wind of change."

The liberation struggle was nearly everywhere directed first toward the achievement of national political independence, yet political change was only one aspect of a three-sided revolution, which had as its other aspects technological and social changes.

Dr. Kwame Nkrumah had this interrelated nature of the political, technical and social struggle in mind when he was tempted to give the injunction to his followers—with apologies to the New Testament—"to seek first the political kingdom and all these things will be added." Since it was the necessity for economic exploitation of natural resources and raw materials which led to political domination by foreign powers, and which also resulted in deliberate retardation of social development, any change in each of these areas must have direct effects in the other areas as well.

The relationship between political independence and economic development must be emphasized. Although, in moments of crisis during the struggle for independence, a nationalist leader might proclaim that "it is better to be independent in poverty than to enjoy economic wealth under political subjugation," yet the underlying motive for wanting independence in most cases is to obtain the freedom of making decisions about the use of the resources of the nation for the benefit of its citizens instead of being forced to share these benefits according to the ideas of the foreign masters.

The mass of the people, in most cases, become involved in the struggle for political independence only because of the promise of rapid and tangible improvements in their private material circumstances. Existing conditions of poverty, illness and a generally low standard of living are blamed on the fact that the people are not free to organize their own national life and to exploit the resources of their country. At the same time, the much higher standard of living in the metropolitan country is explained by the economic exploitation of the colonial territories.

Independence thus becomes not a final goal but in effect only the beginning of a revolution aiming at transforming the whole previously colonial society. The leaders of the newly independent nations find themselves immediately confronted with the equally important need for revolutionary activity to achieve both technological progress and social development.

The objectives in the political sphere, following the birth of the new independent nation, may be listed as follows: to maintain the newly won independence; to frame a Constitution that would safeguard the highest goals for which the anticolonial struggle was carried on; to maintain democratic rights for all individuals and groups in the nation; to provide the machinery and the processes of good government; and to enable the free choice of the people to be expressed through an unrestricted exercise of their franchise under universal suffrage.

The danger of what has been loosely termed "neocolonialism" is very real. This embraces every attempt, overt or otherwise, to bring the new nation under some form or other of political attachment to the previous colonial rulers.

In addition to its political application, the concept of "neocolonialism" also includes all forms of economic relationship that place the newly independent nation in a position of dependence for the continued exploitation of its resources and for general economic development. Such neocolonialist economic power may arise through financial loans or through subsidiary industrial or commercial corporations, which, although they may be registered in the new nation and under its laws, are nevertheless owned and directed by a parent company in the previously metropolitan country.

Another important neocolonialist phenomenon is the creation of associations whose aim is to control the external market for the raw materials and natural and mineral resources of the former colony, which, at the same time, continues to be a ready-made market for the manufactured goods from the metropolitan country. Although some benefit will accrue to the newly independent state, the major financial and economic advantages lie with the controlling groups abroad.

It is only fair to note, however, that in some cases the neocolonialist slogan serves another purpose: namely, to divert attention from inefficient attempts by the leaders of the new nation to plan and to execute programs for the economic development of their country. It is convenient to find a scapegoat, and the old colonial masters are blamed for continuing economic ills and for internal political instability.

Most of the new nations have agreed that their first line of defense against neocolonialism is to adopt a policy of nonalignment with respect to the major power groupings of the former imperial countries and of neutrality in the struggle between the contending blocs.

The objectives of the technological revolution, although equally clear, are not so readily achieved on the basis of independence. The aim of this phase of the revolution is to bring all available knowledge and technics to bear on the problems of health, education and the profitable use of the natural environment, including both natural and human resources. There is almost always an overwhelming lack of the physical facilities through which knowledge and technics become available. High illiteracy rates among both adults and children are characteristic of colonial dependency.

The provision of educational facilities therefore tends to receive almost undisputed priority in the new nations. To give effect to this priority, however, is quite another matter. Not only do schools have to be built but enough teachers have to be found. As only those who have themselves been to school can teach, it soon becomes a serious problem to decide just where the major emphasis should be placed and the maximum of funds expended—on schools or on teacher-training.

The problem is further complicated in that the national technological objectives also depend for their achievement on the degree to which the available knowledge can be passed on to the whole population. The control and prevention of disease, the technics through which the land could be used to produce more and better food and the primary products required by industries and the economic use of local materials for providing such important physical necessities as good and healthy housing all require the communication of knowledge—usually through the written word.

Furthermore, none of these goals can be met without the expenditure of money. There is usually very little spare money available as savings in societies that have almost literally lived from hand to mouth during the colonial regimes. The only sources of capital for technological and social development are external. Often the very nations that have only recently relinquished political domination now become the only immediate source of assistance for further development.

Quite apart from the provision of capital for economic and technological development, the former imperial nations are also often the only source from which trained personnel can be made available for the planning and for the execution of development schemes and projects.

This double dependence on the nations, which, it is legitimately feared, might evolve a suspected neocolonialist relationship with the newly independent states, is one of the most important factors leading to instability in the post-colonial era. The new states are faced with the problem of how to achieve the goals to which they are dedicated in the post-colonial revolution and, at the same time, to safeguard their independence. The solution would be made considerably easier if the new nations could obtain the assistance they need, without mortgaging their nonalignment and their neutrality at the same time.

The problem is, however, only a part of the larger and more universal problem of the relationship between rich and poor nations, although it must be noted immediately that not all newly independent countries fall under the classification of poor nations, and that poverty may be, as in the case of Portugal, a reason for refusal to sever the colonial and imperialistic bond.

As long as some nations remain poor while others continue to increase in wealth, the tensions that threaten world peace will remain unrelaxed. The truism that a nation cannot long survive half slave and half free can be revised and applied in a world-wide context. Universal peace and security cannot be maintained as long as the world is half rich and half poor.

At the same time, however, efforts to put some of the accumulated wealth of the rich nations at the disposal of the poor nations will only lead to failure if they are not rid of the element of charity and if they appear to threaten the human dignity of the recipients of aid in the poor countries.

It is in this connection that the existence of the United Nations is regarded by all the new and developing nations as an absolute necessity. The dangers inherent in bilateral agreements for technical assistance (both for personnel and capital) can be minimized where these agreements are entered into on a multilateral basis, preferably through the United Nations.

Through several of the specialized agencies of the United Nations, considerable results have already been achieved, notably in the fields of the control of disease (World Health Organization), the improvement of agriculture (Food and Agricultural Organization), the development of programs of education at all levels (United Nations Educational, Scientific and Cultural Organization) and the betterment of the conditions of human labor (International Labor Organization).

The results of the past can be matched in the future if the United Nations succeeds in coping with the problems the new nations face in their efforts to transform their economies from being principally those of primary-material production to those of industrial production; from an entire dependence on the industrial nations and the prices they pay for primary products to mutual agreements that would take the interests of the developing countries into full consideration.

The continuing technological revolution in the developing countries, together with the struggle for power and for spheres of influence among the powerful, developed nations, will result in strains and tensions, which constantly threaten to produce physical conflict.

Is it not, therefore, in the best interests not only of the new nations but also of the developed nations that maximum efforts be made to bridge the economic gap as quickly as possible between the developing and the developed nations?

In the light of this urgent challenge, responsible Christian citizenship must urge a serious re-evaluation of the priorities that are currently given to such other uses of national resources as space projects and the development of nuclear weapons as well as conventional defense programs.

The wind of change that swept away colonialism could turn into a refreshing breeze bringing health to all the nations; or it might be fanned into a tempest if all human efforts are not directed urgently toward making the post-colonial era a period of reconciliation, of interdependence and sharing of resources and the enhancement of human dignity for all men.

# 17

# THE SEARCH FOR SUPRANATIONAL POLITICAL INSTITUTIONS

by ALAN BOOTH (Ireland)

IT is not an easy moment at which to define the concept of nationality. For nations are seeking new understanding of themselves, exploring in some cases the nature of their unity, in others contemplating the surrender of their identity to some larger group, and in yet others struggling to be born. It may well be that the very term the "nation-state" is less useful today than it was in the past as describing a phenomenon presumed to be of general occurrence in the social organization of civilized men. What we have to deal with in reality is the fact that certain societies have developed a significant sense of common aspiration and destiny, of belonging together. The interesting question is what the size of such units should or can be in the world today.

Outside pressure, suffering tyrannical oppression or persecution have undoubtedly played a major part in developing the sense of nationality. The bond of common woes, the sense of a shared experience, of righteous indignation against a well-defined injustice, the joining together to throw off an oppressive yoke—all these have gone into the furnace from which has emerged the popular recognition of nationhood. In undergoing together these bitter and painful experiences, men have learned to transcend narrow loyalties of family or tribe, and have rejoiced to hear a brother's voice in the mouth of someone previously considered a stranger.

No doubt, consanguinity and a common tongue have contributed to the formation of certain nations. But a sense of national solidarity is capable of welding together people of diverse origins, as long as they share a sufficiently dramatic or traumatic historical experience that has stirred a common imagination. The same sense of solidarity can fracture a community that had origins in common but responded to historical events differently in different parts. Switzerland, Belgium and Yugoslavia are European instances of multilingualism within a nation. The ethnic, linguistic and religious strata of the Indian nation are plain to see.

Undoubtedly, a nation develops its own myths to strengthen its sense of unity. These may emphasize the physical or intellectual prowess of its members, and lead to the notion of racial homogeneity, which is largely imaginary. As myths, they may do more good than harm, but they should not be allowed to conceal the fact that nationality as opposed to tribalism has been successful in the past in relegating racial differences to a secondary role.

Before asserting that nationalism is part of man's unworthy past, let us recognize the constructive role it has played and, presumably, can still play in establishing positive and creative relations between men. China, the Soviet Union, the United States, India and Indonesia, are human unities of immense range and scope, each providing within itself the possibility of creative human collaboration on a great scale. Within these societies, for all the grave troubles endured by ethnic or religious minorities, the overarching unity has a basis in popular consent and general acceptance apparently more enduring than the forces of division. We are bound, therefore, to see in the development of the modern nation the human discovery on a microcosmic scale that we have a shared destiny, that we are capable of deep common loyalties and that we need each other in spite of differences of ethnic origin, language, religious conviction or even appearance. It is in this sense that we understand the struggle of African nations to be born, overriding tribal loyalties, and, in our wildest moments, we perhaps dare hope that it may be through a deeper patriotism that the racial conflicts of the South will be overcome. But peoples often have to be hammered very hard on the anvil of history before they will recognize as a neighbor someone noticeably different from themselves.

If all this is accepted, it may at first sight seem difficult to justify the denigration of nationalism in certain parts of the world, and often among Christians. But it must be remembered, for instance, that the desire for unity and for the feeling of participation in a large and significant human enterprise has been used to hide exploitation and injustice within the nation. Privileged and comfortable groups have, consciously or unconsciously, welcomed the beating of the patriotic drum as a means of drowning the voice of the poor or oppressed. They have charged a high price for membership in the nation, and their fellow citizens felt that they could make their voices heard only by attacking patriotism itself. Moreover, men have made the nation the ultimate end of their lives, setting it imperiously above religious claims within, and above the rights of all others without.

In Europe, the experience that brought men together in larger self-conscious unities, after the decay of the feudal world of small communities, also set these new nations in rivalry without any arbiter to moderate their conflict. The units in conflict were not new tribes but supertribes, with all the panoply of modern industrial production, and the wars that marked the first half of the twentieth century were both sparked by struggles between these European supertribes. It was clear that the nations must either discover wider unities or destroy each other with their sophisticated scientific and technical achievements.

## The European Dilemma

In postwar Europe, it was urgent to find a solution to the problem of enabling autonomous national sovereignties to live together without mutual destruction. The conjuncture of a number of factors —the desire of certain leading French and German statesmen to make impossible another war between their countries; the possibilities for industrial and commercial integration over most of Western Europe; the fact that the scale of production had reached the point at which a wider common market was urgently demanded; and the sense that European national units were too small to compete with the modern giants—supplied the rational grounds for a new leap of the imagination: the construction of some sort of supranational unit.

The original designers of the European Economic Community had clearly in view the use of economic factors to produce a political result. As the logic of modern industry led toward economic integration, so economic integration would in turn demand common political institutions. The obstinate citadel of national sovereignty would be captured by an outflanking movement, and its inhabitants would be beguiled into surrender by promises of rich economic benefits. Whether the outcome will be simply another superstate or, alternatively, an openended experiment in international organization remains one of the chief elements of controversy among the members of the European Economic Community. France is charged with harboring a vision of a "United Europe" differing little except in size from the outmoded nation-states of the nineteenth century—a fit partner, opponent or counterbalance for Russia and America. The Netherlands has in general never disguised its view that the integration of western Europe should be simply a step toward closer integration of the whole Free World by way of an Atlantic partnership. "From the Atlantic to the Urals" or "from Central Europe to the Pacific"—so the dreams go. But the differences are more than geographical: They involve varying estimations about the evolution of nationalism in the twentieth century.

One view holds that classical European nationalism has become too parochial for the world of today. The European tradition is in danger of being overwhelmed by the new young giants, and much that is of human value may be lost. Since the relatively small but highly developed (and aggressive!) European nations cannot individually make their voices effective in the rest of the world, they should make common cause. It is fortunate that commercial and industrial interests point in the same direction and can be used as a motor for such political development. In this view, the objective is defined as creating "Europe." The implied criticism of "nationalism" is simply that the traditional European national unit is too small.

The other view makes a more radically negative judgment of nationalism as anachronistic. This view sees the formation of the

EEC as an attempt, in one particularly favorable area, to transcend nationalism and to devise workable, trustworthy and irreversible supranational institutions that would provide a model, and perhaps a focus, for a more universal system of international law and order. The emotion surrounding arguments about British membership, an "open" or a "closed" community, and the relation of the EEC to America reflect a recognition that the two ways of looking at the EEC represent significantly different opinions about how best to organize the world community in the nuclear half of this century.

It may be that, in the field of defense, the logic of technology will provide the inescapable answer. Either the Europe of the Six will aspire to become a supernation armed with its own nuclear deterrent (as a diplomatic lever rather than a useful weapon), or will participate in some scheme to share nuclear responsibility within an Atlantic Alliance. Even this could be regarded as only a step toward a universal system of nuclear control, but it would be of value as a pilot project. If, as seems likely, the second alternative proves to be the only one technically and economically possible, the choice will become inevitable, even if it takes some nations time to adjust themselves to this reality. The nuclear bomb has made nations, even the superpowers, out of date, and our problem lies in making political adjustments sufficiently fast to cope with this awesome fact.

The attempt in Europe to supersede the nation-state has been a conscious effort to come to grips with the destructive forces of nationalism. Economic and industrial integration have been the first steps. The Treaty of Rome not only proposed a plan of integration but provided for the formation of a commission charged with the chief initiatives and representing the common interest over and against that of individual nations. This machinery was buttressed by two other common institutions, the European Coal and Steel Community and Euratom (which undertook common activity in developing nuclear power for peaceful purposes). But all this commercial, industrial and economic unification within a sharply defined area is set in a wider context. Member nations of the EEC are also in the larger Council of Europe, and here, too, there have been interesting experiments in limiting and qualifying national sovereignty.

Perhaps the most significant has been the development of the European Human Rights Convention, complete with its court, to which individual citizens of countries acceding to the convention can appeal against the action of their own government. The Preamble of this convention states that "as the Governments of European countries which are like-minded and have a common heritage of political traditions, ideals, freedom and the rule of law, [they are resolved] to take the first steps for the collective enforcement of certain of the Rights stated in the Universal Declaration" (of Human Rights proclaimed by the General Assembly of the United Nations in 1948). It is clear that the convention signals a real surrender of national sovereignty, a passing from declarations to enforcement machinery, taking advantage of the common ethos of a particular area and regarding the whole enterprise as only a "first step," which might be followed usefully elsewhere within such time as it could be universally adopted. Many of these themes will recur later in this chapter.

Thus it can be seen that two sharply contrasting purposes run together in these European experiments in supranationalism. One is undoubtedly that of rehabilitating European wealth and power after the revolutionary effects of the last great war. This would sweep aside old nationalisms in order to create something very like a new but greater European nationalism. It can be rightly regarded by the rest of the world as offering no very noticeable contribution to world peace but as simply shifting the frontiers of conflict away from the center of Europe and augmenting Europe's power to interfere elsewhere. The other is to learn a lesson about nationalism itself, be it large or small, and to begin experimenting in building the machinery to control and resolve the relations of states to each other. If, say some, there is a long, hard road ahead before such machinery will be acceptable on a universal scale, at least we can begin with those nations that have a considerable common tradition (and a unique reputation for quarrelsomeness!), in the hope that what we create may have significance on a wider scale. The proponents of this objective are always alert to see that the circle drawn around Europe is never completed and that openings are always provided for wider inclusiveness. They must recognize, however, that the rest of the world will be skeptical, if not of their good intentions, then at least of their chances of success.

## Other Regional Initiatives

In no other area of the world have circumstances so combined to compel a group of nations to try to overcome their parochialism in this way. However, there have been other experiments in regionalism. None of them, even in intention, are regarded by their members as having significance beyond the regional boundary—they are attempts to reach common policies within an exactly defined area. None of them explicitly look forward to a time when member states will surrender their power of decision in major matters of policy to a majority vote in their common institutions, though voices are heard urging such a direction.

We must leave aside a host of treaty arrangements between nations that are one of the traditional practical devices to make the most of the common interests of states. Regional arrangements are intended, immediately or by stages, to transfer the power to determine policy over a wide field from individual nations to common organs or institutions. The crux of the matter is whether a regional arrangement relies on national consent to agreed policies or establishes institutions that have the power to make and enforce decisions, whether it is essentially consultative and advisory or puts decision-making effectively in regional hands. The one represents an agreement to abate sovereignty, the other its actual surrender.

It is clear, for instance, that one of the oldest existing regional arrangements, the Organization of American States, never contemplated an irreversible surrender of sovereignty by its member states to a central authority. It is an organization but in no sense a federation. It is an excellent example of the classical treaty system whereby contiguous states join together to regulate their mutual relations, to seek means of mutual assistance and to resist outside interference in their common interests. But it is also evident that national sovereignty is, in general, jealously preserved and that there is no intention of developing in a different direction.

On the other hand, the youngest of such regional organizations, the Organization for African Unity, has at least some potentialities of a different kind. Still very much at the formative stage and at present preoccupied with the twin tasks of excluding outside interference in Africa's political conflicts and of removing the last examples of white minority control, it nevertheless maintains a lively debate about a more exciting unity. Important voices are advocating the development of common organs for making and implementing decisions that would represent an irreversible surrender of national sovereignty. Clearly, this does not come from any disenchantment with nationalism as such but rather from the need to consolidate in order to face the rest of the world with greater authority. The problem for Africa is a dual one: to develop national unity transcending local, tribal or linguistic loyalties; and, at the same time, to achieve a supranationalism capable of withstanding the pressures of the world outside. The common man in Africa seems to respond far more warmly to tribal loyalties and to continent-wide aspirations than to the somewhat artificial national entities left behind from colonial days. If that proves true, nationalism in Africa may prove to be a pale and passing experience, perhaps to be superseded by the vigorous assertion of the claims and policies of a whole continent, embattled against the world.

Aspirations toward Arab unity can also come under the heading of regional systems tending to discount nationalism. But it is clear that in this case there is no dream of developing systems with applications beyond the area in question. Arab unity grows from common ethnic and religious roots and is by definition exclusive. Like all other regional systems, it is, in part, a response to outside pressure and an attempt to augment power to withstand the intrusion of "strangers," in this case pre-eminently Israel and her supporters. So far it has achieved no stable form, and has been beset by severe disappointments. But the hope and dreams that it represents are not simply an efficient treaty system for cooperation in specific areas of common concern, but rather a genuine unification, temporarily foreshadowed in the United Arab Republic, whereby existing nations would sink their sovereignty in some form of common federation. Nationalism would be theoretically overcome, but in order to create a more glorious expression of ethnic unity capable of protecting itself more effectively against the rest of the world.

The ancient nations of Asia show no equivalent developments. The inevitably rather artificial experiment in federating the territories of Malaysia arose from administrative necessities consequent upon British withdrawal and the absence of any more persuasive arrangement. It cannot be considered a step in overcoming nationalism but rather an attempt to create nationalism in order to overcome lesser divisive loyalties. If a federation of Malaysia, Indonesia and the Philippines (Maphilindo) were ever born, it would indeed be a significant move in the direction of controlling and regulating potentially competing nationalisms over a wide area of Southeast Asia. But, in general, the great cultures and civilizations of Asia are still trying to find themselves after the somewhat suffocating experience of the imperial period and the disturbing impact of scientific knowledge, so that they are generally too absorbed domestically to feel the need to control nationalism. They first have to seek ways of expressing it appropriate to both their own cultures and the twentieth century.

## The United Nations

Let us turn now to a consideration of the United Nations and its agencies as the most widely respected effort to control the anarchy of competitive nationalism. The United Nations expresses in the most vivid way the discovery, in mid-twentieth century, that humanity everywhere shares substantial common interests, and needs instruments to pursue them together. As nationalism has often drawn strength from common hardship, so this new discovery of universal interdependence derives part of its strength from the sufferings of two world wars. They made clear mankind's common interest in peace, and its demand that the pursuit of peace not be made an excuse for tolerating injustice. Economic equalization, interracial respect, decolonization and the rest flowed from this, paralleled by efforts to find new ways of expressing and nourishing the deepest things men have in common. It is hard to believe that the sense of universalism we have achieved in the regular activities of the United Nations and its offspring, such as UNESCO, FAO, WHO and the rest, can ever be lost.

But, of course, this does not mean that we yet have an efficient institution for settling our conflicts. We have created an organization in which it is possible boldly to advertise complaint and to ensure that oppression by the strong is not hidden from public gaze. We have acquired a forum where no one can easily suppress the opinion of a rival. We have achieved a meeting place where regularly every year and, more frequently in the event of emergencies, national governments can confer without elaborate and special preparation. We have a Secretariat whose loyalty is to the organization and its universal mission rather than to the interests of any parties to a dispute. These are achievements of immense value and it would be criminal to bring into question the survival of so much that is indispensable for human welfare.

However, does the United Nations represent a real delegation of national sovereignty? This is not merely an academic question. Those governments that find that at the United Nations they can gain substantial support for their policies are inclined to maximize its authority and to insist that the majority opinion has at least a powerful moral weight. Those that find themselves in a minority are eager to point out that the opinions of the General Assembly are advisory only, and not compulsive. On the one side are those who earnestly desire a new and better world order and believe that a limited system of central government is imperative and, to a degree, available in the United Nations machinery. On the other hand, there are those who, while desiring institutions of world order, doubt if those now in existence can relieve national governments of their ultimate responsibility to make their own decisions.

The founders of the United Nations were clear that a member nation should be expected to give public adherence to the Charter, but not to surrender any sovereignty. The first paragraph of Article Two of the Charter states, "The Organization is based on the principle of the sovereign equality of all its members." But provision is made, in the specific case of the maintenance of peace, for the intrusion of the organization upon the sovereign rights of a member state. If a nation's actions are judged by the Security Council to endanger international peace, the forces of the United Nations can

legally be set in motion to prevent such action. In this respect
alone, member nations acknowledge the right of the United Nations to intervene directly in their policies. Even then, the five
permanent members of the Security Council were given veto power
over such action against themselves, so that they retained this ultimate bastion of sovereignty.[1]

Such a design evidently intended to provide an international
forum where the pressure of world opinion, the opportunity for
public speech and private diplomacy, and the services of a Secretariat provided nations that, in principle, retained almost their full
sovereignty, with every facility and inducement to adjust their
claims against each other, and to discover common interests, without resorting to military force. It further intended to give the "big
five" a preponderant role, when unanimous, in policing the peace
of the world. By definition, such an institution falls far short of
providing a "government" that can claim a general obedience to
its majority will, but it may be regarded as an intermediate step in
that direction. Those who want to go beyond the original intent
of the experiment will urge that more and more authority and
responsibility should pass from national governments to the center,
and they should feel an increasing moral obligation to "obey the
United Nations' decisions." It is easy to castigate governments that
hold back as old-fashioned and unduly addicted to national sovereignty. It is more important to ask whether there are valid reasons why no nation has so far contemplated handing over its final
powers of decision to the United Nations.

No doubt, the primary obstacle is the doubt whether mankind
yet possesses sufficient common purpose, respects sufficiently common values, and is sufficiently ready to submit particular interests
to a general good for it to be safe for a nation to commit its
fate to the majority opinion of the world. Moreover, even within
democratic nations, there are valued safeguards that protect individuals and minorities from the temporary whim or sudden passion
of a majority. Such a system of law and judiciary, backed by conventions and customs possessing great authority, has yet to be

---

[1] In this brief summary, no account is taken of the controversial issue
dividing the United Nations at the time of writing—whether so formal an
interpretation of the Charter is appropriate any longer.

devised for the international community. The absence of such an "international ethos," or the belief that it is absent, fatally obstructs surrender of national sovereignty at the present time. In a world where there are believed to be "colonialists" and "anticolonialists," "Communists" and "Capitalists," "Stalinists" and "Anti-Stalinists," "Socialists" and "Free-enterprisers," people are not going to let ultimate decisions rest on the random crystallization of a majority in the corridors of power. Both fear and a sense of responsibility inhibit them. The members of a majority may see themselves as expressing the general will. The minorities, which are being overridden more often, see a majority decision as the successful diplomatic maneuver of a special interest.

A common ethos does not grow in a vacuum. Its roots will lie far away from the noisy market place of international political controversy, but it will begin to emerge in part among people who are doing important things together. In common action, men will discover both the limits and the extent of their shared convictions, wherever derived. The United Nations not only reveals the absence of such fundamental agreement but also provides one of the chief places where the maximum available agreement may be discovered. The very fact of common achievement—in a peace-keeping operation, in promoting universal education, in focusing the world's need of food, etc.—provides an assurance to timid men that cooperation is not a forlorn hope and spurs them on to further international adventures together.

## Is Regionalism a Necessary Step?

The ways and stages by which the United Nations might become the sovereign instrument for ordering the unruly anarchy of nations do not yet appear. But we must ask whether the growth of regional unities referred to earlier will tend to help or hinder the proper functioning and developing of the United Nations. Chapter VIII of the Charter of the United Nations specifically recognizes the value of regional arrangements for handling local problems of peace and security. The Security Council is bidden to encourage the pacific settlement of disputes through such regional organs as exist. But of course a regional body is not allowed to undertake the military resolution of local conflicts without the authority of the Security Council. So much for the legal situation of all regional organizations. But the question we are asking goes much further.

It has been a matter of lively debate over many years and has now acquired a particularly acute significance. When the Soviet Republic and the United States glared at each other from behind their nuclear armory, many people felt that the future of life on earth depended on securing a *modus vivendi* between these two terrible centers of power. The prospect of a proliferation of power, by the creation in Europe, Asia or Africa of new regional giants, seemed to complicate the task of reaching stable agreements. Regionalism, in this view, had a limited value in arbitrating national claims among neighboring sovereign states. But if, as in Europe, its aspirations went further toward a real pooling of power, the shadow of new giants would be thrown across the table *à deux*. The curiosity of recent years has been that the Soviet Union has feared this prospect more than the United States. At times, the latter has positively encouraged the emergence of a full-fledged western European partner, able to share her burden and assuage her loneliness. Only more recently has the notion dawned that the emerging power might prove less of a spouse and more of a rival, seriously limiting American freedom to pursue policies in which she believed.

If General de Gaulle has been the European advocate of a new third power in the Atlantic middle ground between America and Russia, China emerges to seek a similar role on the Pacific side. Both hold that the submission of the world to the nuclear hegemony of Russia and America does not promise a stable and just solution to the conflicts of nations. Both, in principle, maintain that the only alternative is the development in the rest of the world of units of equivalent power able to stand up for themselves. China is seeking to sustain similar African sentiments. Presumably, the kind of world order they envisage is one determined by a Security Council that would recognize that the Republic of China is governed from Peking, and would seat, as its permanent members with a veto, four or five political units of roughly equivalent power and with nuclear armament. Can it be supposed that such powers would be any more successful in sorting out their rivalries than the existing permanent members have been in resolving their differences inside or outside the Security Council?

Nevertheless, the protest from France and China does challenge the rigid posture, partly the paralysis of fear, which hoped to leave ultimate military power in the hands of two great powers and to content itself with trying to keep them on talking terms with each other, so that the rest of mankind can at least survive in its own corners. Such a posture does not take into account the two most likely sources of conflict in the future—the discrepancy between the rich world and the poor, and the rivalry between the white and colored races. For, under present arrangements, ultimate power remains with the rich and the white, as China is not slow to point out. And while at the United Nations the Afro-Asian world, together with the countries of Latin America, disposes of a great preponderance of voting power, nations are discovering that the possession of many votes is not a complete substitute for the possession of actual weapons—technological, financial or military.

The argument for pooling sovereignty regionally thus has several elements. It is a step toward reducing international anarchy, immediately at hand because the nations involved share something of a common ethos and therefore believe more readily that they can predict one another's reactions and find common ways of facing problems. It is a means of securing greater influence on international developments insofar as the disparity of size and resources with the great powers is reduced. It can, for these reasons, be regarded as a necessary initiative in creating conditions in which a stable world order could be negotiated between parties on an equal footing.

On the other hand, any serious challenge to the relative stability of the existing arrangements of mutual respect between Russia and America is felt to be intolerable in the nuclear age. Do we have to go through the last twenty years all over again, as new young giants join the party at the top table? Is it not better to press forward the universal solution by way of the United Nations, agreements on disarmament and the elaboration of peace-keeping machinery? There are many who seek a way out in this direction. Others believe it is superficially conceived—a hasty dash for safety, which will fail because the necessary preconditions have not been achieved.

About one thing, all with eyes to see must find themselves agreed: the new patterns of power and aspiration vividly presented by China's re-emergence on the world scene and by Africa's determination to achieve full development tend to make anachronistic the thinking of the 1940's and 1950's on the structures of world order and on the right way to bring the nation state into orderly relations with the little world in which it struggles to survive.

# PART V

## THE CHURCH
## AND THE CHRISTIAN CITIZEN
## IN A SECULAR WORLD

# 18

# THE DEVELOPMENT OF
# MODERN ECUMENICAL
# POLITICAL THOUGHT

by THOMAS SIEGER DERR (United States)

### Theological Introduction

THE stream of ecumenical thought that has chiefly been concerned
with the responsibility of the church to society has always engaged,
at some level, in a discussion of the theological bases of Christian
social policy.[1] Certain basic themes have shown themselves persistently relevant, among them the relation of the Kingdom of God
to the history of the world. In the early decades of this century,
the debate was between a dominant Anglo-Saxon view, full of
evolutionary optimism about the Kingdom's coming on earth, and
a minority continental view, emphasizing the discontinuity of the
Kingdom and the natural order. The theological renascence of the
1930's, led by Karl Barth, plus the historical disasters of that era,
effectively removed from ecumenical thought the idea that the
Kingdom was to be derived from this world. Yet the necessity for
action in history was preserved by the notion of the present reality
of the eschatological Kingdom, which requires men to act in accordance with its demands. Since the war, ecumenical thought has
sought to discern the divine providence working through the secular
movements and revolutions of our time, without making trust in

---

[1] The theological basis is discussed in detail in Volume I of this series.

God an excuse to evade the responsibility for Christian participation in the struggles of this age.

A second theological theme relates the eschatological presence of the Kingdom to the church's concern for the whole life of man, without sharp distinction between secular and religious realms. Before 1930, the ecumenical interest was to deal realistically with the corporate nature of social structures, as against interpreting the gospel's primary concern as the salvation of individual souls out of sinful society. When the theological renewal attacked the human pretensions implied in liberal theology, it did not lose liberalism's sense of the immediate relevance of the faith to the actual communal life of men. Down to the present, ecumenical thought has preserved both transcendent and temporal dimensions in dealing with the social order. The transcendent dimension shows in the repeated judgment on contemporary society for its lack of perspective, of a spiritual center, of a sacred sense of life, as in J. H. Oldham's warnings about the fatal consequences for human culture in a purely anthropocentric approach to the problem of environmental control. The temporal dimension shows in the newer motifs that are derived partly from the ideas of Dietrich Bonhoeffer, speaking of the identification of the church with God's work in the secular world, the servant church, which participates in the common life in obedience to God and in sacrifice and solidarity with men.

A third theme traces the growth of the conception of the church. When, as in the 1920's, the church was thought of largely in sociological terms as an organization with a certain power to influence secular society, like other groups, it was then natural to think of ecumenism in terms of cooperative action among the scattered parts of the church. The reintroduction of the eschatological dimension in the theology of the 1930's, plus the struggle of the German "Confessing Church" to escape the Nazi government's domination, created an awareness of the soteriological, transcendent aspect of the church. Here ecumenism became the life of the one Body—in principle a visible and organic unity—a genuine manifestation of the *Una Sancta*. Today, this concept means that the church is to be freed from its accidental associations with Western cultural and institutional and national patterns, freed by its awareness of its transcendent dimension to act redemptively in the world.

A fourth and last theological concern is the ethical method by which the church shall make relevant social decisions. The most favored system of the earlier years of the ecumenical movements was a modified natural law, where one sought general principles, or "middle axioms," below the absolute divine laws, yet sufficiently broad to cover whole classes of situations and provide ethical guidance in them. The middle-axiom theorists, whose best known advocate was Archbishop William Temple, were subsequently accused of having developed an inflexible system that tended to absolutize the inevitable element of human error present in any formulation of "principles." The attack came mainly from sources informed by Barthian dialectical theology's attempt to understand the Bible as the immediately present Word of God and sought to express an ethic based on the method of dialogue, of response to the divine initiative in each unique situation, where Christian action cannot be stated in an unchanging manner. The "contextualists" were, in their turn, accused by men like Reinhold Niebuhr of producing no social ethic at all, since they excluded the discovery of constant factors in God's commanding and left only a chaotic, unrelated series of particular decisions. Emil Brunner, among others, sought to recover the missing constant without recourse to the natural-law tradition by pointing to "orders of creation," basic structures of the world given by the Creator's will, which can be recognized as unchanging amid the events of passing history.

The debate continues today. John C. Bennett argues that the contextualist emphasis is valuable as a corrective against too easily consecrating specific social programs; but that, in fact, accumulated ethical wisdom of some sort, whether it is called principles or middle axioms or something else, is brought by Christians to each situation. The "responsible society" concept, as described by Oldham at Amsterdam, was a social order with characteristics such as freedom of conscience, respect for persons, restraint on power, and so on, which Oldham himself referred to as "general principles by which Christian action should be guided." In response to the contextualist charge that the "responsible society" is thus a product of the natural-law tradition, not of Biblical theology, the concept was rephrased at Evanston to make clear its nature as criterion for any given social order, not itself a substitute order.

## The Nature of the State

That early ecumenical hope of building the Kingdom of God on earth involved a favorable impression of the potentialities of human nature, an impression that, in turn, helped to shape a positive theory of the state as, in addition to its technical role as the manager of external affairs, the bearer of culture, an instrument for the potential "Christianizing" of national life. The minority, negative view within the movement began with a pessimistic anthropology stressing man's sin, and considered the provision of security the state's principal function, and power its distinguishing mark. During the mounting crises of the 1930's, ecumenical theology came to understand better the extent of human sinfulness, the presence of which had always been at least recognized even by the optimistic majority. This new realism about human nature might have been expected to lead to approval of a more powerful state to control sinful men. But many churchmen, fearing just such a consequence, argued that the *imago dei* had not been entirely destroyed by the Fall, that, whether thanks to the continual and renewed grace of God or to an inalienable structure of human nature, there existed in man spiritual and social faculties that formed a more natural basis for community than the exercise of coercion by the state. For some others, the concept of a universal moral sense smacked too much of natural-law theory. But, however this altered anthropology was expressed, most could agree both that the persistence of sin made a perfect social system impossible, and that the necessary evil of state power must be tempered by recognizing the natural communal elements in man.

The understanding of the sort of state appropriate to such a balanced view of human nature was worked out, as it happened, in tension with the challenge of totalitarianism. The total state claimed to be built precisely on those natural community relations and to have integrated them into a coherent whole. To the ecumenical mind, the fault in that argument was the failure to distinguish between state and nation. The state could not claim to *be* the nation, but only its servant. It was to protect the natural communities in the nation, not overwhelm them. This understanding of the limits on state power was acknowledged even by those holding a negative theory of the state. Outmanned in the early ecumenical debates, they had come back to the fore on the strength of the theological renewal, with its awareness of man as sinner and its distinction between the Kingdom and the world. They fully recognized the ambiguity as well as the necessity of state power, and knew it must not be responsible only to itself. Its role was to act for the common good. Ultimately, its limits are rooted in the sovereignty of God, who sets its function and to whom it is accountable for the exercise of its authority.

The debate between positive and negative theorists in the 1930's was carried on largely in the vocabulary of the divine "order." The negative view, exemplified by Brunner, and current among the churches of the continental reformation, held that the state belonged entirely to the "order of preservation," set up as a dike against sin. The positive theory, represented by Temple and V. A. Demant, among others, and said to be common among Anglicans, Orthodox, and Roman Catholics, saw the state as an "order of creation," representing God's plan for human society's development. On balance, one would have to say that the latter view still represented the ecumenical majority, though considerably chastened by both historical events and Barthian theology. This concept was in accord with the new ecumenical consensus concerning the state's necessity in a world of sin and death, but it went further in granting the state's right to promote and guarantee justice in its function of keeping order and to assist men's common purposes. Force was the instrument of the state, not its reason for being. According to this theory, in a situation of cultural disintegration, the state's duty was to enter the cultural arena to arrest the decline and effect renewal if possible.

From some Anglo-Saxon groupings of liberal theological leanings, there were dissenters even from such a moderate position. They resented the inroads that continental theology and social thought had made in the positive, activist, optimistic view of the state. These churchmen feared that the order-of-creation theory had a possibility of giving divine sanction to *any* state, however unjust, and thus could be used to justify the incursions of a totalitarian regime into all aspects of a community's life. Yet the differences here were partly at least a matter of emphasis. All affirmed that the state's authority is of divine origin and therefore under the judgment of God for its use. Some might emphasize judgment and others divine origin, but all condemned totalitarianism in declaring that the state cannot claim the right to shape the whole life of man.

Faced with the disruptive effects of the postwar world's revolutionary technical and political changes, the ecumenical movement has continued to relate human nature to political organization by rejecting both collectivism and individualism in favor of natural communal relations. The experience with totalitarianism has made clear the need to diffuse power throughout the body politic, and especially to build up a rich variety of associations below the level of the state. Meanwhile, the circumstances of history have given added emphasis to the positive theory of the state. From Amsterdam to New Delhi, ecumenical reports have remarked that the fact of rapid social change means increased government activity for the pursuit of justice, peace and material well-being. The church, it is said, should welcome this active role for the state on behalf of the general welfare.

No matter how positively the ecumenical movement has viewed the task of the state, however, the stance of critical distance has been maintained. In the first instance, to be sure, the authority of the state commands Christian obedience, even if the government is bad. Christians, reads the oldest ecumenical wisdom, should work for change within the established order, the legal system, and certainly not by revolution. Resistance for the sake of conscience existed as an ultimate right, but the state could justly punish such resistance. Nevertheless, the state could normally claim obedience only because it held authority in trust from God; and when historical circumstances, like the rise of Nazi totalitarianism, clearly showed that trust to have been violated, then the "ultimate" right of resistance might become an immediate duty. The Thessalonica Report was reflecting the lessons of the past when it said that Christians may sometimes have to exercise their responsibility to the state by resistance. But this same report was also looking at the present; for, in a revolutionary world, ecumenical thinking has come to entertain more and more seriously the possibility of revolt. It is now even discussed whether violence might not be a provisionally acceptable technique of change, this despite the long history of ecumenical praise of nonviolence, and despite the ecumenical principle of long standing that no private center of economic or social or military power should become stronger than the state. Thus the 1964 Mindolo Conference on race relations in southern Africa, confronting a situation where nonviolent action seemed to have no hope of success, considered whether violence might not be the only recourse for the oppressed. All the cautions are set forth, but in the end the Christian use of violence is not categorically rejected. Such, then, are the facts of the world today that elements within the ecumenical movement can seriously contemplate justifying the forceful overthrow of constituted authority.

The identification of the moment for revolt, of the actual trespass by the state that brings on Christian opposition, has been variously accomplished by ecumenical thinkers. For some, a legal standard served. It might be expressed in the natural-law tradition, where positive law is supposed to reflect eternal principles such as freedom and justice, failing which some appropriate form of hostility is called for. Or the standard might be expressed less absolutely as the necessity for the government to subject itself to the rule of a law at least more permanent than its own will, such as a Constitution, as a safeguard against capriciousness. Beyond the existence of a legal tradition, the Amsterdam definition of the responsible society [2] makes the validity of the state depend on its responsiveness to the wishes of the governed.

The Christian's decision to obey or disobey the state depends, too, on the nature of the freedom he expects. Dialectical theology has stressed the ultimate, eschatological freedom from the power of sin and death, which releases men to act in social life. In the exercise of this freedom, the Christian is determined solely by the grace of God, thus preserving a spontaneity of action befitting the con-

---

[2] "A responsible society is one where freedom is the freedom of men who acknowledge responsibility to justice and public order, and where those who hold political authority or economic power are responsible for its exercise to God and the people whose welfare is affected by it."

textual method in ethics. From the Anglo-Saxon and Orthodox camps came a concept of Christian freedom more ontologically based and hence more constant in its requirements. This freedom was rooted in Christian respect for human personality and was manifested politically in the right to choose and to discuss. Thus man as man had a claim to freedom, and the church could oppose tyranny on behalf of all men. Churchmen such as Oldham and John Baillie feared that a stress on inner freedom came at the expense of liberty of action and so simply contributed to totalitarianism by cutting the nerve of active resistance. Today, it is taken for granted in the ecumenical movement both that the inner, inviolable, eschatological freedom exists, and that it is the source of social, political, and economic freedoms. It must be expressed openly. As Egbert de Vries notes in the rapid social change studies, the freedom from hunger and oppression, which exists potentially in modern technology and ideology, is different from the freedom of the gospel, the freedom from the power of sin and death. But the latter changes human personality and thus renews and changes the whole of human life.

## Nationalism and Internationalism

Political nationalism has never really been popular in ecumenical thinking. Life and Work from the beginning was a champion of a broad internationalism, required by Christian universalism, founded on Christian brotherhood and good will and having its inception in the League of Nations. There were criticisms of this outlook, and some limits were imposed on it even by its advocates. The criticisms were political, mainly from churchmen in the losing nations of the First World War, who feared that internationalism was a cloak for the perpetuation of a vindictive peace; and they were also theological, from those who objected to the optimism that regarded the League as a substantial step toward the Kingdom. The limits, likewise, were principally of two kinds. One was the implicit tension between the internationalist affirmation that national sovereignty must be limited by an international body and the conviction that a state's authority was not to be undermined in its own territory. The other limit was the conviction that variety among peoples and nations was the Creator's will, and that therefore the church should support national self-determination and the unhindered development of ethnic culture. A critical attitude toward colonialism and a deep concern for the welfare of indigenous peoples have, for a long time, been central to ecumenical thinking. Yet, even here, it was thought that the intention of divine providence must be the preservation of national individuality *within* an interdependent world society.

During the nationalist tide of the 1930's, there were more statements from ecumenical quarters appreciating the virtues of national cultural distinctiveness. Men such as Hans Lilje called attention to the prerational givenness of nationality as an inescapable part of an individual's life and admired the stability, loyalty and self-sacrifice that the national community called forth. Yet the reports continued to abound in warnings and qualifications. The uniqueness of a nation could not justify its sovereign isolation from the world it is supposed to enrich by its particularity; nor can this national individuality be made into an excuse for suppression of other nationalities. A sharp distinction was drawn between imperialistic nationalism and the legitimate aspirations of a people for self-determination. The nation must not be made the source of value, nor nationalism a religion in its own right. In sum, the nation was seen to be ambiguous, good for the life of its people but also dangerous to humanity.

Ecumenical internationalism underwent some modification and chastening during this period. Just as thought about the nature of the state changed to accommodate a less optimistic view of man but also to elaborate various theories of limits on governmental power, so thought about the possibilities of an international community de-emphasized optimism about the triumph of good will and made more room for the use of forceful authority in establishing justice among the nations. As for limits on this authority, relations between countries were to be governed by international *law*, while their sovereign freedom in their own land was to be spared from any international collectivism or totalitarianism. Realism recognized that the internationalism currently possible was likely to be based on political expediency, on community of interests, and so was not to be confused with ecumenism, the life of the world-wide church.

The nationalism of the contemporary period gains its force from the interests of the many newly independent countries in establishing and keeping their freedom, as well as from the dislike of the old nations to relinquish their sovereignty. Self-government for dependent peoples has always been a goal of the ecumenical movement; and the postwar documents—the Charter of the Commission of the Churches on International Affairs, and the Amsterdam and Evanston reports, for example—show no exception to this rule. The later reports, like Thessalonica and New Delhi, appropriately stress the preservation of independence already won. Ecumenical thought recognizes the new nationalism as a positive good in consolidating the unity of a new country against disintegrating factors; in creating a sense of dignity, selfhood and pride in indigenous traditions; in overcoming racial subordination; in protecting recent political independence from continued or renewed domination in different guises.

Yet, even though nationalism was useful in the emancipation of a dependent people, and as such worthy of Christian support and participation, it is still a force easily perverted. The Thessalonica Report, and also Paul Abrecht, in his summation of the rapid social change studies,[3] have called attention to one of the current dangers. It is the temptation of a new nation pursuing its own identity to reject everything western as part of its colonial past, even at the cost of losing concepts, such as those having to do with the freedom and dignity of man, which are basic to the gospel, even though they may have reached nonwestern lands in conjunction with the secular, imperialist expansion of the West. There is also the danger that, in turning their backs on western history, these countries will learn nothing from the past excesses of European nationalism and so repeat old mistakes. Another danger is the disruption of the now very complex web of international economic relations. Against selfish defiance of the fact of interdependence, ecumenical reports have called for increasing coop-

---

[3] *The Churches and Rapid Social Change.* New York: Doubleday and Co., 1961.

eration, supporting the technical ventures of the United Nations, expansion of development capital, stabilization of markets for primary products and aid as prolegomenon to trade. But the movement's economic internationalism is certainly not understood to hinder developing nations. The biblical concept of stewardship requires that the riches of the earth, which belong to all nations, be shared with all by those countries best situated to exploit them. Thus the West has an obligation to assist underdeveloped countries and do it without, as the New Delhi Report underlines, any attempt to change the nonaligned political status of the receiving nation, thus limiting its sources of aid.

Beyond the factors of political and economic realism, ecumenical internationalism continues to be driven ultimately by the Christian vision of the fellowship of all humanity. The embryonic form of this fellowship is the life of the church itself, however far it may be from the actualities of world politics. Ecumenical Christianity has in fact shown a capacity to overcome divergences of race, class and nation in many concrete instances. It has helped to create dialogue across the formidable barriers of the East-West Cold War, as in the writings of Joseph L. Hromadka of Czechoslovakia. It has helped the bridge the gap in understanding between old and new nations, as in the work of M. M. Thomas of India. On this primary level of creating an international *ethos,* a prelegal sense of community, world Christianity has a major role to play.

Christians also, however, have a good deal of difficulty in detaching themselves from the ideology of nationalism to see their world-wide solidarity. The major instance of this perennial problem of the relation of Christianity to culture is the famous "Christendom" concept, which has had special discussion in ecumenical history. According to this concept, Christianity and western civilization belonged inevitably together. Western society was Christendom. In the early years of Life and Work the temptation was present to think of the ideal international order as the West writ large, a "Christianized" world. Yet such thinking was never dominant, the major inhibiting factor besides the obviously unChristian, even barbaric, elements that came to the surface in the western world being the conviction that God has ordained the differences among nations and peoples. The distinction between "making western" and "making Christian" has always been understood in the ecumenical movement, from Edinburgh, in 1910, to New Delhi in the present. If a church must be close to the life of the people, and if the people have a right to self-determination and the distinctiveness of their culture, then it follows that the churches of the new nations must not be of European character, nor be agents in the westernizing of indigenous societies. If the trans-national church is to be beholden to no particular culture, then it follows that identification of the Christian mission with the expansion of any one civilization is idolatrous.

Whether the critic is Paul Tillich talking about the shattered illusions of western culture, or Hromadka scoring the church's alliance with prerevolutionary regimes against social justice for the masses or M. M. Thomas pointing out the ideological taint in the missionary movement, ecumenical thinkers from Amsterdam on have agreed that the church is now clearly in a post-establishment, "post-constantinian" era. There are no longer "Christian" and "non-Christian" lands, but mission is the task of all. Christian criteria must be established against destructive nationalism in every country. The alternative to the discredited identification of church and society is a secular social order, the autonomy of the state from the church, a concept that has gained favor as a consequence of the newly emphasized theological significance of the secular. Abrecht and Thomas and others argue that the idea of an authentic secularized society, to which the church stands in a creative and judgmental relation, is an essentially Christian idea. The Thessalonica Report reminds the churches that as institutions they, too, are under God's judgment for their relations with culture, and that the image of Christian captivity to one social order must be corrected by an emphasis on the ecumenical character of the church and the Lordship of Christ over the whole world.

The ecumenical movement's attention to current problems in internationalism is continuous with its earlier interest in creating an international political order. The need is for an international organization able to enforce its will against dissident nations, a body with its own sovereignty, representing more than just compromise among its members. Expectations are perhaps more modest today than in the 1920's. Postwar ecumenical reports back away from calling for a unitary world state, fearing it would be a vehicle for the exercise of big-power tyranny. Instead they speak of cautious progress toward a federal system, expansion of lower-level cooperation among nations, experiments in the limited surrender of particular functions to international bodies, regional unions of various kinds and so on. There has been talk of structural changes in the United Nations. The running thread in the conversations is recognition of a limit on national sovereignty and a search for ways to express and implement this limit. Sober, peaceful, practical gradualism is the motif, a slow evolution toward a world order. This cautious attitude contrasts interestingly with some of the revolutionary urgency heard in other areas of ecumenical social concern. Ecumenical thinking seems to recognize that the greater force at the moment is nationalism, that this force often operates for good in developing nations, but that eventually it must find its place within the larger internationalism.

Similar soberness and caution has marked the course of ecumenical thought on one of the most famous and burning of all issues in Christian internationalism: the pacifist question. As early as the 1925 Stockholm Conference, there appeared the declaration that war is "incompatible with the mind of Christ and thus of His Church." Yet, though this phrase was often repeated in subsequent reports, the movement could never bring itself to declare war "outlawed." Despite the presence of a vocal pacifist minority, the conferences regularly upheld the right of defense against attack and hence the need for appropriate armament. The Oxford and Amsterdam reports recognized three general positions held within the ecumenical fellowship: one was the pure pacifism, which renounced war absolutely and refused to take part in it. A second defended the concept of the just war, undertaken to preserve international law and repel aggression; but Christians were to refuse participation if their country should be *unjustly* at war. The third argued that Christians, having to obey the state, should take up arms when their country so orders, knowing that wars, the product of sin, are inevitable and a necessary part of an imperfect world. While all three were said to be possible Christian positions, the weight of the ecumenical consensus has rested on the second. Since the development of nuclear weapons, however, many Christians have said that no war is defensible, since atomic warfare would destroy rather than save civilization.

A good deal of ecumenical effort has been spent on mutual disarmament. This concern occupied Life and Work from the very beginning; for technical developments in warfare and the exposure of civilian populations were nearly as frightening in the First World War as atomic weapons have been in the contemporary period. The approach of the reports and conferences in recent years has been through limited arms control as a first step, a constant probing to find ways, however slight, to break the impasse among the nations, even urging them, in the words of the New Delhi Report, "to run reasonable risks for peace." The movement has stressed that war is always sin, even when necessary; has fought resignation to the inevitability of war as blunting sensitivity to its dangers; has warned against hate propaganda and vindictiveness; has proposed various uses of governmental and nongovernmental channels to seek peaceful settlement of disputes; and has emphasized the ideal of reconciliation and removal of the causes of war. Thus, while unable to take a completely pacifist position, the ecumenical groups have been seriously engaged in creative peace-waging.

## Political and Economic Systems

The original ecumenical judgment on the internal ordering of the state was a strong bias in favor of democracy, meaning rather generally government by the repeatedly expressed will of the governed. This position was based on the diversity in human life, on a feeling that strongly centralized government was less responsive to the varied needs of its people and less responsible in the exercise of its power; on the need for freedom in political as well as religious choice, which inheres in the Christian respect for personality; and on the greater hearing accorded the church's views in a free society.

In the contemporary period, criticism of the religious sanction for democracy has come from Christians both in communist lands and in newly independent countries. Hromadka at Amsterdam challenged the moral, spiritual and intellectual prestige of western democracy, charging that it had been blind to the evils of eastern

European feudal regimes; that its own ideals were likely to be cloaks to cover the entrenchment of a privileged class; that its parliamentarism and much-vaunted freedom of thought have not contributed sufficiently to social justice and peace; and that discipline and dedication are superior to formal freedom when the social problem is to rebuild a shattered nation. Roughly the same argument can apply to an underdeveloped country; and there have been churchmen who have criticized democracy as unable to provide the strong central government needed to build a new nation. It is argued that centralized political unity may be necessary to achieve economic and social progress.

Such a change in historical circumstances has not, however, caused the ecumenical movement to hand over democracy to authoritarianism. The report of the Thessalonica Conference on *Christian in Rapid Social Change* (1959) notes that the problem is to keep several values in balance. A concern for freedom for the individual, for active personal participation in political life, leads to democracy. When social and economic development needs to be done quickly, decisive government action may be required. Freedom, justice and order are therefore partially in conflict. What has been happening in this and other reports is a reappraisal of western political ideals and their alleged derivation from Christian faith. As in the 1930's, the word democracy is used in different senses. In nonwestern lands, it seems to mean roughly government on behalf of the people by a regime that embodies the national ideals and therefore has popular consent to rule. "Dynamic democracy" is a form of government that has the capacity to effect social changes, even by state-imposed discipline, for the sake of the general welfare. But the ecumenical consensus still accords Christian support to such ideals as equality under the law for all groups and peoples, personal freedom, and open criticism and discussion of government policy. If education is lacking, said the New Delhi Assembly, it should be rapidly improved, so that all the people can participate responsibly in political life. Nor have the dangers of authoritarianism been ignored, as if the ecumenical movement could forget the lesson of the 1930's. Repeatedly, the reports condemn the sacrifice of individuals to the good of the state, the totalitarian control by the state of all aspects of life, and the subordination of means to ends in social change. They warn of the danger of corruption inherent in arbitrary power, and urge the development of a pluralist society, so that even a one-party government may be held in some way responsible to the people.

In other words, though modern circumstances may have called into question such forms of western democracy as opposition parties and parliamentary rule, the ecumenical movement still holds to democracy as an ideal, and defines it in a way roughly continuous with its customary meaning in the history of the West. It may be that, in many new countries, the most basic requirements for free popular government are lacking, and that the state may have to create the social prerequisites from above. But such arbitrariness can only be temporary, and the purpose of forced development is to attain a level where the more desirable democratic practices will be viable. Underlying this view is the conviction that in the long run a free cooperative society brings out the latent good in man and also affords protection against the rise of tyranny. Here is mirrored faithfully the dominant theological view of man as both creative and destructive by nature, capable of advanced community or of brutal despotism.

Little need be said here about the ecumenical position in the ideological debate that arose in the 1920's between *laissez-faire* capitalism, socialism and communism, since this is dealt with in another volume of this series. Since the Second World War, the principal ideological interest of ecumenical thought has been the stance of the churches toward revolution. Repeatedly, the ecumenical conferences have noted and regretted the historical tendency of the western churches to be allied with the vested interests, with the economically powerful and against the working classes in many areas. Their status in society, their traditional preference for order and their belief in the sanctity of private property have rendered them incapable of appreciating the forces of revolution, even when revolt is in the name of justice. Worse still, the churches are most numerous in the wealthiest nations. The Thessalonica Report, in calling attention to the "most bitter fact" of the division of the world into a white-rich majority and a colored-poor minority, lamented the circumstance of the Christian Church's being found mainly among the former and, as western, not being sufficiently sensitive to this "offense to God." The ecumenical movement has strongly regretted the socio-economic status of the churches and has urged upon them the need to transcend this background and participate constructively in the revolutionary struggle for social justice around the world.

Russian communism was intensely disliked in ecumenical circles in the 1930's, partly for its theoretical atheism, partly for its persecution of the church, partly for its advocacy of violence and class war and, in general, for its revolutionary threat to ordered society. Churchmen defended socialism and the approach to the labor movement but were opposed to communism. The Oxford Report is critical of communism's utopianism, materialism and disregard for the dignity of the individual, though it does not make a sweeping condemnation of socialism. The conference, moreover, seeing the danger of self-righteousness among western Christians, asked the church to acknowledge its own share in the rise of anti-Christian movements.

The realism and fair-mindedness of the Oxford approach to communism has been the mark of subsequent ecumenical thinking. On the theoretical level, Marxism has been opposed for finding the meaning of life wholly within man's earthly history; for reducing the motives of man's actions to the compulsions of social structure; for offering man a complete scheme of salvation; for its elimination of individual freedom in collective necessity; for its doctrine of the sinlessness of one class; and for its atheism and evasion of transcendent judgment. But also, on the theoretical level, Marxism has been praised by Christians for its idealism, its desire to improve the lot of the poor and its vision of equality and brotherhood. On the practical level, the ecumenical movement has had some harsh words for the actual consequences of Marxism as seen in its communist establishment in Russia and elsewhere. Its totalitarianism, its violence, its ruthless subordination of means to ends, its terror and the new forms of injustice and oppression to which it has given rise have all been denounced. Yet, also on the practical side, there have been appreciative words for communism as a necessary expedient in a severely underdeveloped country, as a useful judgment on the West for its complacency about economic injustice and as an effectively serious spur to genuine social reform. The Evanston Report warns the West of the dangers in pursuing a persistently antirevolutionary policy all over the globe, in the name of fanatical anticommunism.

Such ecumenical realism about communism has had the effect of keeping the movement from being identified wholly with either side in the Cold War. But there is also here reflected an early, continuing and apparently indestructible ecumenical social principle—the nonidentification of the Kingdom of God with any political or economic order. Such an identification would have been impossible for practical reasons, of course, given the conflicts within the movement. But the real reasons for refusing to consecrate any given order are deeper and include awareness of the eschatological dimension of the Kingdom, of the created differences among nationalities and their ways of life, and of the ideological taint resulting from human sinfulness. The outcome is, however, more than bland neutrality. The thrust of ecumenical thought has been toward wide reforms and change for the benefit of the whole life of man, expressed so as to be charged with possibilities for specific applications in varying circumstances, even in social revolution.

### The State and Its Christian Citizens

The ecumenical interest in the internal order of the state has often focused on the rights of individuals in society. Whether stemming from a natural-law concept of the rights of man or from a more explicitly Christian source in the dignity of all men as loved and redeemed by God in Christ, or from the necessity that man be free to respond to God's calling, to give full expression in his own life to the truth of the gospel, this championship of human rights has been characteristic of the movement. The struggle with totalitarianism strengthened its defense of personal freedom; and its critiques of social systems, whether communism, capitalism, or socialism, frequently focused on the suppression of individual development. Since the creation of the United Nations there has been a trend toward regarding the rights of men everywhere as an international concern, not just the affair of a nation toward its own nationals. The ecumenical movement, through the C.C.I.A. and its director, O. Frederick Nolde, has contributed to this trend and was an active participant in the development and enactment by the United Nations of the Universal Declaration of Human Rights.

Conference reports have ranged over a number of different rights —freedom of speech and assembly and association; freedom of political participation; freedom of parents to choose the type of education their children will receive; freedom from arbitrary arrest; freedom for conscientious objectors to elect alternatives to military service; and various social and economic rights—but over the years have paid special attention to racial equality and religious liberty. The race issue is one of the most urgent of contemporary problems. Recently, because of the effect of rapid social change in raising the expectations of the hitherto poorer races, the problem of race relations has become global. The interrelation of race and new nationalism, the link between the Negro struggle for freedom and the death of colonialism, and the widening gap between rich and poor nations propelled the race question to prominence in international politics. But, within the ecumenical movement, this concern has a long history. There has been much criticism of the offenses of whites against colored peoples and denigration of feelings of racial superiority, from the earliest days of Life and Work to the present. Anti-Semitism has come in for special attack, spurred in the first instance by reaction to the Nazi race myth, but repeated as recently as New Delhi's special resolution. Christian protests against racial segregation have been encouraged, with the Evanston Report even calling disobedience of racially discriminatory laws a Christian *duty*.

The ecumenical movement has been at pains to deny support to those who would justify legal separation of the races—separate facilities for education and the like—on the grounds of the created variety of peoples. Diversity is the Creator's will, but so is equality in spiritual status and in access to justice. Both the 1960 Cottesloe Declaration (which resulted in some South African churches leaving the World Council in protest) and the New Delhi Report say that the unique contribution each race has to make can be realized only in community with others of diverse gifts. The doctrine of "separate development" defies the Christian view of man and the nature of the church, and the concept "separate but equal" is, in practice, actually a contradiction in terms. Ecumenical reports struggle to apply these insights to the life of the church. Itself unhappily often the victim of a segregationist culture to which it has conformed, the church should renounce all forms of racial discrimination in its own life and take the lead in abolishing such forms in secular life, even identifying itself with the oppressed race in the struggle. In so doing, Christians and their churches will discover anew the ecumenical perspective of the one church with its diversity of peoples in a single fellowship.

Protest against religious persecution or unjust restriction has been axiomatic for the ecumenical movement, whether aimed at Soviet or Nazi governments in the 1930's or at contemporary nationalisms based on one religion to the detriment of others. Various conference reports have spelled out the details of religious freedom: the right to worship; to train clergy; to give religious education to youth; to preach publicly for conversion; to change one's religion; to determine the group's own conditions of membership; to do missionary activity at home and abroad; to publish literature; to declare the application of faith to public affairs; and to be able to hold such material means as are necessary for this work. If the church is not free in its own life from government control or interference, then ecumenical thought affirms it may resist, just as may individuals when the state has given cause. The reports have emphasized that the church may not claim for itself rights that it would not freely accord to other religious groups. God's redemptive dealing with men, said the New Delhi Declaration, is not coercive but is based on free response; therefore human attempts to coerce or eliminate faith are violations of God's way with men. It is clear that religious liberty is a basic human right, a necessary freedom of conscience, linked inevitably to the cause of human freedom in general.

The ecumenical movement has rather consistently held that a church's freedom from state interference extends to the right to criticize and to attempt to influence government policy, but that the state may not similarly interfere with the life of the churches. The difference lies in the distinctive nature and function of the church. The developing understanding of it in its soteriological, as opposed to sociological, dimension coalesced with the decline of the Christendom concept to produce, in ecumenical thought, the norm of a church operating in a secularized culture with less concern for its privileges as an institution than with its freedom to perform its essential work as the bearer of redemptive life for the world. The secular and even anti-Christian character of the state has been increasingly recognized as a fact, underscoring the independence of the church and its freedom to act apart from government.

The nature of Christian action independent of, but directed toward, the state, has undergone some shifts of emphasis and style in the course of ecumenical history. In the 1920's when the majority in the movement were committed to corporate concepts of salvation to bring the world ever closer to the Kingdom, direct joint action by all the churches on the social order was the obvious need. The church as a body worked directly on national governments and international organizations, dealing with matters affecting the whole life of man. In the 1930's, the emphasis shifted more to the church's own integrity in worship and teaching, so to provide a foundation for its political judgments and support for the work of its laity in secular life. Despite the changed emphasis, however, ecumenical thought envisioned and defended all kinds of direct church action, from the public pronouncements of conferences to representations to governmental bodies.

Since the Second World War, the style of Christian action, as conceived by the ecumenical movement, has been considerably affected by contextualism in ethics. There has been a rejection of systematic social program-planning—drawing the Christian blueprint for the ideal society. Consequently, the conference reports renew what is actually an old ecumenical motif, namely, opposition to Christian political parties, partly because of their divisiveness within the church, but also partly because of an unwillingness to identify the church with the ambiguous programs and policies of a party. A second consequence of the contextualist antiprogram attitude is the raising of doubts concerning the church's institutional involvement with the world through schools and hospitals and the like. Abrecht and others have suggested that the church's role is to *pioneer* in social service; therefore, it should not fight to maintain its established service organizations if the government wants to take over their management. Instead, the church should be flexible, ready to respond to demands for new ways to serve, ways in which the state cannot or does not act. A third consequence is an increased emphasis on the role of the laity, on the "indirect" action of the church through its members, who are instructed in Christian truth and responsibility and actively supported by the corporate body.

None of the foregoing consequences mean that the ecumenical movement has given up direct action. On the contrary, it is perhaps more active than ever. But here also the effect of contextualism has been felt, in the style of such action. Against the promotion of a long-range Christian program, the movement has favored the prophetic way in pronouncements, speaking to special situations, naming names. Concentrating on the concrete instance, the church agencies can deal realistically with the problem, knowing how to compromise for the sake of progress without surrendering the tension between the absolute and the immediately possible. The church can act for limited accomplishments without being so bound to the world's standards by its institutional baggage that it surrenders its faithfulness to the Word of God.

Contextualism, then, has shaped the manner of Christian social action, while the fact of such action has remained an ecumenical constant. In endless variety the work of the church in society is carried on through ecumenical groups today, by independent work in places of need; by cooperation with secular agencies; by seeking legislation; by promoting mediation; by protest, public and private. Indeed, the conviction of the ecumenical movement that political action is necessary for the church is the inevitable end product of its theology of church and society. Here is the result of a belief that the Kingdom is fully relevant to the historical present, that the labors of men are significant, that sin and salvation have corporate dimensions, that all of the social and cultural life of the secular world is the arena of redemption, and that the one Church of Christ is called to witness to and work for that transformation. This faith is the constant form with which increasing experience, precision, sophistication, and resolution has shaped the main thrust of modern ecumenical political thought.

# 19

# CHRISTIANS AND POLITICAL LIFE IN A DYNAMIC ASIA

by YOSHIAKI IISAKA (Japan)

A FUNDAMENTAL question for the Christian as a citizen is that of loyalty. The Christian has a loyalty to God and a loyalty to man, and sometimes the two conflict. The loyalty that man owes to human groups and associations is always conditional and never absolute; his loyalty to God, in all circumstances, is unconditional and absolute. Not even the state has the right to demand absolute loyalty from its citizens, although it has often tended to do so.

It follows that man's loyalty to man and to groups must always be evaluated in the light of his loyalty to God. There are two poles between which human loyalty operates. On the one hand, there is an "either-or" relationship between loyalty to man and loyalty to God, which was expressed in the *clausula Petri:* "We ought to obey God rather than men" (Acts 5:29). There may be circumstances in which loyalty to a human group has to be denied for the sake of loyalty to God. This was the situation of the many Christians who resisted the diabolically perverted totalitarian regime of Nazi Germany. On the other hand, there is a "both-and" relationship, when loyalty to God can be focused and expressed in an act of loyalty to men or groups. This is the essence of the new commandment that Jesus gave to his followers: To love one's neighbor is to love God, and vice versa (see also Matt. 25:40). In such a case, the believer who gives his loyalty to man makes a decision of faith and a response to God in a particular situation. Thus we have to recognize that there may be times when "to die for one's country is to die for God," though such a case is rare. More often, this identification of loyalty to the human with loyalty to God is utilized by blind patriotism or extreme nationalism for its own purposes.

In the world today, questions of loyalty often become acute. Loyalty to the whole of humanity may conflict with loyalty to one's own nation. In a world of sovereign states, politicians and diplomats are legally obliged to be loyal to their own nation and to consider its interests before all others. Again, loyalty to a particular class may conflict with loyalty to the nation, or loyalty to a religious group with loyalty to the government, especially when the former is banned by the latter. Whenever loyalties conflict, the Christian has to make a choice, testing his loyalties in the light of his ultimate loyalty to God. No one human loyalty has precedence over others; each can be justified only when rooted in loyalty to God.

## Christian Participation in Politics

One area in which conflicts of loyalties are likely to arise for the Christian citizen is politics. To participate in politics is to exert some degree of influence on the making of policies and decisions. There are many established methods of doing this: election, referendum, recall, party membership and so on. There are others of a fluid and transient character, such as demonstrations, protest meetings and the collection of signatures. Even political apathy and indifference can be a form of political participation, exerting a negative influence. Politics are universal, involving everybody to some extent.

As a social organization, the church forms a potential pressure group in politics, although its main concern is not political. The principle of separation of church and state, which is embodied in many modern Constitutions, is not to be understood as an absolute dichotomy. Nor should Christians be discouraged from becoming professional politicians, for this is only one method—though a significant one—of political participation. Amid conflicting interests, the Christian's concern is how to obey God. In seeking to be obedient, his narrow self-interest will give way to a wider perspective within which he can consider the interests of others. Crass self-interest will be transformed into the enlightened self-interest that is the basis of political compromise. Such compromise is possible where there is a broad basis of agreement between the different parties on the goals and values of society. Thus one of the most important tasks of the church and of individual Christians is to broaden that consensus through preaching, education, training and participation in everyday social life.

The principle of separation of church and state is rightly understood to mean that each shall be true to its respective tasks and perform its proper functions, without trespassing on or interfering with the other's domain. There is a danger in the church's becoming the state, and in the state's becoming the church. If the church is concerned with politics for the sake of politics, it will become perverted; and if the state demands worship from the people and absolutizes its own ideology, it will become the demonic monster of Rev. 13. But separation does not imply indifference: An institutional and functional separation does not preclude friendly relations and close cooperation. The church's concern for the state is based upon its mission to protect human life and to care for the human soul. When necessary, therefore, it will assume a watching role, interceding, warning, criticizing, protesting and even resisting, according to the needs of the situation. On the other hand, the state has a right to administrative supervision of the church—as of other social organizations and associations—within the limits set by law. It also has a duty to secure the greatest possible freedom for the church.

The Christian citizen belongs to both church and state. He has to represent and to participate responsibly in both. He has to exercise his citizenship according to the decisions that he takes as a member of the believing community, and he will play his part in the church's mission in the world of politics through a serious assumption of his citizenship. Thus, though there is a strategic organizational separation, there is no existential separation, because responsible church membership cannot be divorced from responsible citizenship.

Another false conception arises in this connection—that of a separation between the church and the individual Christian. Those who hold this concept would limit political action and participation to the latter and deny to the church *qua* church any corporate action in the political field. This view is based on a false individualism which weakens the dynamic and organic bond between the church and its members. Whether to act individually or corporately in the political sphere is a strategic decision that must be made in the light of particular situations. Moreover, if the corporate decision of the church in political matters is to be prompt and relevant, it has to be made by a few who hold positions of leadership in the church and represent it legally. On the other hand, an individual Christian or a group of Christians may make a resolute political witness, acting according to faith in Jesus Christ, seeking to hear God's call in a particular situation and placing themselves under his judgment. Such a political witness made in faith by a minority—in an extreme case, a minority of one—may be regarded as the witness of the whole community of faith, for this minority represents the church and its mission.

Among the questions that arise in connection with responsible Christian participation in politics, there are three that we would mention here: political apathy, resistance and conscientious objection.

### The Problem of Apathy

In modern democracies, the ordinary citizen's active participation in politics is presupposed and encouraged. But, in recent years, this presupposition has not always corresponded to reality. Two kinds of political apathy have appeared, which we may call "structural" (arising from the nature of the political structure itself) and "organizational" (resulting from the organized effort to manipulate it). Such apathy even appears to be inescapable in a "mass democracy": As the possibilities for political participation at the grass-roots level increases, so does the political apathy of the masses.

There are several possible causes of this apathy. It may result from the complicated organizational and technological character of our society, or from the general preoccupation with economic affluence and immediate interests. Or it may express satisfaction with the *status quo*. In extreme cases, it may be a sign of resignation.

Religion can be a cause of apathy if religion is merely a means of emotional gratification and of other-worldly expectation. Whatever its case, permanent political apathy is a menace to democracy; for criticism and opposition are integral to it.

The problem of political apathy is particularly difficult for those countries that have recently emerged from colonial and traditional bondage. Long subservience to colonial and feudal authorities has made their citizens apathetic; often they believe that politics is not, and should not be, their business. Citizenship is conceived as cooperation with the authorities within the limits set by them; beyond these limits lies the beginning of subversion. Sometimes traditional religions contribute to political apathy by advocating other-worldly salvation at the cost of "this-worldly" participation. Such religions have a close connection with the state and degenerate into an aspect of the ruling ideology.

The various manifestations of apathy pose an important problem for responsible Christian citizenship. The Christian faith should not stimulate either political indifference or political fanaticism, for both spring from an inadequate understanding of the Kingdom of God. That Kingdom should not be an excuse for escaping from "this-worldly" involvement, nor should it be confounded with the rash realization of ideal social plans. It is the *telos,* as well as the test, of present society. It provides a guide for Christian social action that must be translated into decisions in a given situation.

## The Question of Resistance

The right and duty to resist have, in the past, been prominent in Christian social thinking. In our century, two factors have brought this problem into the foreground of Christian political ethics—the emergence of totalitarian states and the violent resistance of subject peoples to colonial powers during their struggle for emancipation. In the light of these new developments, the traditional doctrine of the right to resist has to be drastically revised.

Traditionally, Christians have been inclined to view the state as a dam against chaos and a guarantee of order, and have treated rather negatively the problems of resistance and revolution. Order has always been preferred to war and anarchy, which allegedly represent the power of sin, and from this preference for order, the duty of obedience to authority has derived.

In human history, however, no order can be perfect nor any chaos permanent. There is a state of peace and order in which freedom suffocates and injustice thrives; there is a state of war, when men are determined to free themselves from unbearable tyranny, which looks forward to greater freedom. Peace can reign when the privileged are maintaining the *status quo* against the dispossessed. In extreme cases, peace and order may be maintained by a dictator or a tyrant. Thus there is no moral ground for saying that tyranny is always preferable to anarchy, or that patience to endure the wrongs of tyranny is always a greater Christian virtue than courage to resist unjust powers. Moreover, the maintenance of peace and order depends upon power, which is characterized by moral ambiguity and ethical ambivalence.

If we are to deal adequately with the problem of resistance, there are two preconditions to be met. First, we have to guard against forming a metaphysical concept of the state and government on the basis of the Bible. Such a concept, whether we call it a "theology of the state" or by some other name, will hinder a realistic approach to the problem of the state in the context of our time. The Bible is not concerned with formulating a theory of the state. The New Testament contains no general and objective statement about the "state" or about authority but only concrete suggestions that were relevant to the specific problems arising out of the life of New Testament Christians in the body politic, which was totally different in nature and structure from our own. Thus, while the Bible can tell us *how* Christians in those times judged their political problems, we have not merely to follow *what* they did; in the light of this *how,* we have to find our own approach and solution.

The second precondition is that we should not allow ourselves to be too much influenced by Reformation thinking on this problem. The Reformers, too, were children of their time. Their attitude toward the state was limited by the political situation of the day; and there are important differences between their political situation and ours. In particular, there is a difference in the extent to which the masses can participate effectively in politics. In former days, they had very few means of influencing political action, and it was natural for an ethic of endurance and submissiveness to develop. Today, however, democratic Constitutions provide opportunities for the masses to organize themselves and to exert effective pressure on politics—even to the point of overthrowing the existing regime. There is also a difference in the amount of political information available to the people and the means by which it reaches them. At one time, it was safe to limit resistance to a certain group or class, taking for granted the political ignorance and poor judgment of the people. This assumption no longer holds good. Information is available through diverse media and channels, and any person or group is thus in a position to make political judgments.

Today, the churches have departments of international and domestic affairs, staffed by specialists. They organize study programs and seminars and can sometimes offer information and judgments that are more impartial and penetrating than those provided by government organizations. Thus the Reformers' distinction between those who could resist (for example, a particular social class or men in public office) and those who could not (for example, individuals and private persons) has become obsolete.

All this calls for a pragmatic approach to the question when and in what circumstances resistance is justified. For instance, if we seek to justify resistance to Nazism or communism because of their nature, our resistance is ideological but not Christian. Our concern is to judge whether and at what point such a system has become so oppressive that it constitutes a denial of humanity and turns into a demonic monster, irrevocably perverting justice and freedom, and against which no action other than violent resistance is conceivable. The important point is not our own interest or safety but concern for our neighbors; not our own rights but the justice of God; not our own heroism but obedience to the Lord. If resistance is not to be blind and opportunist, some thought must be given to the resources and organizations available; and the prospects for success should be realistically assessed. If one attempt fails because of poor preparation and bad organization, the next may be more difficult and even hopeless, for the existing regime will be more cautious and better prepared to meet it. Moreover, in the world today, if drastic political action leads to a change in power at the national level, there are bound to be repercussions of all kinds at the international level.

So-called "Christian motives" provide no justification for political undertakings that fail because they were badly prepared, though we must admit the possibility of an extreme case, when there is no alternative to resistance, even though it has scant prospect of success. Then, the value of the act is symbolic rather than practical; it is an indication that man's ultimate loyalty is to God and that this loyalty transcends relative judgments about the outcome in and for history. Even if it fails, the act will inspire others and draw their attention to the issues at stake.

Thus the political act is to be seen in two dimensions: its trans-historical significance and its historical consequences. On the whole, political witness in the form of resistance is borne by a minority that believes that it has been called by God to take this step. They may or may not be joined by others; but, in either case, they will constitute a minority group within the whole Christian church. Yet, in the act of resistance—as in all other political action taken by faith in Jesus Christ—the minority will existentially represent the whole church, and the political witness of the whole church will be made through this minority.

At this point, it may be useful to consider the question of differences that arise among Christians on political matters. They may arise from the way in which different Christians have been brought up and from the unconscious social and economic assumptions that they have absorbed, or they may be the result of conflicting interests and values. The Christian faith provides believers with common ground on which to judge man's self-centeredness, rationalization and aggrandizement in politics. Christians should discuss their differences of political judgment, examining themselves in the light of their own faith, and thus seek to reach greater agreement. Differences will remain; but normally they need not be a threat to the unity of the church. In an extreme case, political differences may lead to a split in the church, because the loyalty and conscience of some members do not allow them to remain with the others merely for the sake of unity. The issue at stake here is not merely political but goes far deeper; it is the choice between the true and the false church. A significant example of this was provided by the *Deutsche Christen* under the Nazi regime.

## Conscientious Objection

"Passive resistance" is usually taken to mean the deliberate disobeying of a particular law or order of the state. The most remarkable instance of this today is conscientious objection: a refusal of military service on religious and ethical grounds. It raises many questions, particularly in view of the experience of two world wars and the changes that have taken place in the structure of the state and of the world.

In modern states, universal conscription and the death penalty appear to be signs of the state's almighty power over the lives of its citizens. The former has been reinforced by the state's increasing control over men's minds and thoughts by its use of modern techniques of persuasion and brainwashing. Cheap patriotism has been extensively manufactured, and precious lives have been claimed by the state for its dubious undertakings. In this situation, conscientious objection was intended to be a protest against the false pretensions of the state, a warning that it should recognize the limits of its rightful powers and a reminder that freedom of conscience is outside state control and, in fact, constitutes the basis of loyalty without which no state can be expected to last long. Though individual acts of conscientious objection cannot change the course of events, they have tremendous implications. They constitute not only a reminder of the deeper level of human freedom but also an anticipation of things to come; that is, universal disarmament and a world without weapons.

With the development of the techniques of nuclear warfare, the distinction between "absolute" and "relative" pacifists seems to have become blurred. A total nuclear war would bring the destruction of human culture and society upon the victors as well as the vanquished, and therefore all have to be "absolute" pacifists. The traditional concept of a "just war" is no longer tenable.

So far, conscientious objectors have had to engage without complaint in "substitute services" instead of military service, and these are usually unpleasant or tediously laborious jobs. The churches, rather than the government, should assume greater responsibility for deciding how they should serve and what kind of jobs they should do. Conscientious objectors must learn how to organize themselves into a wing of the peace movement. The ideal of disarmament is nothing but conscientious objection on a national and international scale. Conversely, as an integral part of their strategy, peace movements should protect and propagate the principle of conscientious objection.[1]

The conscientious objector should heed one warning: if he is to be consistent in his ethical decisions, his conscience must keep him as responsible in other matters as he is in the question of military service. Preoccupation with one issue is no excuse or compensation for neglecting others.

If Christians are to be effective in politics, they must cooperate and form a common front with non-Christians. The political realm is not concerned with the ultimate but with the immediate; it is a realm of relative and temporal achievements. Christians cannot compromise on the absolute truth of the Christian faith, but, in a relative sphere, such as politics, there is room for concession and compromise. Those who, like many idealists, seek the impossible or improbable in politics will be led into blind radicalism, and their ensuing disillusionment will make them, in turn, reactionaries and supporters of the *status quo*. Those who take part in politics, whether they are Christians or not, should make a realistic assessment of what is possible and probable. Their attitude should be pragmatic: They should make their judgments on particular issues, not according to absolute and eternal standards but according to immediate or intermediate results.

Thus Christians can and should cooperate with the state, pro-

---

[1] Though the Constitutions of many countries contain guarantees for conscientious objectors, the Constitution of Japan is unique in applying this principle to the nation itself. Article 9 of Chapter II, "Renunciation of War," reads: "Aspiring sincerely to an international peace based on justice and order, the Japanese people forever renounce war as a sovereign right of the nation and the threat of force as a means of settling disputes.

"In order to accomplish the aim of the preceding paragraph, land, sea and air forces, as well as other war potential, will never be maintained. The right of the state to belligerency will not be recognized."

Thus, the constitution enjoins conscientious objection on every member of the nation. Japanese Christians are seeking to preserve this article unchanged, against those who are pressing for its revision.

vided that it is sincerely striving to accomplish the tasks of nation-building and human welfare, even if it is not always friendly to the church and Christianity. This is often the situation in communist countries or in those countries where the dominant religion is not Christianity. An unfriendly attitude toward Christianity is certainly to be deplored, for it suggests a threat to religious liberty and, ultimately, therefore, to all other human freedoms and rights. Yet, in itself, it is not necessarily a reason for Christians to refuse to cooperate in or to resist efforts to improve conditions and to promote better social standards.

Several points should be noted about the attitudes Christians should adopt in cooperating with non-Christians.

1. Many newly independent countries have not yet attained even a minimal standard of social justice and welfare for the mass of their people. In such countries, Christians should set aside their controversies with non-Christians over the ultimate question of God or atheism and should engage at once in the urgent task of nation-building. This is not to say that apologetics are unimportant —far from it. Christians need to remember, however, that if preoccupation with dogma and ritual prevents their paying attention to the needs of the people, their negligence will be a denial of the love of God.

2. To fulfill the urgent tasks of state is, in itself, a witness, since it expresses Christian love in service to others, and deepens the fellowship between Christians and non-Christians. But Christians have sometimes felt inhibited in sharing in common tasks or adopting a common front, either because of their ideological understanding of the Christian faith or because of some nonessential excrescences that, strictly speaking, have nothing to do with Christianity as a faith but are rather the product of a particular cultural environment. If need be, Christians should be ready to sacrifice these and to assume a new style of Christian life—religionless Christianity—which, freed from traditional ways of life and thinking, owes to others nothing but love. This would mean the end of the church's privileged position in the West and of its hermitlike position in the East.

3. Christians are not concerned with ideologies and their promises and programs as such, nor should Christianity be confused or

identified with any ideology. Ideologies express the basic values of those who hold them, often reflecting their social and economic position as well as their hopes and aspirations. They embody views of the world and programs that promise the realization of these aspirations. Christianity judges all human ideologies, for its knowledge of human self-centeredness exposes their limitations, and its eschatological insight enables men to distinguish true promises from false. It makes it possible for Christians to use these ideologies, which have thus lost their power, by treating their absolute claims as relative. Christians are not bound by the program of any "isms," and therefore can freely use any program in the service of men, without regarding it as having absolute validity. The test of any ideology or program is its usefulness for the humanizing process. Christians are the servants of men, but they are the masters of ideologies and programs. Thus they should adopt a more positive attitude toward political ideologies, and so be able to cooperate with those of a particular ideological background.

4. In politics, as in other realms, Christians are the light of the world and the salt of the earth. The light exposes, illumines, enlightens and brightens the political world. It cannot be hidden, for it is a reflection of "the true light that cometh into the world." It will lead and guide men amid the encircling gloom of the political situation. Light symbolizes the distinctive and overt aspect of the Christian way of life. On the other hand, salt signifies the hidden and covert aspect. Penetrating the depths of things and losing its distinctive form and color, it preserves the political world from corruption. Distinctiveness and hiddenness, manifest and incognito —this was the dynamic rhythm of our Lord's life as the servant of men. This rhythm must find an echo in the political witness and service of Christians today. The distinctiveness of the political witness of Christians against Nazism was certainly one form of Christian citizenship; the hiddenness with which, without losing their savour, they serve in some countries today is another.

## The Lordship of Christ and the Kingdom of God

Human politics is characterized by ambiguity. Christians, however, do not become cynical, because they know by faith that

Jesus Christ is Lord over the political realm, and that God's rule, the Kingdom of God—which is the ultimate hope, the hope for a consummation beyond history—will reveal and fulfill the meaning of history and of human politics. They will not be embarrassed by the precarious nature of the political situation but will try to discern the signs of God's planning and working. For them, the Lordship of Jesus Christ and the Kingdom of God signify not merely a negative transcendence of the political situation but positive guidance in it.

The Lordship of Jesus Christ covers the whole world and all in it. False dichotomies, as between the church and the world; the religious and the secular; the ministry of the laity; Christendom and pagan countries; the realm of grace and the realm of sin, are therefore excluded. These different realms are all under one and the same Lord, and there is no excuse for limiting our responsibility to the one realm and rejecting the other. His Lordship reveals the common factor that binds together the different realms: their humanity. The human is the measure of all things, because God became human in Jesus Christ. In the political realm, therefore, our concern is with humanity. This is the orientation of the Christian's concern for politics.

The Kingdom of God also has a positive implication for politics. To the eye of faith, it provides not only judgment, but also guidance. We try to trace the reflection of the Kingdom of God in history. It is only a reflection, not the Kingdom itself; but it makes us realize the closeness of the reality. and its contours tell us something of the pattern and features of the Kingdom. We can seek to reproduce these contours on our earthly canvas: The Kingdom, God's rule, can be the pattern and example for human kingdoms and rule. When the church proclaims the Kingdom of God, it is inevitably concerned with human kingdoms and with politics.

# 20

# A ROMAN CATHOLIC VIEW OF POLITICAL RESPONSIBILITY

by Michael P. Fogarty (United Kingdom)

A number of countries can look back today on upward of a hundred years of participation by Catholics in modern forms of political life. The direction of movement over these hundred years is clear. Then, a Catholic politician, or at least a consciously Catholic politician, was a churchman in politics. Now, he is a politician who is a member of the church. Then, he was the leader of a distinctive minority, often socially or politically underprivileged, in any case, outside the mainstream of political and social progress. He was fighting a defensive battle, a rear-guard action, for that minority's specifically ecclesiastical interests. Now, he has become the leader of a national party with positive, not merely defensive, policies covering the whole range of public issues, placing little or no special emphasis on ecclesiastical problems and belonging clearly to the same category as other parties even when it still bears the seemingly distinctive label "Catholic" or "Christian." By virtue of this change, he is called to national leadership in western Europe, in the Anglo-Saxon countries and lately in Latin America and Africa to an extent beyond the dreams of his predecessor of a century ago. He has come to see himself and to be accepted as a colleague to whom others, as well as enthusiasts of his own religion, can look for leadership, a man of broad public responsibility, not merely the defender of sectarian interests, an honest partner and fair competitor, one who respects the rights of others and will not twist the Constitution to put Popery in power. He has become a leader among fellow citizens.

Such a generalization is necessarily less than the truth. It is not hard to think of exceptions and qualifications both now and in the past. But, as an impression of the trend, it is correct. Why has movement gone this way? What position, in more detail, has been reached? In what sense can one still speak of a Roman Catholic view of political responsibility, as apart from a view of political responsibility that happens to be held by, among others, some Roman Catholics?

## The Reasons for the Trend

### A. The church meets the problems of the modern world

The first reason for the trend is simply that the Catholic Church has run into the problems of the modern world and has had to develop policies and organizations for handling them. In the countries with a relatively long Catholic political participation, three phases can be distinguished.

The first, from before the French Revolution up to around 1880, might be called the fight for survival. All over Europe, the Catholic Church, under heavy attack from nationalists and secularists, dug in to defend its own essential freedoms: freedom to manage its internal affairs, to teach, recruit, found new institutions and play a part in secular fields most directly related to its work, such as schools and social welfare. In several countries, this led to the foundation of Catholic parties within a more or less democratic political system. Catholics in a number of countries began to accept that the tolerance of other views, whether or not it was to be approved in itself, was an essential element in the sort of political framework in which alone the church could expect to survive and flourish.

In the second phase, from around 1880 till the Second World War, the Catholic Church came more generally to grips with modern social and political problems. Understanding and sympathy for democratic politics increased as a result of experience in the United States, the British Commonwealth and Ireland, as well as in western Europe. The Catholic parties in western Europe acquired, after hard infighting, strong "social" wings, based on Catholic or interdenominational trade unions, workers' educational movements and youth movements such as the Young Christian Workers. The Popes poured out a stream of encyclicals on political and social issues. Ecclesiastical issues, notably that of the schools, remained an important element in the political activity of Catholics, but were now equaled or overshadowed by issues of a more general kind.

The first two phases, though involving relations with groups outside the Catholic Church, were primarily a matter of the church's internal development, a case of Catholics coming to grips with themselves. They were also confined, with minor exceptions, to Europe and European-populated countries overseas. In the third phase, in which we now are, the church has turned its full attention to the problems of coexistence and collaboration with other ideological groups in a plural society, and to Catholics' contribution to the development of the world as whole. John XXIII's encyclicals *Mater et Magistra* and *Pacem in Terris* add little to the content of the church's teaching. But they lay new stress on dialogue and collaboration with people of other beliefs, Christian or not, on the rights and equality of *all* men, and on the need to seek mutually acceptable grounds of obligation. For the first time, the light in encyclicals on the social order falls on countries everywhere and at all stages of development. In one field after another of the church's activity, more and more of the new growing points are proving to be international or, at any rate, in countries other than the main traditional centers of Catholic activity.

B.  *The church learns to manage innovation*

It is a commonplace of management today that an organization wishing to cope successfully with the swiftly changing conditions of the modern world must do two things. It must encourage a high degree of enterprise and initiative on the part of its subunits and individual members, for only they can keep closely enough in touch with the problems with which each is concerned to understand them fully or see their full significance for the organization's work. But it must also ensure strong central leadership, able not only to stimulate members' initiative and equip them to use it but also to summarize its results and weave them into a coherent whole. We have learned only too well in recent years, and notably since Keynes' work in economics, how easily a social system that lacks this central steering can spin out of control to destinations its members neither intended nor like.

One of the devastating effects of the split in the church in the sixteenth century was to raise a wall of separation between these two elements of management precisely at the moment when, because of the accelerating speed of social change, it was vital for the church to develop both together. The Catholic Church retained from the work of its great medieval thinkers a capacity for synthesis, for summing up discussion within the church, drawing conclusions from it, and giving central leadership. This later bore fruit in the great political and social encyclicals of the nineteenth and twentieth centuries. But Catholics also developed a defensive, fortress mentality, which discouraged individual sorties. They were notably slow to show their initiative in the new, pioneering fields of modern science and technology or of democratic politics. They could synthesize what was discussed if they were in touch with it, but too often were underrepresented where the most active and promising discussion was going on. In pioneering, in dynamism, in launching the ordinary member of the church into action, the advantage was heavily with the Protestant side. But, to offset this, large sectors of Protestantism showed an almost pathological fear of central leadership in the church. They bought their superiority in initiative at the price of lagging behind in synthesis.

Through the last three or four generations, both sides have been recovering from this division. On the Protestant side, there has been the search for the church. On the Catholic side, a "theology of the laity" has developed, and more initiative has come to be expected from laymen as well as clergy within the church's own machinery as well as outside. There has also been a vast improvement in the channels by which the results of this initiative are drawn together and influence the action of the church as a whole, although they are still often imperfect. Quantitative methods of analyzing opinions and situations, for example, as developed for church purposes by the institutes belonging to FERES,[1] are still too little used. Laymen are often inadequately trained for their role inside the church or are reluctant to fill it fully. But with all

---

[1] International Federation of Catholic Institutes for Social Research.

its limitations, the change has been immense. Centrally, or through its individual members, the Catholic Church is today in far less danger of being shut inside its traditional frame of thought and out of touch with the full and changing reality of the modern world than it was one hundred years ago.

## C.  *Adjustment by other groups*

Another important development has been the growth of a readiness among non-Catholic groups for a dialogue with Catholics and of a sense of fellow-citizenship. It is a century since a Protestant mob tried to lynch the parish priest of my own city of Cardiff. But it is only within the last generation, in many parts of Britain, that it has begun to seem normal for Protestant clergy to treat a Catholic priest as an equal colleague deserving their friendship and confidence. Central European Socialists, not much over a generation ago, ceremoniously joined crematorium clubs to underline their rejection of Catholicism; for them, Catholicism and socialism were mutually exclusive. Today the Socialist International accepts Christianity, including Catholicism, as one of the ideological foundations on which its supporters' adherence rests. Socialist parties, one after another, have announced that they accept the right of Catholic parents to choose church schools and that they see Christian-Democratic parties as political competitors and not as ideological rivals.

The inmates of a beleaguered fortress have some excuse for developing a fortress mentality. If the fortress mentality has declined among Catholics, it is largely because, and insofar as, the enemy is no longer at the gates. Not surprisingly, it is precisely when Catholics' right to live in their own way and organize their own institutions—schools and colleges, trade unions, political parties—has begun to be freely admitted that a number of them have begun to ask themselves whether some of these institutions are not primarily of use for defense and might now be dispensed with. Like the traveler in Aesop's fable, they lower their defenses more easily to the sun than to the storm.[2]

---

[2] The sun and the wind argued which was stronger. They agreed to test their strength on a traveler who was walking along a road wrapped in his coat. Whoever first got his coat off him would win. The wind screamed

## Toward What Sort of Society?

Recent Papal encyclicals hold out the vision of a "Responsible Society." I deliberately borrow this term, which is more expressive than anything in official use in the Catholic Church, from the World Council of Churches.

A "Responsible Society," as the encyclicals see it, is a society that takes responsibility for its people. It understands that, without a strong state and a close-knit network of social relations, it cannot achieve the conditions of life at which Christians should aim. It plans for technical advance, economic growth, social security, a fair distribution of income and property and progress in health, housing, and education. It sees to it that all groups and areas within the country progress together and that no sector is allowed to drop behind, and it joins in efforts to the same end internationally. It uses direct state enterprise and public ownership where necessary. It insists that individual and group interests are subordinated to the common good of the whole, and that individuals and groups are trained to act with social responsibility and not simply for their own ends.

But a "Responsible Society" also is a society of responsible people, educated, socially skilled, with access to knowledge and money, able and ready to make the widest possible range of decisions for themselves. At the center of any consideration of political and social organization must stand human personality with its needs and abilities. Human beings need the opportunity to develop and use their gifts to the full. They are also society's most valuable resource, and, particularly in a changing world, it is vital to use their powers and initiative to the limit. Planning must therefore be designed to enlarge the limits of freedom. It must have a subsidiary function, not that of supplanting individual or group effort but of encouraging it, providing resources for it and supplementing and steering it insofar as it needs a larger framework or proves inadequate.

---

down in a hurricane, tearing at the traveler's coat; but the more it tore at him the tighter he wrapped his coat around him. Then the wind retired and the sun came out, warming the traveler; and in five minutes his coat was off.

The state must protect human rights such as those defined in the United Nations' Declaration of 1948 and ensure that citizens have the necessary freedom to act. This includes the freedom to exercise responsibility in business. Economic initiative should come in the first place, though never exclusively, from individuals and voluntary groups, and the state must respect "the right and duty which normally belong to every man of providing for the needs of himself and his dependents" (*Mater et Magistra,* 55). Where organization is needed above the level of the individual, the slogan should not be nationalization, which strengthens the hand of the state to the exclusion of lower-level groups, but socialization, which strengthens the whole network of social relations, including those that people can influence more directly for themselves. The church's vision is one of people managing their own civic, social and economic affairs as directly as possible through organizations on the human scale: clubs, cooperatives, enterprises, trade unions, political parties and groups. The state must see to it that citizens have not only the legal rights necessary for this but the necessary knowledge, skills and finance: knowledge and skill through research, education and training; finance through a high and secure standard of living and the personal and group ownership of property. It must recognize that direct state enterprise, controlled at a relatively long distance from the citizen, is always a last resort. Where large-scale organization of any kind is used, those engaged in it should participate in its control according to their education and developed ability. In modern societies, *Mater et Magistra* notes, their degree of education and ability is or should be increasing all the time.

This implies, among other things, that democracy will more and more be the normal form of a modern state. There is an old Catholic tradition (Aquinas: *Summa Theologica,* I., ii., 105) that a "mixed" constitution should be preferred: one with a personal, strong executive head, office-holders making up an aristocracy of merit, and election of the government by and from the people. Leo XIII, in 1885, noted that "at certain times" popular participation in government "may even be of obligation." The last three Popes have made it progressively clearer that in modern conditions, "at certain times," is coming to mean in general or as a rule.

The case for the rule of subsidiary function is not merely that it ensures more adequate scope to individuals and smaller organizations. It is also that large-scale organizations, including the state, can do their essential work properly only if they do not have to waste their resources on tasks that could be performed by individuals and smaller groups, or on ferreting out problems to which these lower-level groups could have drawn their attention. There is always a risk of overloading the top levels of large-scale organizations so that decisions cannot be taken rapidly enough or with full enough consideration of all the relevant facts. The worst effects of substituting overcentralized control for free initiative and competition tend to be seen (*Mater et Magistra,* 57) in the supply—or lack—of consumer goods "and still more of things which serve the needs of the mind rather than those of the body."

The state and lower level organizations alike must cover their fields not only completely but with a wide sense of responsibility, for collaboration between them must not be merely mechanical. Catholic theory rejects not only the thesis that individuals or lower-level groups are subordinate to or derive their authority from the state but also that of separate compartments, the so-called "mechanistic" approach to government and management—the idea that looking after the common good is the responsibility of the state, and that individuals and lower-level groups need look out only for their own interests. The management of society must be participative. Higher-level leaders must act with consideration for the judgments of individuals and lower-level groups, and these in turn must act with consideration for the judgments of leaders who operate at higher levels and have a wider view. However, this solidarity and mutual responsibility of individuals and groups at different levels or in different fields must not be carried to the point where national and local leaders concern themselves indiscriminately with each other's sphere of activity. There is a striking parallel here between Catholic political and social theory and the findings of recent management research on how best to manage in a dynamic and progressive firm, the problems of the "management of innovation."

The social and political pattern outlined in the encyclicals is an ideal one. Societies that fall short of it cannot necessarily achieve it in a day. Marxists suggest that a developing society is likely to pass through three phases:

1. The first is a phase of disorganization, when the problems of industrialization are new and poorly understood, technical and administrative skills are lacking and capital (and particularly a centrally available pool of capital) is hard to come by. A government may be able to do little beyond removing obstacles to those entrepreneurs or organizers of cooperatives or voluntary social services who happen to have the will and the means to take the lead.

2. In a second phase, poverty remains serious: Only the most urgent needs can be satisfied, and capital, education and technical and social skills are still scarce. But enough resources and skills, including administrative skill, are now available to make possible general solutions to elementary economical and social problems provided what is available is carefully planned and rationed. At this stage, the best approach may be by strong central leadership, organizing production on standard lines and ensuring to each person at least a minimum standard ration of necessities, including basic social services such as education or social security.

3. In the third phase, when education and technical and administrative skills are more freely available, people are better trained and equipped to make their own decisions, and resources are relatively abundant. At this stage, coercive, standardized, central planning can be replaced by individual choice or selfadministration through voluntary groups, though central coordination of the decisions emerging must remain. Indeed, coercive central control not only can but must fade away, because in an abundant and educated society the range of choices to be made becomes too great for it to master.

Phase three corresponds to the ideal set out in the encyclicals. But nothing in the encyclicals denies the possibility of a society being in either of the previous stages and needing more coercive government and management, and less participation, self-administration and personal choice than in phase three. The Catholic Church has always made it clear that there is no absolutely preferred form of government. Each country must choose a form suitable to its own stage of development. If, for example, an African country beginning industrialization considers that it must have a one-party government because it is not yet ripe for full democracy, the church will not quarrel with this. It will, however, say two things:

First, nations in the earlier phases must build toward the more ideal society of phase three. At each stage, every opportunity must be taken to apply the rule of subsidiary function, and to offer citizens the chance to participate where they can and to equip them for this. Trade unionism and sharing in community development are possible even where government and management in general must remain authoritarian. The phases are never absolutely distinct. Each always includes elements of the others, and maximum encouragement must always be given to the more advanced elements characteristic of and paving the way for phase three.

Second, the transition from one phase to another must normally be a matter of evolution, not revolution, as must progress within each phase, and even the most authoritarian government must make this possible. John XXIII underlines in *Pacem in Terris* the theme that, nationally as well as internationally, real progress is peaceful progress, and good government consists in talking through problems, not shooting a way out of them. This does not exclude forceful argument, backed in special cases by methods such as strikes or, more extremely, civil disobedience. But it does exclude violent revolution and repression except in the most extreme cases where no other solution remains.

## How Shall a Christian Take Part in Politics?

The obligation to take part in politics arises not because people are Christian or Catholic but because they are members of a political community. The form of a political community is a matter of choice, and *Pacem in Terris* lays down that those with good reasons have the right to migrate from one political community to another. But involvement in *a* political community and the duty to take part in it are facts from which no person can escape. Man is a social being who can realize his full potential only in and through society, including organized society and, in particular, the state. Therefore, he must play his part in shaping society and must accept its directives except insofar as they are clearly contrary to the moral law. And, in this respect, there is no distinction between those members of a political community who are baptized or are members of the Catholic Church and those who are not.

Catholics are reminded in the encyclicals that the church's doctrine provides them with extra guidance on how to fulfil their political obligations and that they should be active in fulfilling them. But they are also reminded that the source of these obligations is common to all, in or out of the church, namely the facts of the political situation as understood by reason and evaluated by conscience. There is a "pattern of order imprinted by the Creator himself" (*Pacem in Terris,* 5) on the facts of the situation, and, from this, any man of good will can read out a natural law, the reflection in created things, including human society, of God's eternal law.

The natural law in all its complexity is not easy to discover, for it takes into account the whole context of each situation. A true interpretation of it has to steer a careful course between the many pairs of deviations toward which natural-law theories have been misdirected at various times. Eighteenth- and nineteenth-century liberals overstressed individual rights and obligations at the expense of social; twentieth-century Marxists overstress the social at the expense of the individual. One school swings toward scientism: It confuses the natural moral law with the natural laws studied by scientists, treats it as if it could be discovered solely from the scientific study of facts and fails to recognize that, as an ethical law, it has at its roots value judgments, few but vital, which are related to human nature and experience but are not derived from it in a scientific way and are not verifiable by science. Another swings toward intuitionism: the idea that judgments are intuitively grasped and unverifiable, even when common sense shows that they contain a large element of factual assessment of what the state of affairs actually is. Some natural-law theories are relativistic: The natural law as they see it has no fixed principles, and the whole pattern of ethical obligation changes from one culture or phase of social development to another. Others insist on treating as fixed principles rules of behavior that are clearly related to the way of life of a particular people or age. Some natural-law theorists have seen war and conflict as the dominant feature of society; others have dreamed of a utopia where cooperation and good will would reign, understanding would be perfect and conflict would cease. Some overstress the future at the expense of the present; others concentrate too much on the here and now.

History shows that a true appreciation of the natural law can only be arrived at through a slow and painful process, with many setbacks and pendulum swings from one extreme to another. It is an immense advantage that revelation and grace are available as additional guides. Revelation not only does contradict the natural law—both, after all, are messages "imprinted by the Creator"—but it casts additional light on it. It illuminates natural truths before natural reasoning could reach them, and, along with grace, helps natural reasoning to avoid error.

Nevertheless, Catholic theory on the one hand insists that the natural law is in fact accessible to people of good will even without the aid of revelation and, on the other hand, agrees that, even with this aid, Catholics may not be the first to arrive at it. *Pacem in Terris* notes that people outside the church have often grasped particular areas of the natural law more quickly and effectively than Catholics and have led the way in political and social progress. Therefore, says John XXIII, Catholics should not only build their own political and social doctrine on the natural law but also watch for the good points in the political and social doctrine of people of other beliefs and be ready to cooperate with them in civic matters, in some cases even where their social and political theories are wrong. (Perfect understanding of the natural law is in any case unlikely. Catholics must therefore be practical, down to earth and reluctant to let the theoretical best become the enemy of the good.)

Until as recently as a generation ago, official statements of the Catholic Church gave at least the appearance of a blanket condemnation of the major political and social movements that have shaped the modern world.[3] Strictly, what was condemned was the

---

[3] Pius XI, in *Quadragesimo Anno,* noted that his predecessor Leo XIII "sought help neither from Liberalism nor from Socialism: the former has already shown its impotence to find a right solution of the social question, while the latter ... offered a remedy much more disastrous than the evil it aimed to end." He spoke himself of the "idols of liberalism" and "the tottering tenets of liberalism," and said flatly that "no one can be at the same time a sincere Catholic and a socialist properly so-called."

abstract principle deemed to underlie socialism and liberalism, and this condemnation did not exclude collaboration in practical action in cases where it could be advantageous: for example, in the formation of a coalition government including Christian Democrats along with Liberals or Socialists. But it was left to John XXIII to insist on the need for a sophisticated distinction between the elements in each theory of which Catholics can or cannot approve and on which collaboration can or cannot be based. If, he says, socialism is tied to an atheist philosophy such as Marxism; if it means technocracy —an engineers' world where family life and other civilized values are sacrificed to production; or if it means state control beyond the limits justified by a country's current phase of development, then the church opposes it. But if it simply means planning for full employment, economic growth or regional development, for better social services, or for more effective trade unions and shared responsibility in work, then the church is strongly for it. If liberalism means abandoning moral standards, or a *laissez-faire* economy in which planning for growth and balanced regional development is neglected and the weakest go to the wall, then the church opposes it. But, if it means such things as political democracy, respect for the rights of conscience, or free choice for consumers and a chance for people to share in the decisions affecting their own lives, the church strongly favors it. Catholics are reminded not to compromise their principles, but it is increasingly accepted that, except in extreme cases such as communism, they are free to support a political or social movement even if certain of its principles are, from the Catholic point of view, unacceptable.

The additional guidance that a Catholic politician can expect from revelation is all the more effective in supplementing and clarifying the natural law because it is not only recorded in Scripture but is clothed in the thought of the church—in the efforts of Christian thinkers and practitioners, summed up by the church's teaching authorities, to understand it more fully and show its application to particular situations.

In tracing the relation between revelation, the natural law, and the decisions a Christian has to make in particular situations, political or other, the Catholic Church makes three distinctions.

1. In reaching his practical judgments, a Christian starts from a position of encounter, not only between a man and a situation but between a *Christian* and a situation. He has to assess the facts of the situation in the light of such knowledge as he has, that is, according to their natural law aspect. But he has also to judge with the extra understanding and grace that come to him as a Christian.

2. The encounter is not merely between a Christian and this situation: It is between a Christian and this situation *among and in the light of all others,* particularly in the light of the experience derived by Christians and others from related situations. Understanding of the natural law, and the Christian's grasp of revelation and its relevance to practical decisions, grow through experience and reflection.

3. The encounter is not merely between *a* Christian and this situation or pattern of situations, it is between a situation and a Christian *who is a member of the church.* All action, political or other, has a social as well as an individual dimension, and no one can act effectively or develop as a human being except in solidarity with others. What is essential for the Christian is that he is a member, not of *any* social organization, but of that social organization that is Christ's Church and the mystical Body of Christ. At the natural level, the church is an important piece of social machinery through which experience is exchanged and accumulated. It is an important part of a Christian's responsibility to take part in and learn from this exchange. But over and above this purely natural function, the church as a corporate body has a special responsibility for preserving the Christian revelation and developing an understanding of it and of its applications and has a special grace and guidance in doing this. The Christian who forgets these social dimensions of his action, his need to think and act in and with the church, is throwing away an important part of the guidance and support available to him.

One of the points made most strongly in John XXIII's encyclicals is, accordingly, that the church—not merely individual Christians—has accumulated a body of doctrine on social and political action, worked out from the natural law lighted up by revelation and by the church's reflection on both, and that it is the duty of those engaged in social and political action to study this doctrine as intensely as they might any other professional study. They are to treat it not simply as abstract knowledge but as a branch of technology, an area where it is as important to acquire skill in practical application as to grasp the knowledge itself.

In what way is this accumulated doctrine, with its current developments, binding on a Catholic politician? Some of the formulas current in the church are less than helpful. It is sometimes said, for example, that tactics and strategy are for the political practitioner, but that the church has a decisive word to say on value-judgments. The honesty, skill, far-sightedness and respect for others with which day-to-day political problems are handled determine a political system's moral character. Such strategic choices as the major problems on which to concentrate in the next decades or how far to slant solutions toward a future phase of development necessarily reflect value systems. Conversely, the choice of ends is a matter for the church rather than the politician only insofar as the church as a whole, or its teaching authorities, is able to consider all the factors involved and to arrive at a solution within the time available. In a rapidly changing world, these conditions will not often be met.

The right formula would once again seem to be that of subsidiary function. The church must, to the best of its ability, aid and support the politician by suggesting directions of movement within a sphere of discretion of just that size which he can manage. But it must not remove his discretion to make those decisions, including value judgments and the determination of ends, which he can in fact handle, nor must it try to control details that only the man actually facing the situation can fully grasp. Either of these things will be bad for the politician, who is deprived of the chance to use and develop his abilities fully; bad for the country, since decisions will be made by those less qualified to make them; and bad for the church itself, since its decision capacity will be overloaded, its leaders will lack the time and energy to do their proper work well, and the ill-feeling and mistakes resulting from the whole situation will bring the church into disrepute.

Whether the church does all it should to guide the politician depends on the efficiency of its own machinery. I do not think that in my own country any church has staffed or organized itself to provide Christian politicians with the guidance which they have the right to expect; to debate political and social issues fully in the light of Christian doctrine; to accumulate the knowledge needed for this; or to develop its own doctrine fast enough or in enough detail to keep it fully in touch with the current state of affairs. A Catholic can find in the encyclicals and other teaching documents of his church a broad consensus about the general direction of political action, but this is not at all the same thing as having the public and teaching opinion of the church brought to bear with precision and understanding on the actual issues facing a country at a certain time. It too often happens either that there is no effective discussion in the churches at all or that the issues discussed are those that are newsworthy. But it does not follow that issues that are less newsworthy are less worthy of debate, and often it is precisely these that the churches lack the machinery, formal or informal, to discuss.

There is a traditional and justified suspicion that, if the church, clergy and laity together, is encouraged to come to grips with and to offer guidance on political and social problems, it will be tempted to overstep its competence; to reach decisions without full knowledge; ignore relevant circumstances; override the views of outside groups; and judge on the basis of outdated stereotyped doctrines; and that, having thus reached defective conclusions, it will, in the case of the Catholic Church, impose these on its members by authority.

It must be admitted that at times the Catholic Church has given ground for suspicions of this kind. But there are at least three reasons that suggest that the danger is less than it was:

1. *The improvement in the church's learning process.* The church today comes to grips more quickly—though still not quickly enough—with important political and social issues. There is also less justification than in the past for accusing it of coming to conclusions without full knowledge of the facts or a full consensus.

2. *The increased self-confidence of the lay element in the church,* and particularly of practitioners in the political and social

field. Already, in the nineteenth century, the Catholic Center Party in Germany, though founded for the defense of ecclesiastical interests and engaged in a major political battle over them, flatly rejected an attempt by the Pope to direct it. Today it is common for Catholic politicians, including those in formally Catholic or Christian parties, to insist that they are only bound by the church and its authorities within the limits just defined. It is inconceivable today that even a Catholic party should accept the sort of clerical direction that was taken for granted in Italy at the beinning of this century.

3. *The abandonment by the church of claims to special political favor.* Until recently, the attitude of many Catholics justified the view that the Catholic Church operates in politics on the basis "heads I win, tails you lose." In a plural society with a non-Catholic majority, the church was likely to appeal for tolerance and the separation of church and state. In one with a strong Catholic majority, it might well demand that it be established as the state church and that political power be used to favor it against other beliefs. It is only by going well behind the face value of the text that it is possible to understand Leo XIII's encyclical *Immortale Dei,* "On the Christian Constitution of States," in any other sense. But this attitude was never universal among Catholics in modernized societies, has been crumbling for some time and recently has been disappearing in a landslide. The church would seem to be tending toward the following position though the issue is still unsettled.

First, each person has the right to follow his conscience in judging the truth of different beliefs and deciding his ultimate purposes in life. He has also the right to express his judgment in action, including action to persuade others, publicly or privately, as an individual or with others of like mind, so far as this does not interfere with the similar right of others or involve practices condemned by common morality apart from their association with particular religious beliefs. These rights have often been defended by Catholics on political grounds. Only if they are guaranteed can there be easy and equal collaboration between citizens and can the state pursue effectively the common good. But they are now also increasingly defended, by Catholics and others, primarily on the ground that they are essential to human personality and its development.

The church has always insisted that a man can obey the law of God only as it presents itself to him through the judgment of his conscience, and that therefore, in matters of religion, no one should be forced to act against his conscience. The practical implications of this for external and political action have emerged more clearly in recent years, notably at the Vatican Council. Freedom of conscience in religion must include freedom to express religious beliefs in public. Man is a social animal, whose social activity is inseparably linked to his inner life. He must therefore be free to express his religious beliefs not only individually but communally, as a member of a religious group, and not only for purposes of worship. People commonly form their conscientious judgments best through free, unrestrained discussion, and the opportunity for this must be available if people are to be able to reach sound judgments about religion.

Second, the state is not directly concerned with what the beliefs or ultimate purposes of its citizens are for it—these are simply a fact. Its business is to realize them insofar as this entails the pursuit of a common good. In doing so, it has to take account *both* of the rights of individuals and groups of different belief *and* of the predominance of one or other belief.

So, for example, it will be normal for a state with a mainly Moslem or Jewish population to adjust its legislation on holidays and days of rest, or on marriage and divorce, to what is acceptable to the majority, and likewise in a state where most of the people are Protestant or Catholic. It will be normal on a ceremonial occasion for the Moslem head of a predominantly Moslem state to attend the mosque and for the Catholic head of a predominantly Catholic state to attend the cathedral. But this recognition of the claims of a majority in no way abridges the rights of minorities. The state must maintain these rights, and, if necessary, it must create regions of exception in specially sensitive areas, for example, by recognizing the right of minority groups to their own rules for marriage and divorce, to be absent from work on religious feasts or to financial support for schools acceptable to them in terms of religion. In matters less directly related to religion, it must see that citizens are treated strictly alike.

It will often be convenient to register the relations between the state and the churches within its territory simply in terms of the state's ordinary law and Constitution. The 1937 Constitution of Ireland is an excellent example, by a country with an overwhelmingly Catholic population, of the practical application of the newer approach to the church-state relations just described. But it may also be convenient to make a special agreement between the state and the church—a concordat. Modern concordats have covered notably:

- The right of the church to worship and teach freely and to manage its own internal affairs; to appoint to its own offices and establish and manage its own orders and foundations; to raise funds and hold property; to publish books and papers.
- The civic qualifications and disqualifications of the clergy; for example, the requirement that the holders of certain church offices be nationals of the country concerned, the exemption of the clergy from military service, or restrictions on the political activity of the clergy (the Catholic Church, as a matter of internal discipline, in principle approves of restrictions of this kind).
- Catholic schools and colleges and facilities for Catholics in the state educational system.
- Catholic movements for charitable and social purposes and for adult education: Catholic youth movements and women's movements; facilities for Catholic members of state movements (for example, for members of state youth movements to attend Sunday Mass).
- Facilities for Catholic members of state services, particularly chaplaincy services in the armed forces.
- The marriage and divorce (or prohibition of divorce) of Catholics.
- Catholic feasts and their relation to public holidays.

Concordats of this type involve no particular privilege for the church; they are simply a codification of what in other countries appear as scattered items of the general law.

Such formulas are a very long way from traditional ideas of church establishment; they also quite specifically reject the conception of a "wall of separation" between church and state or of religion as a private matter. It is one thing to deny, rightly, that it is the state's business to determine the beliefs and purposes of its citizens. It is another, and quite wrong, to say that the state is to ignore what these purposes as a matter of fact are. Indeed it cannot do so, for it must act to *some* purpose. The question is simply whether it acts to promote the purposes of *all* its citizens, considered both in their majority and in their diversity, or more or less arbitrarily accepts some particular set of purposes it will favor above others.

## Christian Parties

In the light of what has just been said, when and how far is it justifiable for Catholics or other Christians to appear on the political scene with their own parties, whether or not they bear a Christian label? Clearly there is no assumption in current Catholic thinking that Catholics as such have a right to lead in politics or are necessarily or even probably more correct in their political views than other citizens. Catholics are directed to collaborate with others on equal terms, not to patronize or assume superiority over them. There is thus no general principle requiring a Catholic or Christian party: The case for such a party must be judged on the facts of each situation. In the light of the very wide experience of Christian parties in Europe and Latin America, there appear to be three major and two secondary considerations in deciding whether such a party is justified or not.

A. *What is the relative strength of Christians compared to other groups?*

Successful Christian parties have tended to arise in countries where practicing Christians are a minority (if they were a majority they could control the country without organizing apart) but one substantial enough to be a major political force if, and only if, it concentrates its strength behind one party.

B. *How far do the conflicts most important for political and social action follow the division of fundamental beliefs?*

Are the issues of major current political importance directly related to the activities of religious bodies or especially sensitive in terms of religions or philosophical beliefs, for example, issues about state control over churches, or about education or marriage and divorce? Or do major current issues, though not especially distinctive of any religious belief, happen to be more clearly perceived, through a historical accident, by Catholics or by Christians generally than by other groups? There is no particular reason why non-Catholics or non-Christians should disagree with the ideal of a "Responsible Society." It is a natural stage in the development of any society, and there is nothing distinctively Christian about it. But certainly, at particular times and places, this ideal has been grasped by Christian political leaders more clearly than by the adherents of other ideological groups. In such circumstances, Christians in general or Catholics in particular may have, so to speak, an educational ground for organizing on their own, for in this way they can define the image they present to the citizens more clearly and bring home to them more sharply what the ideal target is.

This educational case is particularly likely to arise in situations of rapid and fundamental change, such as that of newly industrializing countries. In any society at any time, action is guided by ideology, but ideology can operate at different levels. It may be based simply on custom and practice, and this may be adequate so long as a society is stable. But when a society is faced with rapid, bewildering and fundamental change such as overtook western Europe in the nineteenth century or Latin America, Africa or Asia in the twentieth, ideology needs to be made more explicit and to be rooted more deeply. Custom and practice become obsolete, and it is necessary to refer directly and specifically to basic and general principles for a guide. A group that proposes to lead in these conditions needs clear, coherent, explicit and, above all, deep-rooted principles. It does not necessarily follow that such a group will lead best by organizing apart, under its own banner. But it will certainly be under a special obligation to act politically and socially in such a way as to make its principles clear and educative to others. The best way to do this has often proved to be, to supporters of certain principles, to form a separate party with a distinctive program and name. This point does not of course apply only to Catholics or Christians, but it does apply to them among others.

C. *How far have different groups of citizens progressed toward maturity in their capacity for problem-solving and especially for solving problems that may involve groups with other beliefs?*

Is there, for example, a blockage of communication, a barrier of prejudice that prevents easy collaboration between Catholics or Christians and other groups and encourages discrimination or even persecution? It is sometimes possible to open a dialogue only by hitting one's partner on the head with a club. A trade union may have to strike in order to force the opening of negotiations. Christians have found in a number of countries that they must organize their own political force if they are to be taken into consideration at all.

Or is the danger not so much prejudice as confusion, in which no group of citizens has acquired enough political and social skill to handle the major issues of the day effectively? If Catholics or other Christians have reached a high level of political skill and maturity, they may simply take the lead in politics without forming specifically Christian parties. Why, for example, did Christian Democracy of the West European and Latin American kind never take hold in Britain? A main reason is that, by the time of modern mass political parties, large sections of the middle and working class were receiving, in the movements associated with the Evangelical revival, a training not in most cases directly political but one that equipped them to make their Christian principles effective in politics as individuals. Therefore, they had no need of a specifically Christian party.

But it may also happen that Catholics or Christians are not yet mature enough politically to lead effectively as individuals but have come far enough to be able to present an effective front if brigaded together under a strong central command. In these conditions, it may be best for them to organize themselves in a Christian political party.

The two minor considerations are:

D. *The cost of change*

A working political system represents a heavy investment of time and effort. There will always be a prima-facie case for continuing the pattern of parties until strong reason can be shown for change.

E. *Repercussions in other fields*

Political parties usually constitute only one element in a network of related political and social movements. There may well be advantages in keeping similar lines of division throughout the network and in not changing them in any one part of the network, for instance in politics, unless there is good reason for making a similar change in the whole.

The conditions that justify Christians in organizing apart in politics are more likely to be found in countries undergoing rapid change than in those that have reached a certain stability and maturity. In the former, there is likely to be confusion over objectives; issues controversial in terms of fundamental beliefs are likely to be thrown up; partial and onesided views will be common; and ability to solve the newly emerging problems may be only poorly developed. In more stable and mature countries, the more controversial and fundamental issues are likely to have been disposed of; political leaders are likely to have acquired a reasonably comprehensive view of the problems to be solved; and problem-solving ability is likely to be well developed. But the two secondary conditions may be relevant here. If a stable, mature country has a Christian party that is part of an established complex of Christian institutions, strong positive reasons will be needed to justify replacing it.

In a number of countries, the question of breaking up existing Christian parties or social organizations has in fact been raised. In Germany and Austria, Christian trade-union movements were not revived after the Second World War. In no country has it yet seemed worthwhile to break up an existing major Christian party, though an increasing number of active Catholics and other Christians have shown themselves willing as individuals to consider the case for voting for "neutral" parties. But the Christian parties have lost more and more of their specifically church character, and, at the same time, "neutral" parties have been dropping their anti-religious or anticlerical policies. It may well be that this double evolution will, in the end, have much the same effect as formally breaking up the Christian parties, but without the strains, disputes and ill-feeling that a direct attempt to break through the existing structure would involve.

# 21

# CHRISTIANS AND POLITICAL RESPONSIBILITY

by EDWARD ROGERS (United Kingdom)

BY the will of God, the church has been planted firmly in the midst of a turbulent and troubled world, with a mission to fulfill, under Christ, that is directly related to the world's turmoils and troubles. The complex question of the relationship of the church and the Christian to the manifold problems of secular society raises issues that cannot be evaded. Even when, in some parts of the church at some periods of its history, there has been a deliberate attempt at withdrawal, the withdrawal has, in fact, been no more than a variant in the pattern of relationship. In its local manifestations, the Church of Jesus Christ is, and always has been, set in the context of the secular. To communicate the saving word of the gospel, it has adapted itself, not always consciously, to meet the needs of an apparently permanent social order or of the powerful and bewildering changes of a social transition. It follows that this question is not one to which a simple, single answer can be given. We are not dealing with fixed factors but with the infinitely varied and perpetually changing interactions of living—and dying—institutions.

We must begin by accepting facts as they are. We shall get nowhere if we start, for example, by assuming that the actual church corresponds perfectly to the ideal. If we are to face the immediate issues of relationship with the secular world, we must admit what we know well from our own experience: that the particular institutional church to which we belong is not an integrated community of fully committed Christian believers, joined in perfect love and utterly obedient to the leading of the Holy Spirit, which witnesses without flaw in word and deed to an unregenerate world. In the church, as well as in the secular world, there are fallible institutions and performances that do not match promises and professed ideals. There are national churches, minority churches, divided churches, deeply affected in custom and outlook and in the opportunity to exert perceptible social influence by internal and external variations in their historic development.

From nineteen tangled centuries, at least one clear lesson can be learned: that the Christian church is not indissolubly bound to any one form of political system. The tremendous missionary surge of the eighteenth and nineteenth centuries came from western nations that were either committed to a democratic political system or struggling to attain one; and it came to be assumed that Christianity's political expression was democracy.

Other things being equal, a strong case can be made for political democracy. Every adult in a democratic franchise has an opportunity and a responsibility to exercise effective political influence, and responsibility is essential if there is to be genuine involvement. Democracy is probably the most acceptable form of government to the people of a nation with reasonably good living standards, education and means of communication. But the simple rule, "one man, one vote," does not provide a foolproof road to wisdom or justice, nor is it irrefutably the most efficient in every social situation. A democratic electorate can be bribed by appeals to self-interest, and a majority can tyrannize over a minority as sinfully as any oligarchy. A developing nation, longing to break free from the crippling shackles of poverty but unprepared for the discipline and hardship involved, may move more swiftly under dictatorship or single-party rule.

A political system must be judged by its efficiency and righteousness in dealing with the realities of a given situation,[1] in defending the citizen against external aggression and internal lawless-

---

[1] Bishop Zulu of the Anglican Church in South Africa suggests the addition of the following phrase: "in defining the rights of citizens and in reverence for their personality."

ness, in fostering conditions that can provide the material bases for a good life, in guaranteeing justice and order and liberty. In an imperfect world, there are situations where a government must emphasize order rather than liberty. Generally speaking, there must be stability, peace and a modest affluence before liberty can take precedence over order.[2] Democracy is probably the best system that man has yet devised. But this does not mean that a universal franchise is to be equated with the rule of God.

Through the centuries, the church has often been absorbed into a political system, but has never yet been totally identified with any, and has witnessed to the saving grace of Christ and to the essentials of Christian conduct through organizational structures variously based. The church's grasp of the implications of social change is always a slow process; it is often agonizingly slow to its prophets and reformers. To exaggerate in order to point a truth: It seems that at every critical period of revolutionary change in society the church is a couple of generations in arrears. Yet, when a new discovery—such as gunpowder, or ocean navigation, or power-driven machinery—has destroyed a social or political order, somehow the church survives.

For, although the church is inextricably involved in the turbulence of the secular world, it is never wholly accommodated to the temporal and the transitory. The church is in the world and beyond the world. The purpose of the honest politician is to try to create the conditions for the material welfare and happiness of his people. It is a worthy aim. But the purpose of the church is to show the children of men that the true meaning of life is to be found outside or beyond the world of their achievements and their disappointments. This is, in fact, the true "prophetic note," and it is the factor that prevents involvement with the transitory from becoming identification.

At the same time, this slowness in adapting itself to changing situations gives a disturbing impression that the church is always being overtaken by events—pursuing, but never quite catching up. It is pushed into social action by pioneer humanitarian reformers

---

[2] Bishop Zulu suggests that this statement assumes that liberty will follow upon "stability, peace and modest affluence"; the truth of this statement depends on the nature of the Constitution.

more often than it leads them. If we believe that the will of God is manifest in the flux of history, and that his will should be most clearly perceived in his church, ought we not to be doing more to direct the course of change? Ought not the church, for example, enunciate on the basis of Holy Scripture its own social and political policy?

Indeed, some have tried to devise such a comprehensive and final pronouncement, inside and outside the church, and they have failed miserably. A bold confidence in one's ability to pierce the mists that hide the future is not enough. We must be realistic and admit that there are too many variables to permit precise prediction. Even if it were possible to design an ideal pattern for mankind in society now and to allow for developments on lines already evident, a new discovery or a global war would sweep the hand of history through the bright neatness of the design.

Again, we flatter ourselves and forget the inevitable consequences of our imperfection if we imagine that we can design the political system that totally accords with the will of God. There are too many things we do not know. More important, until we have the mind that was in Christ Jesus, we cannot imagine the nature of the ideal.

But there is no cause for despondency. There is nothing in the New Testament to suggest that planning the grand design for man is our responsibility. There is much to suggest that our part is to walk by the light we have and to take by faith one step at a time. The urgent social and political problems of an unregenerate world confront us immediately: poverty; hunger; disease; illiteracy; distorted sexual relationships; delinquency; greed. We know that there is a task at hand to create better human relationships in the working structures of industrialized communities and to eliminate corruption from the bureaucracies of nonindustrialized communities. We know that war has reached the depth of evil and that better ways of resolving international tensions must be pioneered. There is enough here to be going on with. If, by God's grace, we are enabled to solve or to help in solving these present problems, we know that the solutions will in their turn create new problems; but as each new problem is a new opportunity, each step takes us a little further on the way.

What, then, is the manner of the church's involvement in the problems of our time? Will it not be most effectively influential if it is an active but specifically Christian participation in the world of affairs? If Christians are not to hover ineffectually on the outskirts of politics or industry, should there not be Christian political parties, Christian trade unions and Christian employers' associations?

Such organizations have been and are being tried, and they are not lightly to be dismissed. Parties like the Christian Democrats in West Germany or Austria or Italy may best be understood and assessed as responses to specific situations.

In Europe, after the collapse of Roman civilization, the flickering light of learning was kept alive by the church in the midst of barbaric ignorance. The clergy held almost a monopoly of the arts of reading and writing and, because they were literate, they acquired administrative authority in the secular world. Having power, they sought to hold onto it when the monopoly of learning had ceased. In some countries, they slowly and reluctantly surrendered this power; in others, they clung to it with a grip so firm that anticlericalism became a notable element in the doctrines of rebels and social reformers. In western Europe, in particular, socialism was avowedly anticlerical. The rise of political parties specifically opposed to the church created, by direct reaction, political parties that claimed to be specifically Christian.

But when a political party has the responsibility for government, it continually has to decide on matters which are morally neutral or on which there can be genuine and conscientious divergence of Christian judgment. For example, during the abortive negotiations over the possible entry of the United Kingdom into the European Economic Community, there was long haggling about the import of temperate foodstuffs. It is presumptuous and dangerous to assume that on such matters there is a judgment that can be described as *"the* Christian judgment." It is wrong to claim the sanctions of the gospel for speculative opinions on economic or financial questions. It inhibits the mission of the church to enclose it within one section of the community. It is healthier for the community and truer to the genius of the church that political parties should be formed around reasonable and legitimate diversities of political judgment and that Christians should be able, with good conscience, to serve within the differing parties.

It will be noted that we began by speaking about the church, and we are now referring to Christians. In this shift of emphasis lies a clue to the church's involvement in the secular world.

I began my own ministry in the dock areas of London. My people worked in the docks and on the river, in gas works and on the railway, in shops and offices. I moved to a village where my people were shepherds and miners. I left there to go to Birmingham, where most of them worked in heavy engineering or in a rubber factory. In all these churches there were teachers and nurses and local government officers. This situation is not extraordinary, but world wide. Though their particular occupations will vary according to local circumstances, the majority of church members throughout the world earn their daily bread in the secular world.

In every field of human endeavor, effective action depends upon people. Plans and ideas come to life only through people. One of the disconcerting facts that the new tribe of "social engineers" tends to overlook is that there are not enough of the right sort of people to carry out their bright ideas. Thus the basic responsibility of the Christian in the secular world is to be the right sort of person. The man in my church who was a skilled and conscientious shepherd, the man who was respected in his engineering works as a trade unionist who would not stoop to deceit, the woman who taught little children in a slum school and loved them —these preached the gospel they believed by deeds and brought saving grace into their environment.

The trouble is that many still separate their work from their worship. Certainly in industrial communities, work is regarded as energy and skill and time bartered for money. The attitude is understandable. The artisan is not likely to take much notice of sermons on the dignity of labor when, as still too often happens, he is hired and dismissed and ordered around as though he were a "labor unit" or a piece of animate machinery. Yet the whole basis of the intricate system of industry is the provision by human beings of the goods and services that other human beings require. In this realm, perhaps more than anywhere else, the fact of our interdependence is manifest. Here is a place where the guidance of the church should be much more clearly given. Management consultants and industrial psychologists are now begnning to say what the church should have been saying long ago: that work is satisfying and meaningful only when those engaged in an industrial enterprise are treated at every level as intelligent human beings and are consciously aware that they are participants in a group undertaking with an end product that benefits the community and is worthy of their labor. This will mean changes in the pattern of employment and changes in the internal structure of industry. But, if it thereby becomes possible to create a genuine sense of vocation in daily work, it is the responsibility of the church to be thinking hard about it.

It will be no quick or easy task to bring moral theology to bear relevantly on the techniques and processes of industry. But there is a way of Christian involvement that can be explored without delay. In nations at every stage of development there are key posts unfilled; perhaps because the financial reward or prospect of promotion is small, perhaps because the work is particularly exacting, perhaps because the job is low in social estimation. In the western nations, for example, the extension of valuable social services is retarded because other occupations pay more and demand less. In the developing nations, too many of the intellectual elite want to be lawyers, not enough want to be engineers or accountants. The churches would be serving the present age, and affecting for good the communities in which they are set, if they encouraged and helped their young members to fill the gaps.

Similarly, in most nations, there is an opportunity for people to offer some of their free time for voluntary social service. In some, where help of this kind traditionally used to be given within the extended family but where the impact of new ways of life is destroying the old patterns, there is need to pioneer the establishment of such voluntary service.

In both these fields of service, however, there is a subtle danger. The only valid motive is love for one's neighbor. The call is to activity, in daily work or leisure time, that is inspired by response to an observed need and undertaken for the sake of others. If the dominant motive is self-regarding and the service rendered with the primary object of enlarging the power and influence of the church, it will be labor in vain. There is a salutary warning in Matt. 6 about those who do good to enhance their own prestige, and a divine commendation in Matt. 25 of those whose compassion is the fruit of love.

Though our emphasis is on the activity of Christians within the secular world, they do not act as isolated individuals. There is need for a ministry of support and guidance and advice. The range of that ministry is necessarily conditioned by local circumstances. Some churches are in situations where public critical comment on political and economic developments is impossible. Others are too small and poor, their resources stretched to the limit in maintaining the witness of worship, to be able to do much in this difficult field. But, if they can do no more than train and teach their members, within the fellowship of the church, that, in the fullness of faith, there is a "this-worldly" aspect made explicit in honesty and sobriety and compassion, the ministry will be invaluable. Most churches, however, do enjoy the liberty of comment that ought invariably to be a constituent element of religious liberty. The statements and resolutions of ecclesiastical courts and assemblies may directly influence political and social action. They should certainly, through the guidance and information given to their own people, exert a perceptible indirect influence.

While it is true that church pronouncements tend sometimes either to be flavored with an unconvincing grandiloquence or to be so vague and general as to give little clear guidance, it must be added that, on many occasions in this present generation, the church has spoken with clarity and expert knowledge on social or international issues in a way that has deserved and received attention inside and outside its own fellowship. This has happened, almost invariably, when a group within the church has given intensive study to a particular problem. The establishment and growth in recent years of boards of social responsibility or departments of Christian citizenship as integral parts of the structural organization of churches is a most welcome development. Departments of this kind discover a twofold function. First, they can call into the service of the church, through working parties and special groups, the professional expertise of Christian laymen. Such groups can do stimulating work even when there is no official department or board of their church to which their findings can be related; but it is obvious that wider and more authoritative publicity can be gained when there is a clear channel or communication to the official organization. Second, departments can cooperate smoothly with similar departments in sister churches. I write as one who has had charge of a Christian citizenship department since 1950. In almost every major activity concerning this department in recent years—housing, constitutional developments in Zambia and Malawi, aid to developing countries, the technicalities of nuclear policy, penal reform, the law of divorce, assessment of the social consequences of industrial technological change—there has been consultation with the Anglican Board of Social Responsibility and with the Baptist Department of Christian Citizenship. This consultation proved so beneficial that it is now taken for granted. The pooling of resources and information adds greatly to the value of the judgments we present for the guidance of our people and strengthens the impact of any comment presented to government or to official social authority.

The concerns mentioned in the preceding paragraph should make it clear that guidance of the kind needed cannot be provided solely by poring over the pages of the New Testament or manuals of theology. And these are only a few of the concerns affecting one church in one nation; a world-wide survey would reveal many more. The valuable studies of the World Council of Churches on areas of rapid social change provide a profusion of hard questions for us to answer: Dare a small and struggling church, set in the turmoil of a nation newly come to independence, spare some of its best ministers and laymen for political service? Dare it not spare them? Is it wise to cooperate for social reform with non-Christian majority groups? If so, on what terms should cooperation be offered and accepted?

Such questions cannot be fully answered from within the church. Part of our present difficulty arises from the fact that to most of the clergy and ministers, who are generally and naturally regarded as the leaders of ecclesiastical action, the detail of pragmatic politics or applied sociology or industrial structure is an unknown language. A broader basis of training in the theological colleges would modify this ignorance, but even then the quicker awareness would be external. The ignorance would disappear if pastors and clergy were to earn their own living by labor in the secular world, but that drastic solution to one problem would inevitably create other and greater problems. Certainly, much more use must be made of the wisdom and experience of our laymen. They are the men who, in daily living, wrestle with the problems, too vividly conscious of their reality to be content with the glib answers that are no answers and strong enough in faith to believe that, if they wrestle in study and in prayer, answers will be found. But it will not be enough if the ministry is prepared to listen humbly to the voice of the Christian laity. The satisfying answer will not come from within the church alone.

The church has insights and wisdom without which the secular world can never fully live. It has learned through Christ the true glory of the nature and destiny of man. It knows that man cannot live by bread alone. It does not judge schemes or policies purely by a coldly clinical assessment of their material efficiency. It is bound by divine command to point out and to condemn the unjust and the cruel and the merciless. But those who are outside the church, yet at the heart of the pain and tragedy of secular society, have valid insights and wisdom too.

The late Archbishop William Temple, who did as much as any man to bring the challenge and promise of the gospel directly to bear on urgent social and political questions, steadfastly enunciated the theory that it was the task of the church to state clear, general principles. It was then the responsibility of the politician or trade unionist or employer or social worker to translate those principles into rules of practice. William Temple rarely followed his own counsel in this respect. Rather, he plunged without reserve into the thick of the debate.

It must be so. The church, on the whole, has neglected the study of moral theology, to its own disservice. We find ourselves armed with insubstantial general principles with which to withstand the sharp attacks of personal and social immorality and amorality. There is no list of general principles from which we can extract the appropriate one to deal with a particular situation. There are only two basic principles: the dominical laws of love to God and love to one's neighbor.

Love is possible only in action and relationship. The church and the Christian citizen who are obedient to these fundamental laws cannot sit on the judge's bench, as it were, dispensing aloof and impartial judgment on an erring world. They must be involved in the sin and sorrow and uncertainty. They must be prepared to listen and to learn from the secular world. They must earnestly seek for the mind of Christ—and realize that they may find some part of it in the specialized skill of the economist or the sociologist, in the impotent frustration of the man at the assembly line, in the questionings of the worried statesman or military strategist, in the bewilderment of the peasant as his settled way of life disintegrates. "Dialogue" has become a maid-of-all-work in ecumenical discussion, but a genuine dialogue between the church and the world is the way to the answer. It may be that, if we come asking for help as well as offering advice, and if we are honestly and manifestly anxious to discuss rather than to assert, the secular world will not only be ready to talk, it will be willing to listen.

# 2 2

# THE CHURCH AND THE
# CITIZEN IN A SECULAR WORLD

by GERHARD BASSARAK (Germany)

THE new thinking of the church concerning the Christian responsibility in the world, including the world of politics, is revealed in a new understanding of the "holy." Alfons Rosenberg, one of the Roman Catholic speakers in the radio series of the South German radio on "Religiosity in a Worldly World," says that "until now, every age, almost every human group, had its own ideal of holiness. In the early days of the Christian Church, all disciples of Christ were covered by the all-embracing name 'the Saints' while the designation 'the Holy One' was applied to one person only, Christ the Lord." Later on legends of the saints set forth archetypes, symbols and images of the Christian way of life and thereby transformed the *communion sanctorum* into "a pantheon for heroes of virtue, into a school of virtue." Rosenberg asks whether in these days—"except for religious genii and men passionately inflamed by God—holiness is still possible in the midst of the high pressure of technical operations and the rush of secular life, in the clangor of machines and the entertainment industry." He answers the question by exploring the modern dimension of holiness and discovers that all attitudes to holiness in the past have had infinitely more in common with one another than with our view of holiness today: "It is evident that traditional asceticism, based on the formulas 'God and your soul' and 'Save your soul' has as a way of holiness eventually led to the development of religious individualism. Today and in the future holiness will be experienced through holy community. ... We are charged to integrate Christianity into life. ... We need the sacrament of the neighbor, which at the same time is enacted as the sacrament of every moment. A new religious-social structure of Christian existence is beginning to take shape." This is how a Roman Catholic articulates the problem.

A Lutheran says: "One cannot find any rule [viz., of discipleship in the New Testament] that lays down: Christ has done this and that for us, now we are to do the same for him in like manner. Rather the rule is this: I have washed your feet, you ought to wash one another's feet. Don't direct your service towards me but let it go forth and go on! ... Christ's action is aimed at you, your action is to be aimed at your neighbour." [1]

Thus holiness has become transformed from an ontological quality or perhaps a vertical relation God-soul into a structure of horizontal relations—it has become "socialized" and secularized. We shall find that many Christian "values" have, in like manner, been secularized, by being related to the world. The encounter with the world has transformed them, and frequently the Christian community cannot recognize them again as genuinely Christian. This is the permissible, the bidden way of secularizing Christian concepts (including spiritual ones!). Privileges pass from the "possession" of the church into the possession of the world. The church does not cling to them as if it is being robbed, but divests itself of them. The church has lost them once and for all. It must not hold on to them or try to regain them. ("What things were gain to me, those I counted loss for Christ," Phil. 3:7.) Paradoxically, this loss is not making the church poorer but richer: Its Lord is making it rich. The "seed" is given not in the first place to provide for the church's own need of food but—as shown by the parable of the sower (Mark 4)—to be scattered lavishly, uneconomically. In evaluating this phenomenon we need not even go as far as Von Oppen, who asserts that the gospel has effected a revolution in human history, the direction and manner of which may be read very accurately in the text of the Sermon on the Mount, and who tries to establish "structures of the Sermon on the Mount" in the reality of the modern world. [2]

---

[1] GUSTAV WINGREN: THLZ. Col. 385ff.
[2] *Das Personale Zeitalter*, 1960.

The American theologian Harvey Cox, who spent a year study-ing the situation of the church in the German Democratic Re-public, interprets the situation there as "radical secularism." [3] To-day, the main offensive against the church in eastern Germany is conducted not by communism but by a rapidly advancing secular-ism and the equally forward pressing rationalization of a world that was formerly strongly attached to traditional ways. In this respect, the situation is not unlike that in western Europe and in the United States. Only it is much less concealed.

Few theologians in eastern Germany make great lamentations over the advance of secularism. For most of them, secularism is something we must learn to understand, sociologically and theo-logically. Many of them see in secularism the opportunity of calling on the church to leave the stifling atmosphere of a "Christian" Egypt and to go into a land God has promised but not yet shown. The need for a theology of secularism is becoming urgent. Such an attempt, which would have to combine the traditional exactitude and thoroughness of German theology with a refreshing "this-worldliness," cannot, even in outline, be undertaken in this paper. But my observations on "church" and "the Christian citizen" are presented against the background of this larger issue.

## On the Church

In our situation, the church's duty to proclaim the gospel re-mains unchanged. This statement sounds trite, yet it is not; for while the duty is the same, the problem of carrying it out is not. That is to say, the church is not the same as in the past. Perhaps, the shape of the church in the secular world of today will have to be more like that of the church at the time of the New Testa-ment than that of the Middle Ages, in spite of the fact that our tra-ditions derive from the Middle Ages and have that stamp upon them. We shall deal with only a few aspects.

The *Confessio Augustana,* Article VII, describes the church as an act: that of gathering. We know today that gathering and send-ing belong together, as two consecutive steps, as breathing in and out; and of the two, breathing in is primary! Jesus' disciples meet

[3] *Christianity and Crisis,* 13, 1963, p. 652ff.

their Master in the world. He gathers them, but he does it only in order to send them forth into the world, into the dispersion (Diaspora). The church of the Middle Ages—and even the Reformation church—did not know mission. For the Reformation, the church was the gathered congregation. This is the origin of our present-day predicament: the mark of Christian existence is church attendance; however, the coming together of the congregation does not mean community but a noncommittal "attendance." One is no longer at home in the church, in the congregation. People don their Sunday best and pay a visit. Even at the Lord's table, one is a guest. But we are not guests and strangers in the world; rather we are at home there. One goes to church as one does any other activity. The church even speaks of "church activities." Our Christianity is measured by the frequency of attendances at divine service or Holy Communion.

Admittedly, it is expected that faith will be tested in daily life. But as the clergy, charged with preaching and with instructing the congregation, can no longer comprehend the differentiated, specialized, multiform processes of economic and political life in the secular world (something that the clergy in the Middle Ages were well able to do in respect to feudal estates and craft guilds!), little help in mastering the problems of daily life can come from the pulpit. Owing to a lack of contact with the exciting, pulsating life of the present, the compelling and integrating character of sermon and worship is vanishing. People are not sent forth, because a congregation "attending" divine service is not mission, nor is it really a "gathered" community.

A congregation gathering spontaneously and voluntarily, understanding mission as a normal state, experiencing dispersion as "sheep among wolves," and flocking together with a burning desire to discuss the victories and defeats of the gospel in the world and to praise God for the mighty deeds they have witnessed in their daily lives through him and with him and in him—that is the biblical image of the church. (Matt. 10).

Fritz Führ, until his death in 1963 General Superintendent in East Berlin, describes the "church in the beginning of a new age" [4]

---

[4] *Theologische Existenz heute, N.F. Nr 66.*

as a church of the dispersion (Diaspora) but not in the "old style"; he thinks, however, that Diaspora among the confessions may offer a model for today.[5] It is held today that mission is the true and only dimension of the church: The church is mission and only as mission can the church be the church. This may imply that for centuries a false accent has been laid on "gathering."

In this situation, the church has to realize that it is the Church of Jesus Christ—and nothing else. This may appear obvious but in fact it is not. Too frequently and too predominantly "church" means still the national, territorial or official state church; or it means "local congregation," which suggests a church body or association, an assembly of consumers for satisfying their religious needs. It is not the church's task, however, to advocate certain religious or theological doctrines (I am well aware of the criticism this statement invites: For it, too, is an expression of a certain "doctrine"!). The church is not responsible for defending certain ethical teachings; the church is not commissioned to be God's watchdog or police in the world; it is not the church's duty to tell the world "the truth"; the church must not fight for the privilege to do service or to have a hand in all the business and busyness of the world; the church is no rival enterprise competing with the world; it is not a state within the state.

The church has received the gift of the Holy Spirit and, with it, the ability to see the crucified and risen Christ present and at work. He comes into the world today. He is present and enters into the social structures as fellow man. He wants his church, which he always precedes into the world, to discover and proclaim him. The church must not imprison Christ behind church walls. He breaks out from every self-chosen ghetto. He is sending his church into the world so that it may be, according to John 6:55ff., life-giving food for the world, the salt of the earth or sheep in the midst of wolves.

---

[5] In German (and Continental) usage, the term "Diaspora" (dispersion) has long been used for confessional or denominational minorities, i.e., Lutheran (Evangelical) minorities in Roman Catholic countries or a predominantly Roman Catholic population in a given district or town, and vice versa. It is this usage that underlies the terminology here and in other places above. It is typical for the Continental and general confessional situation in days past that the biblical term "Diaspora" could be used for Christian living among Christians.

As Christ is giving himself to the world—secularizing himself—so his church has to give itself to the world. Such self-giving is precisely the opposite of adaptation in the sense of "being conformed to this world." A church that is against the world in defiance, fear, despair or pharisaism is conformed to the world. Selfless giving is distinguished from the world even in the act of secularization. Perhaps the Pauline expression "to the Greeks as a Greek, to the Jews as a Jew" may be apposite here. That the church is not of the world is obvious. It need not be concerned about it. It is its Lord's concern. But this does not lessen the urgency of the church's going into the world. The consequences of what is demanded cannot be in doubt. Discipleship not only leads to the Cross of Jesus but often enough to one's own cross. What makes the situation of the suffering disciple ironic is that it is not the world alone that crucifies but the world and the church together. He who hangs on the Cross was derided particularly by the pious. For to this very day the knowledge that God himself is hanging on the Cross has remained purely academic for the church, in the same way as it knows that Jesus receives sinners, tax collectors and harlots. "Church" has come to mean a group of respectable petty bourgeois. It was very different in the Corinth of St. Paul! Not that the respectable members of the church should become disreputable in order to be like the church in Corinth. But under the oppressive weight of the morally respectable, where is there any room left in the church for the others? Where is the church a sign that its Lord has died for all so that there is room for all in the church? Finally: "We should tell the devil that Jesus did not call to himself saints but sinners and that—in spite of the devil—we want to remain sinners so as to be with Jesus rather than as saints with the devil" (Dietrich Bonhoeffer).

How can one formulate the dialectic, the double aspect of secularization? The church has not to draw the world into itself, or imitate the structures, conceptions, constellations, methods, organizational forms, power and authority of the world. The church must not ask the world to identify itself with it. The world is not a material of the church. It does not belong to the church and must not become subject to it.

But the church has to go into the world, to inject itself into the world without forcing on the world its forms, shapes, images, dogmas, charisma or services. The church has to enter into solidarity with the world in consequence of the Incarnation of him whom it confesses as Lord. It must not become subject to the world but it may, and must, belong to the world.

This applies not only to the apparently still "Christian world" but also to the world of non-Christian religions and to the world of atheism, because all these worlds are certainly not devoid of Christ.

There should be no uncertainty about the specific task of the church in our secular epoch. Dr. Schmidt-Clausen said: "Two long centuries passed after the Reformation before the first Lutheran missionaries were sent out. After that it took another hundred and fifty years before the churches discovered their responsibility in the sphere of *Diaconia* and social service." We may ask how long it will take until the churches recognize their responsibility for political and social peace in this secular, post-colonial epoch, with its vast atomic armaments and unimaginable differences in the standard of living, and when our churches will realize their responsibility for reconciliation. Let us hope it happens before there is an atomic catastrophe.

### The Christian Citizen

"The layman is meant to demonstrate Christ's solidarity with the world in every-day life. He is 'worldly.' He is the bearer of the apostolate. The layman, the 'laikos,' is a representative of the missionary People of God, the 'laos toy theory.' To do this will most probably require a conscious distance from the ecclesiastical sphere." [6] The Christian citizen must not be considered or treated by the church as its possession or property. He belongs to it as little as the child of full age to the parents. The Christian who has come of age belongs to the world. Insofar as the Christian citizen is not a cleric but a layman, he is in a difficult situation, which he cannot fully perceive. In his capacity as a citizen, he lives in a secular world; he has rationalized his life, even in the most in-

---

[6] HOEKENDIJK: *The Future of the Church and the Church of the Future.*

timate, private sphere. Now and then, he may feel uneasy over the
perfection of technics, over man's ability to make things and to
manipulate men and to achieve nearly everything he desires—an
uneasiness fostered by his church attendance. Perhaps he thinks
it curious that everywhere, with the exception of the church, room
for God has become scarce. Is God to dwell only in the irrational
realm? The day-to-day experience that machines are running without God has demythologized history. The awareness that the harvest is gathered in without God and sunshine has desacralized nature and even thanksgiving for harvest is questioned. Faced with
the evident powerlessness, and even absence of God, how shall the
total claim of the Lord of lords, the Lord over nature and history,
as asserted by the church, be believed?

This is where help is needed.

First, we can help by showing that logical contradictions need
not be real contradictions. It seems logical that we cannot do justice to two claims to totality. This is borne out by the biblical saying: "No-one can serve two masters." In this case, however, the
two masters are mutually exclusive. Today, everyone must struggle
to do justice to the claims of many roles: the role of father; hus-
band; church member; and citizen. Indeed, rival claims may overlap as regards time, but there are also fortuitous coincidences and
overlappings of interest. It may yet be possible—to set one biblical
text against another—to render to Caesar the things that are Caesar's, and to God the things that are God's. For the modern secular state and society are only interested in what bears their image
and their superscription. Time and strength do remain for what
we love. There is a private sphere. He who conjures up the menace
of the totalitarian demands of modern societies desecularizes and
demonizes them and does the very opposite from what the Church
of Jesus Christ has to do: It has to drive out the demons!

Second, help may be offered by secularizing the Bible, ridding
it of its sacred character, "profaning" it. According to Luther, the
Bible is the hay and the straw, the swaddling clothes of Christ.
We must show that the Bible is not a sacred, inviolable law. Once
awe for the Holy Book has been removed, all kinds of things may
happen: People may become curious and bold to read; they will
take the Incarnation seriously; they will be freed from the fear of

the "papery pope"; they will be released from the killing letter of the law into the joy of the life-giving gospel.

Third, help may be provided by locating heaven properly. God is not where heaven is; but where God is, there is heaven. But God has come to the world and still is coming. He is where two or three are gathered together in his name. He is in the midst of the earth to the end of the world. The reality of the congregation materializes in the gathering of the two or three rather than through church-going. We might strain the exegesis here and ask whether the mention of the two or three might not be understood to mean that where two are gathered in his name he is present as the third: the crucified and risen Christ. With regard to the reality of the "congregation," Luther's complaint that we have not the people is still being heard today. This, however, is resignation and un-belief. Christians are because Christ is. To be a Christian is not merely a matter of awareness but of being. By definition, the rela-tionship between a Christian and Jesus Christ is comparable to that between two lovers. Christ is the Christians' life, their new exist-ence. They are gaining both by looking not to themselves but to him. Their salvation is outside themselves. Their comfort and their strength is that Christ is near them, with them in their daily lives, that he is round about them, that he encircles them behind and before and lays his hand upon them (Psalm 139:5).

Fourth, it might be of help to understand faith as a living rela-tionship to him who is present, whose presence is being experienced in the nearness of the neighbor, in his word, in his gesture, in his signs (the Sacraments). In his presence, all predications of a Lord over nature and history are fading into meaningless hypostases. They fail also when faced with the reality of the New Testament that, at the time of a slave-keeping society, knew the personal relation of slave to master. An attitude that bore witness to the presence of the Risen One, that signified a relationship with him, would be informed by a Christian ethos. This attitude would aban-don the paragraphed rules of ethics that are either casuistic or legalistic. Where personal insight proves insufficient to find the right mode of conduct, a kind of protestant principle of subsidiarity is needed, including the contribution of experts to replace the con-science, which belongs to a past social reality.

It might be a decisive help to the Christian citizen if the theologians descended from their hymnic heights and stood with both feet firmly on the secular earth; if they proclaimed with scrupulous honesty only what they themselves believed; if they weighed every pious word they uttered; if they offered and distributed as bread of life only what they themselves were able to chew, eat and digest; if they left the *deus absconditus* in his darkness to himself and devoted strength and time to describe and proclaim the glory of the revealed God in the face of Jesus; if they learned to relax their hold on the monopoly of the monologue sermon and to expose themselves to question, dialogue and discussion.

... the clergyman is a servant of the layman. His work is intended to make the missionary People of God abide by their commission. He himself, however, does not appear on the stage of the world. What is being performed there is a "Laienspiel" (the laymen are the actors) in which he has no part. Now and then he may be the producer but in the main he is the prompter. Unfortunately the pulpit has all too little resemblance to a "prompter's box," and he who stands in it is embarrassingly visible. (HOEKENDIJK)

The secular world has dethroned the ancient authorities. Authority no longer derives from age, office or dignity; new authority derives from the strength of conviction and action, and also the giving of help. Churches and Christian citizens will remain churches and citizens in the secular world, too, if they do not cease to love the secular world as God loves it.